WITHDRAWN

THE GUEST-HALL OF EDEN

THE GUEST-HALL OF EDEN

Four Essays on the Design of Old English Poetry

by Alvin A. Lee

New Haven and London: Yale University Press

1972

Published with assistance from the Humanities
Research Council, Ottawa, Canada.

Library of Congress catalog card number: 76-151581
International standard book number: 0-300-01441-4

Designed by John O. C. McCrillis
and set in Baskerville type.
Printed in the United States of America by
The Vail-Ballou Press, Inc., Binghamton, New York.

Distributed in Great Britain, Europe, and Africa by
Yale University Press, Ltd., London; in Canada by
McGill-Queen's University Press, Montreal; in Mexico
by Centro Interamericano de Libros Académicos,
Mexico City; in Central and South America by Kaiman
& Polon, Inc., New York City; in Australasia by
Australia and New Zealand Book Co., Pty., Ltd.,
Artarmon, New South Wales; in India by UBS Publishers'
Distributors Pvt., Ltd., Delhi; in Japan by John
Weatherhill, Inc., Tokyo.

To the memory of

SUSANNA ELIZABETH

Contents

Preface

In the course of an investigation some years ago of the elegiac strain in Old English poetry, I found myself drawn into an attempt to describe the overall imaginative order presented in the extant Old English poetic records, an order within which elegiac themes are only one, albeit a major, form of expression. In the intervening period, partly through the stimulus of teaching undergraduate and graduate students, I have come to see more clearly how principles of literary symbolism and biblical typology function in curiously compelling ways in this body of poetry. The description of a particular historical period's poetic mythology offered here is by no means intended as a total critique of Old English poetic texts; rather, it is an invitation to readers to consider in some detail how the inherited biblical and Christian view of reality was transformed by its meeting with the poetic forms and language of Germanic tradition and how, in the process, new metaphors and poems were shaped or designed.

My thanks are due to all those who have helped me. They include my former teachers Northrop Frye, Lawrence K. Shook, and Jess B. Bessinger, Jr.; my colleagues, especially Thomas H. Cain and Maureen Halsall; my students, especially Douglas Letson and Graham Caie; my wife, Hope, whose devotion and patience are admirably coupled with good literary critical sense; the Pontifical Institute of Mediaeval Studies in Toronto, for generously placing their library and faculty resources at my disposal; the Canada Council and McMaster University for a Senior Fellowship and a sabbatical leave, respectively, both of which together made possible much of the work involved; the Humanities Research Council, Ottawa, for a grant in aid of publication.

The titles of Essays One, Two, and Three are taken from Burton Raffel's translations, *Poems from the Old English* (Lincoln, Nebraska, 1960).

A. L.

McMaster University
Hamilton, Ontario
January 1971

Introduction

This book offers, in the form of four interlocking essays, an account of the design of Old English poetry. It is the result of an attempt over a period of about twelve years to domesticate myself in the imaginative world of the Anglo-Saxon poetic records by viewing the imagery of the poems as a structure, as a consistent and coherent environment into which one's mind moves in reading, regardless of where in the canon one's attention focuses at a given time. Such a procedure begins with rhetorical and structural analysis of particular poems but does not stop there; for this would be to see *Andreas,* or *The Dream of the Rood,* or whichever poem is under scrutiny, as a cultural isolate or separate verbal artifact removed from the poetic environment in which it was composed and which, in large measure, provides its meaning. While reading it is necessary repeatedly to ask the question, How does this poem or passage correlate with other Old English poems? but also to keep in mind a second query: In what ways is this particular composition distinctive in its use of the images drawn from the whole poetic environment?

The use of the complete corpus of extant Old English poetry as the main informing context for perceiving the structure or design of each particular poem leads inevitably to a concern with the kind of imaginative logic and sustaining metaphors that shape this particular body of poetry. Since it is the metaphorical process, the manner of establishing identities of one image with another, that shapes or holds together a poem, any critical concern with design or structure in either a small compass or a larger one must concentrate on the major recurrent metaphors; for it is here that the critic can see working the imaginative logic which underlies even the most intricate or obscure of the "curiously inwrought" poems found in the Anglo-Saxon poetic records. Focusing on this process of identities leads in turn to a sense of an overall poetic mythology or verbal world in which certain patterns of images appear re-

peatedly and particular themes recur frequently enough to be
recognizable as preoccupations of the poets involved. Having
become aware of the major recurrent metaphors and how they
work, and only then, one is justified in drawing certain generalized conclusions about those distinctive imaginative characteristics which set Old English poetry apart from other
bodies of literature. At the same time, however, the completion of such an investigation should enable the critic to recognize some of the ways in which Old English poems reach
out into a broader verbal universe for part of their meaning.

During the past one hundred and fifty years a large number
of Anglo-Saxonists have turned to the Venerable Bede's account of the beginning of Cædmon's poetic career as a basis
for making some general point about the particular major
development in Old English poetry they wish to discuss. I
shall follow in this honorable convention. According to Bede,[1]
the nativity of Christian poetry in the English language took
place at night in a cow shed. The new poetry came as an un-
solicited gift of divine grace to a humble but receptive man
called Cædmon who already, by refusing to play the harp as
a secular entertainer at the *gebeorscipe* (beer-fellowship, beer-
drinking), had unwittingly indicated his readiness to be a
vehicle of revelation.[2]

    1. *Venerabilis Bædæ historia ecclesiastica gentis Anglorum*, ed. Charles
Plummer, vol. 1 (Oxford, 1895), pp. 258–61; English trans. by Leo Sherley-
Price, *Bede: A History of the English Church and People* (Harmondsworth, 1955), pp. 245–48.
    2. Cædmon's reason for refusing to sing and for leaving the hall is
not given in Bede's Latin text. A motive is provided in King Alfred's Late
West Saxon version; where Bede, in the Latin, says "surgebat a media
cæne," Alfred has "aras for sceome." C. L. Wrenn has seen this additional
information as one of several evidences that the Alfredian version represents "a distinctive English tradition" of the text not reflected in Bede's
Latin: see "The Poetry of Cædmon," *Proceedings of the British Academy*
32 (1947): 281. Wrenn also gives Bishop Percy's explanation of the
phrase *aras for sceome:* "that is, either from an austerity of manners; or
from his being deficient in an accomplishment, which so generally pre-
vailed among his countrymen" (quoted from *Reliques of Ancient English
Poetry*, 3d ed. [London, 1775], 1: li-lii). G. Shepherd, in "The Prophetic
Cædmon," *Review of English Studies*, n.s. 5 (1954): 120, says, "It is likely

Prior to Cædmon's dream experience he had heard but had not performed compositions in the poetic language, meters, and formulas of an earlier tradition, but now the entire purpose and content of English poetry were to change. A new kind of verse was to take its impetus from religious themes, with the purpose of moving the hearts of many men to despise the world and to aspire toward heavenly things. Each particular song was to be thought of as part of a total pattern already set down in scripture, in what literary critics would now call the Christian mythology. In short, Cædmon is the figure in whom two verbal cultures meet and fuse, one of these reaching back into a poetic tradition largely unknowable to literary historians, the other into the many centuries of recorded biblical and Church history.

What is important for Bede in the story is that the *Hymn*, miraculously sung by Cædmon, and the repertoire he shortly developed indicated a revolution in English poetry: the aristocratic, heroic diction and techniques of the Germanic tradition now were to be put to use in a new poetry inspired by scriptural history with its morally and spiritually intelligible scheme for interpreting human life. Without going into the question of the degree of literal credibility in the story of Cædmon, I should like in the four extended essays of this book to explore some of the ways in which the Christian mythology outlined by Bede appears to have inspired and shaped a large and central portion of extant Old English poetry—to have provided, in fact, an imaginative context that altered fundamentally the poetic uses of the traditional "word-hoard" inherited from a Germanic past.

The four essays, each one capable to some extent of being

---

enough that Cædmon's inability to sing, together perhaps with some scorn for wordly merrymaking, troubled his mind as he went to rest. . . . Certainly it is in such circumstances as these that prophetic visions were commonly received." F. P. Magoun, Jr., "rationalizes" the whole Cædmon story to make it "a case-history, of an oral singer living in a lettered community" and denies that it tells anything "about the birth of Anglo-Saxon poetry of any kind." See "Bede's Story of Cædman: The Case History of an Anglo-Saxon Singer," *Speculum* 30 (1955): 49–63.

read by itself, are arranged so that any poem or group of poems under discussion at a given point (after the first such discussion) has both a backward reference, to a critical context already established, and a forward one, to the poems yet to be considered. The exception is, of course, Essay Four, which is concerned with *Beowulf* and looks back to all three preceding parts of the book. Essay One, although it deals with a large number of individual poems and seeks to respect their particularity, is an attempt to trace an overall poetic mythology which may, historically, have functioned in many more poems than those we now possess. The emphasis in this essay—on the mythology first and on individual poems second—may well lead some readers to a feeling that the unifying and recurrent structural aspects of the group of poems under discussion are being stressed at the expense of differences of detail and texture.

A similar criticism might be made of parts of Essays Two and Three, though with somewhat less justification. This would be a reaction for which I have a good deal of sympathy, but there are two reasons I have not let it determine the character of this relatively short book. Old English poetry in its main images, themes, and structures *is* highly repetitive, and any critic who tries to pretend otherwise falsifies his account. Secondly, and because of this high degree of recurrence, it has seemed intellectually desirable to try to explain the main principles of design in the poetry under scrutiny by means of a theory that finds its major supporting evidence deeply embedded in the verbal culture in question, that is, in the pervasive presence in Old English texts of a Germanicized Christian symbolism and mythology. Clearly a full documentation of this idea would involve a much more detailed account of the poems (and prose writings) in their historical context than that presented in these four "essays" or "attempts" to describe the design of Old English poetry. I would suggest, in fact, that one of the most pressing needs in the criticism and understanding of Old English literature is the writing of a history of its imagery.

However, in support of any attempt such as that made in

this book to take an "overview" of Old English poetry in the hope of seeing its structural contours, it should also be remembered that most of the extant poems have been repeatedly analyzed as works in themselves, some of them many times; [3] yet relatively few efforts have been made to think of each one in the light of the whole corpus. When such overall treatments are undertaken, they not infrequently demonstrate a pronounced tendency to fly apart into generic categories: epic, religious heroic tale, elegy, mnemonic verse, gnomic verse, didactic verse, allegory, and so forth. At a certain stage in a total critique such generic analysis undoubtedly is necessary— for defining the particular literary species in question or for describing recognizable strands within a longer poem or group of poems—but this kind of analysis cannot account fully for those recurrent structures of images in the given body of poetry that cut across or imaginatively precede the generic differences. What is needed, then, is a theory that goes beyond questions of genre and the related attempts to catalogue Old English verse to matters of basic structure or design. Once such critical work has been done and the outlines or profiles of poems have become clear, detailed exegesis should be able to proceed on a more confident base.

The larger context, then, relevant throughout this book but

3. The relatively light documentation used in these essays, limited in the main to citations of texts, indications of editions, and to articles or books directly influencing or involved in the development of the argument, in no way implies a willful or disrespectful ignoring of those many works that have preceded my own. Although I hope that other scholars and critics of Old English literature will find something to interest them in this book, it is intended mainly for an audience of students and general readers, especially those who combine an interest in the way mythical structures work themselves out in poetry with a desire to read and interpret particular Old English poems. For such readers a recapitulation of the often lengthy scholarly discussions of each of the large number of poems dealt with here would be an intolerable burden. It would also be redundant, inasmuch as there is an abundance of excellent bibliographies and literary histories to turn to. I ask my own classes to use regularly S. B. Greenfield's *A Critical History of Old English Literature* (New York, 1965) or C. L. Wrenn's *A Study of Old English Literature* (New York, 1967).

described most fully in Essay One, is that of biblical or
Christian mythology. The suggestion is made, and examined
in terms of a broad selection of actual poems, that recognition
of the structure of this mythology as it was working in the
early medieval Church is the first and indispensable critical
conception for an understanding of Old English poetry as an
imaginatively unified order of words. There is, of course, no
a priori critical necessity for assuming that this body of verse
is an imaginatively unified order of words. Certainly many,
perhaps most, scholarly interpretations of it have proceeded
on the basis of the opposite assumption—that is, that the
extant poetic manuscripts present us essentially with a very
heterogeneous and fragmentary corpus to be interpreted
largely in terms of "Christian" versus "pagan," or of "secular"
versus "religious" poetry, and catalogued under more or less
inadequate generic terms. The result of this overriding assumption has been, in my view, that much of the study of Old
English poetry has now been stalemated to an unhealthy
degree, on the basis of a far from proven hypothesis. At the
very least it is arguable that the use now of a hypothetical
principle of unity in our approach to the poetic canon may
afford fresh insights.

Rather than speaking, in what follows, of Germanic paganism and secular heroic poetry, on the one hand, and Christian
didactic verse, on the other, I have preferred to attempt a de-
lineation of the dominant overall mythology and symbolism of
Old English poetry. I proceed on the basis of the hypothesis
(flexibly, I hope) that most Old English poetry reflects, in varying degrees, an imaginative unity—not a uniformity or a
monotony—that is at once heroic, Germanic, didactic, *and*
Christian. The total argument of the book is an attempt to
demonstrate how the extant Old English poetic corpus has as
its major function in Anglo-Saxon England the re-creation, in
poetic terms, of the biblical vision of human life. The hypothesis is advanced that, even though somewhere in prehistory
the ancestral word-hoard of the pagan Germanic peoples had
taken into itself formulas, conventions, legends, and narratives
from what J. R. R. Tolkien has called a "darker" and "more

desperate" mythology, the vast majority of Old English poems exhibit a very thoroughly baptized use of the old materials. This does not imply imaginative degeneration from a formerly splendid and fateful paganism; it does mean that as England slowly but surely became Christian a whole new source of poetic metaphors was poured into the ancient word-hoard of the scops, with imaginative consequences for English poetry extending well beyond the Anglo-Saxon period of history. Those thirty thousand lines of Old English verse that have survived both the ruins of time, through many winters, and the ravages of the race of Cain may not be more than a small fraction of what once existed as a flourishing art of words, but the variety and comprehensiveness of what remains are much greater than often is recognized.

Eternal, Unchanging Creator of Earth
An Old English Poetic Mythology

It is seldom taken into account by historians and interpreters of English literature that a significant number of our earliest poetic texts are "myths" in the precise and commonly accepted sense of the word. They are imaginative fictions in which the main actions are the activities of divine beings, sometimes with direct consequences for the world of men but sometimes also restricted to the confines of heaven or hell. In these poems any really effective sense of the laws of nature as we know them is absent, with the result that the figures participating in the poetic action described are, to a modern reader, fictional in the extreme. When, in *The Dream of the Rood,* we read,

> Weop eal gesceaft,
> cwiðdon cyninges fyll.   Crist wæs on rode.[1]

[All Creation wept, lamented the King's death. Christ was on the Cross.]

or, in *Genesis,*

> Her ærest gesceop   ece drihten,
> helm eallwihta,   heofon and eorðan.[2]

[At this time the eternal Lord, Protector of all creatures, first created heaven and earth.]

and realize that the actions told of are in the fullest sense

1. Lines 55b–56, p. 62, of *The Vercelli Book,* ed. G. P. Krapp (New York, 1932). Unless otherwise indicated, quotations from Old English poems throughout this book are to the standard collective edition, *The Anglo-Saxon Poetic Records,* vols. 1–6, ed. G. P. Krapp and E. V. K. Dobbie (New York, 1931–53), hereafter cited as *PR* with the appropriate volume, page, and line numbers.
2. *PR* 1.6.112–114.

those of a divine being but at the same time of central significance in the particular poems, it is clear that we are dealing
with myth.

A second commonly used meaning of the term *myth*—a
classical, biblical, or northern story with an early and authori-
tative place in our culture—is also relevant in understanding
Old English poetry. Biblical myths are, in both a historical and
an archetypal sense, of central importance; classical and
northern myths leave only occasional historical traces, such
as the reference to Woden in *The Nine Herbs Charm* [3] or the
use of a classical myth in *The Phoenix*. In both these poems
the pagan materials are decisively submerged and subordinated
to the Christian ones. Since even any such occurrences as these
are rare, correlation of an Old English poem with a classical
or northern myth, if engaged in at all, will probably take the
form of analogy.

A third sense of *myth*, frequently encountered in contemporary literary criticism, is that of symbolic metaphor or the
living design of poems whereby certain writers, often visionary
or apocalyptic ones, manage to suggest that the linear narrative
of their composition, if it exists at all, is less important than
the sense of a single simultaneous pattern by which the reader
is meant to be aware of past, present, and future all converging
in one moment of apprehension. When the poet of *Exodus*
brings references to Noah, Abraham, and Solomon into his
description of Israel's Red Sea crossing, he is suggesting, by
means of myth or symbolic metaphor, that the climactic events
(the Deluge, the Covenant, and the building of the Temple)
in the lives of all these Old Testament figures have an identity
of meaning: in the historical journey of the Israelites, itself a
traditional Old Testament type of the life of man as a spiritual
pilgrimage toward heaven, the poet has a richly symbolic metaphor for his spirited version of that epochal event, the Old
Testament Exodus, and for his Christian theme of salvation
through God's mighty acts of deliverance. We shall see that
this kind of symbolism is both very pervasive in Old English
poetry and a major source of imaginative unity.

3. *PR* 6.120.32.

Numerous attempts in the early decades of Anglo-Saxon scholarship to associate the name of Cædmon with this or that poem were at least partly based on a romantic interest in the artist as an individual creative genius rather than in the communal traditions used by him. The failure to assign any text other than Cædmon's *Hymn* to the cowherd of the Abbess Hild, along with the now general decision to designate one or more of the four poems in the Junius MS as "Cædmonian" but still to continue the discussion of these poems largely in terms of what somebody did to biblical or later source materials, has tended to obscure what seems to me to be a central point. The poems of the Junius MS are the largest body of direct evidence in English poetry for the way the Christian mythology first took hold of the imagination of poets in Anglo-Saxon times and, by so doing, helped them to present the Christian ideas of man and society in the language and trappings of the heroic world of the *comitatus* or *dryht*. In fact, the manuscript contains the earliest biblically inspired poetry now extant in any vernacular language. Adam becomes an unfaithful thane who breaks his oath of loyalty to his heavenly Gift-dispenser, Noah a brave seafarer piloting his hearth-troop through the treacherous sea flood, and Moses a mighty warrior leading his Israelite folk away from a very Germanic Pharaoh. As has long been noticed, the image or icon of human society in this first known "Englishing" of scripture is a curious and intricate fusion of Germanic and biblical elements. In terms of what it represents of the central shaping and informing role assumed by the symbolism and myths of the Bible in early poetry in the English language, the importance of the "Cædmonian" achievement can hardly be overemphasized. Nor is this achievement restricted to the poems *Genesis A* and *B, Exodus, Daniel,* and *Christ and Satan,* all found in the one manuscript.

In this essay I describe what I consider to be the most important motifs of a body of Old English poetry that can most adequately be discussed as myths, in all of the three senses previously mentioned—stories of divine beings, early traditional tales of special cultural authority, and symbolic metaphors or abstract, vital shapes of poems. Such stories, tales, and metaphors, taken together, constitute a coherent, imaginatively rich Anglo-Saxon poetic mythology. The subsequent three essays attempt to show how this mythology determines much of the structure and meaning of other less clearly "mythical" poems in Old English. Certain preliminary comments are necessary, however, before discussion of actual texts.

In Anglo-Saxon times the part of society which became the main social content of that poetry we now have was organized around two central human figures, the *dryht-guma* or noble thane and his *dryhten* or lord, the two of them sharing bonds of mutual loyalty and protection. This relationship provided the basic unit of a social and political order that sometimes included but normally went beyond tribal or kinship relationships. Ideally, the obligations of the order of the *dryht,* in both actual Anglo-Saxon history and in literature, took precedence over those of kinship. According to Dorothy Whitelock,[4] the two tended to complement each other harmoniously more often than they served as a basis of conflict. While the bond between lord and thane was intensely personal in its ideal manifestations, it also contained within itself sufficient energy to provide the most comprehensive social pattern of the period, that pattern normally indicated in modern times by the term *comitatus.* This Latin word, used of the Germanic tribes by Tacitus,[5] is, of course, accepted as the designation of the social and political organization of the Germanic peoples both on the Continent and in Anglo-Saxon England.[6] But in Old English literature, both prose and poetry, connotations accrue to

4. *The Beginnings of English Society* (Harmondsworth, 1952), pp. 37–38.

5. See Rodney P. Robinson, ed., *The Germania of Tacitus: A Critical Edition* (Middletown, Conn., 1935), pp. 289–91.

6. Ibid., pp. 13–14. For a modern description of the comitatus, see Frank Stenton, *Anglo-Saxon England,* 2d ed. (Oxford, 1947), pp. 298–303. Of the impact of the comitatus on literature, he says: "Much that is characteristic of the oldest Germanic literature turns on the relationship between the companions and their lord. The sanctity of the bond between lord and man, the duty of defending and avenging a lord, the disgrace of surviving him, gave rise to situations in which English listeners were always interested until new literary fashions of Romance origin had displaced the ancient stories. There is no doubt that this literature represented real life" (p. 299).

the term *dryht* that in some ways remove it far from its original cultural setting, even as the essential bond of lord and thane remains an integral part of the meaning.

It is especially in poetry that the concept changes. Here the order of the dryht becomes, in fact, a major source of imaginative figures and organizing patterns. As the Germanic social ethos meets the Christian mythology and its attendant symbolism, the order of the dryht comes to mean the Christian community or *ecclesia*—particular Christian communities, the whole Church on earth, the community of the blessed in heaven, or all of these in mystical harmony. At times, then, in Old English poetry an earthly dryht is given an added dimension of meaning through its metaphorical identification with the heaven of Christian mythology; at other times the mutual loyalties of the dryht are parodied and made demonic through their identification with the society of hell, even though they are still described in terms of the conventional patterns. *Comitatus,* in view of these facts (to be elaborated as this study proceeds), is a word with too many possibly exclusive Germanic meanings to include what happens to the concept in early English poetry.

On a literal, basic level the dryht is an indifferent social unit, a social pattern that in itself is neutral and free of emotional associations, but in the hands of homilists and especially of poets it becomes a major complex of images, ideas, and moods, with ramifications, as we have noted, in heaven and hell as well as in the kingdoms of "middle-earth." The term may designate the most ordinary human society, it may signify a society in the grip of devil worship, it may point to an idealized, even romanticized "gold-hall" world wrapped in poetic nostalgia, it may connote that utter perversion of all true loyalty and love that is the Anglo-Saxon hell, and it may symbolize the perfect, unchanging society of the heavenly Dryhten and his angels. This complex pattern of images may function poetically, in accordance with the prevailing cosmological sense of a three-tiered universe, on any one or all levels of the cosmos. On the uppermost level there is what I shall call the dryht of heaven—that is, the ideal, eternal order of being as this is presented in the images of Old English poetry. In the middle area there are two possibilities: on the one hand, the paradisal or golden gift-hall of the new Creation symbolized in Eden and, on the other, the ruined *dryhtsele* (dryht-hall or dwelling) found when death and destruction hold sway in middle-earth. Occasionally an ambiguous mixture of these two can be found, appropriate to fairly realistic descriptions of earthly societies caught in the war between heaven and hell. On the bottom level there is the parody of heaven, which I shall call the dryht of hell.

In the introduction I mentioned Bede's account of the over-all biblical shape and content of Cædmon's poetry and suggested that the full implications of this concept of the new religious poetry in English now need to be explored in terms of the modern concept of a poetic mythology functioning in Old English poetry rather than being viewed as the somewhat naïve or credulous imaginings of an early society incapable of distinguishing fact from miracle. Although we cannot attribute any extant poem other than the *Hymn* to Cædmon, there is ample evidence in the surviving poetic records of a complete mythology closely analogous to the one sketched in Bede's list of the cowherd's compositions. We have a Creation myth, told directly and alluded to many times, we have Fall and Flood myths, we have etiological myths, and a highly recurrent myth of the end of things. After listing these, with specific references to surviving poetic texts, I shall go on to select from the poems under consideration those recurrent images which appear, both in these poems and others, to be used with metaphorical significance and hence to be instrumental in the formation and consolidation of the Old English poetic mythology. I use the terms *myth* and *mythology* not because I am a critic who would rather talk about myth than about literature but because they seem to me necessary for the purpose of establishing an organizing critical principle with which to understand, in modern terms, a body of poetry from an archaic, prescientific, religious culture. At this point I shall limit references to the poetry itself, since the concern is with the poetic uses of the inherited biblical story, and I shall disregard the ample evidence in sermons, commentaries, historical writings, and even in charters that the Bible functioned in Anglo-Saxon England as a containing verbal form of Christian tradition capable of expressing the aspirations and sense of reality of the whole society.

The poetic records now extant provide the complete story of God and man as it extends from Creation to Doomsday. In my listing of the crucial episodes in the Anglo-Saxon poets' account of that story, each description encompasses both the terms of general Christian traditions of typological symbolism and words more reminiscent of the actual Old English poetic terminology. The myths singled out here and commented on briefly in the remainder of Essay One will serve as a symbolic groundwork for the poems discussed in Essays Two, Three, and Four.

1. The Celestial Kingdom: The Transcendent *Dream* (Joy) of the Heavenly Dryht, of the *Ordfruma* (Creator) and His Thanes (*Genesis A*, 1–14).
2. The Fall of the Angels: Rebellion in the Dryht of Heaven (*Genesis A*, 22–77; *Genesis B*, 246–441a; *Christ and Satan*, 22–364).
3. The Cosmogonic Myth: The Creation of the Hall *Middangeard* (Middle-Dwelling, i.e., Earth) and Its Inhabitants *(Genesis A*, 92–234; *Christ and Satan*, 1–21).
4. The Fall of Man: The Disloyalty of Adam and the Beginning of His Fate as Exiled Wanderer (*Genesis B*, 442–851; *Genesis A*, 852–964).
5. The First Murder: The Slaying of Cain, the Tree of Blood, and the Beginning of *Fæhðe* (Feuding) (*Genesis A*, 965–1262).
6. The Deluge: Noah, the Seafarer, and His Treasure Ship (*Genesis A*, 1263–1601).
7. The Tower of Babel: The Shining Fortress of *Wlenco* (Pride) in the Green Plain of Shinar (*Genesis A*, 1649–1701).
8. The Faith of Abraham: Abraham the Wanderer and the Sacrifice of Isaac (*Genesis A*, 1702–2936).
9. The Egyptian Captivity and the Exodus: The Dryhts of Pharaoh and Moses (*Exodus*, 1–590).

10. The Assyrian Captivity: Judith's Slaying of Holofernes and the Defeat of Assyria (*Judith*, 1–349).
11. The Babylonian Captivity: The *Wlenco* (Pride) of Nebuchadnezzar and Belshazzar (*Daniel*, 1–764).
12. The Advent of Christ: Christ Comes to the Ruined *Dryhtsele* (Dryht-Hall) of Middle-Earth (*Christ I*, 1–439).
13. The Temptations of Christ: Defeat of the Accursed One by the King of All Creatures (*Christ and Satan*, 663–729).
14. The Crucifixion of Christ: The Battle of the Rood (*The Dream of the Rood*, 1–156; *Christ III*, 1081–1203).
15. The Harrowing of Hell: The Dryhten Extends the Feud to Hell's Fortress and Rescues the Faithful There (*Christ I*, 145–63; *The Descent into Hell*, 1–137; *Christ and Satan*, 383–511).
16. The Resurrection and Ascension of Christ: Triumph in War, in Middle-Earth and Hell, and Banqueting in Heaven (*The Dream of the Rood*, 101–103a; *The Descent into Hell*, 17–23a; *Christ and Satan*, 512–596; *Christ II*, 440–866).
17. The Acts of the Apostles: The Battles of the Twelve *Domfæste Æðelingas* (Heroes Firm in Glory) (*The Fates of the Apostles*, 1–122).
18. The Last Judgment: Doomsday and the Triumph of the Golden Dryht of Heaven (*Christ III*, 867–1664; *Christ and Satan*, 597–664; *The Judgment Day I*, 1–119; *The Judgment Day II*, 1–306).

This list might suggest a more straightforward narrative movement through the various stages of the Christian story than actually appears in the poems. Even so, the Junius MS poems, *Genesis A* and *B*, *Exodus*, *Daniel*, and *Christ and Satan*, do set forth the overall biblical structure, indicating, apparently, that someone, scribal or otherwise, thought it fitting to recognize the essential symbolic unity and pattern of the collection. If we consider along with these works a handful of others— *Judith*, *Christ I*, *II*, and *III*, *The Dream of the Rood*, *The*

Descent into Hell, The Fates of the Apostles, and the two
Judgment Day poems— we have a rich, complex gathering
of Old English poetic mythology derived, ultimately, from the
Bible.

To consider these poems as an interrelated group with an
overall shape is not to assume that any one person or group
of persons in Anglo-Saxon England knew all these actual
texts and thought of them in this way (though theoretically,
one supposes, this is not altogether impossible). But the essential imaginative unity of the poems, coupled with the near
certainty that Bede, in his description of the content of Cædmon's repertoire, reflects a widespread conception of the
Christian stories, indicates that they were not simply a collection but a real mythology that had emerged in early apostolic times with a single, definitive, and consolidated form.
This mythology—not that Bede, who talks of *sacrae Scrip-
turae historiis* (history of sacred Scripture, scriptural history),
would use the term—centering on the person and acts of
Christ, contained the meaning of the universe in all its parts.
Its unity was so complete, according to early Christian belief,
that the person of Christ or the full meaning of any part of
the Bible could be revealed through any single passage in it.
As we look more closely at the poems listed above, it is possible
to recognize that this is in fact the way the early poets appre-
hended the biblical revelation, the way in which they re-
sponded to the overwhelming immediacy of the person of
Christ through the Word impinging on their lives in middle-
earth.

In Cædmon's dream, a man stands beside him and says,
"Cædmon, sing me something." The response to that invitation is filled with significance in any account of the origins
of Christian poetry in England. Each particular myth must
now be examined, however, as it functions in actual poems.

1. The Celestial Kingdom

Genesis [7] begins with a doxology or hymn of praise and love
describing the eternal King of glory in the midst of his troops
of angels (1–14). It presents a vision of the interior of heaven

7. *PR* 1.3–87.

where God, the mighty King and "Head of all the high Creation," who has no beginning and no end, enfolds in his arms
(*sweglbosmas heold*) the thrones of heaven and the kingdoms
of the sky. The company of thanes glorifying their Prince are
part of the unitary joy emanating from their *ordfruma* or
divine source. Such images, involving suggestions of a one-body
metaphor for the heavenly society, indicate a pattern that
underlies the whole of *Genesis* and keeps reappearing throughout the poetic records, that of the transcendent heavenly
dryht or ideal form of human society, the Prince of heaven and
his thanes enveloped in a *dream* (joy) mythically anterior to
any strife in heaven, middle-earth, or hell.

2. THE FALL OF THE ANGELS

In *Genesis A*, 22–77; *Genesis B*, 246–441a; and *Christ and
Satan*, 22–364,[8] the myth of the Fall of the Angels is imagined
as rebellion within God's dryht, a turning away from *siblufan*
(the close bonds that exist between kinsmen). Initiated by the
archrebel who later becomes Satan, the conflict as presented
in lines 22–32 of *Genesis A* takes its rise in *æfst* (envy) and
oferhygd (pride) and is accompanied by *gielp micel* (great
boasting). "Thirsty for malice" (niþes ofþyrsted," 32), God's
prince, a "mar-peace" like the fractious Loki in the *Lokasenna*,
disrupts the joy of the hall by "weaving evil counsel" ("þone
unræd . . . wefan," 31–32) and with his fellow traitors sets
up a rival throne and kingdom in the northern region of
heaven. With the occurrence of this first demonic act in the
Christian mythology, a kind of dark, revolutionary, antithetical force begins to work, undermining temporarily the
ideal structure described in the first twenty-two lines of
Genesis A. To use these terms to describe the rebellion of
part of the dryht of heaven is not, I think, to suggest a meta-
physical dualism in the theology underlying the poem. The
inclusion in the myth of the idea of a war in heaven certainly
implies that there is imperfection in heaven, however briefly,
prior to the Creation. But this apparent contradiction of
orthodox doctrine would pose no insurmountable problem for

8. *PR* 1.135–47.22–364.

a medieval exegete intent on seeing truth in the story. In fact, Augustine [9] did explain this aspect of the Fall of the Angels: God had providential foreknowledge of Lucifer's turn to wickedness, as well as of Adam's, but permitted it for the good of the whole Creation. There are many such illustrations of the struggles of theological logic to digest the myths and metaphors of the Bible in the writings of the Fathers, as anyone who has studied the history of the credal controversies in the early centuries will know.

As soon as Lucifer and his followers break the bonds of the original unity, the theme changes (34–35) to God's *yrre* (anger) and *wrað* (wrath), and retribution follows swiftly. A house of torment, enveloped in endless night and pierced by fire and sudden cold, is prepared in the depths of hell, as "grim reward" ("weorce to leane," 37) from the gift-throne of heaven for those reckless, proud angels who desired to share power with God. The poet makes extensive use of the device of variation as he describes the divine revenge in terms of actual physical wrestling (60b ff.), thus deftly recalling the body-of-heaven metaphor used earlier. The primal crime is the disruption of the body of heaven. The myth of the fallen angels represents symbolically what is left of a temporarily diminished totality, what results from the violent division of an originally unified body.

In this respect *Genesis B* is consistent with the brief *Genesis A* version but elaborates the basis of Lucifer's rebellion. The archangel acts in the name of freedom:

> Ne meahte he æt his hige findan
> þæt he gode wolde   geongerdome,
> þeodne þeowian.   [266b–268a]

[In his mind he could not imagine that he desired subjection, to serve a lord.]

Moved by a narcissistic sense of his own excellence—"cwæð þæt his lic wære leoht and scene" (265, "he said that his body

9. *De civitate Dei* 11. 14–15, 17–18 [ed. *Corpus Christianorum, Series Latina XLVIII Aurelii Augustini Opera XIV*] (Turnhout, 1955).

was radiant and beautiful")—the archangel cuts himself off
from what he thinks of as despotism: "Ic mæg wesan god swa
he" (283, "I can be God as well as he can"). In his dizzying
sense of *ofermod* (pride), Lucifer's presumption reaches out to
include his rebel comrades:

> Bigstandað me strange geneatas,   þa ne willað me æt þam
>   striðe geswican,
> hæleþas heardmode.   [284–285a]

[Strong comrades stand by me who will not betray me in
the struggle, stouthearted heroes.]

Like Beowulf with Grendel, God (in *Genesis A,* 6ob ff.) seizes
his foes with hostile hands, crushes them in his bosom, and
drives them forth from their "glorious possessions" into a
"long journey":

> Sceof þa and scyrede   scyppend ure
> oferhidig cyn   engla of heofnum.

[Then our Creator thrust out and set apart from heaven
a proud race of angels.]

The rebels' failure to uphold their earlier proud boast means
the end of "loud laughter" (73) and the beginning of an exile
which is eternal. As the poet succinctly explains the situation,
"heo ongunnon   wið gode winnan" ("they began to contend
against God").

Whether by pure chance, a compiler's planning, or a poet's
deliberation, *Christ and Satan* picks up (22 ff.) the myth of
the Fall of the Angels where *Genesis A* and *B* leave it and
considerably expands the idea of hell's torments. Before it
does so, however, it provides a brief account (1–21) of the
Creation of the world, God's establishing of the regions of the
earth and his creation of man, to whom he doles out lavishly
the joys of the *middangeard. Christ and Satan,* as a complete
poetic structure, covers the overall biblical scheme, though not
all parts of it, from Creation to the defeat of Satan by Christ.
Beginning with a description of God's Son surveying the newly
formed world and the ocean depths and numbering every drop

of the showers of rain, it moves to its conclusion some seven hundred lines later in the figure of an anguished Satan, at Christ's command measuring with his hands the height, depth, and width of hell. In the intervening parts of the poem we have an elaborate reworking of the mythical war between heaven and hell, commencing with the first demonic act, the rebellion in heaven, and culminating in Christ's triumph over Satan, in the passage about Christ's wilderness temptations.

The account of the establishment of hell makes use of a complex of images that can appropriately be called "the dryht of hell," in that they represent a demonic perversion of the heavenly society described at the opening of Genesis A and elsewhere. The essentially demonic act is the attempt to supplant God; accordingly, hell is a grotesque parody of the society faithful to God. Where heaven is symbolized by joy in the high halls, hell is misery and lamentation "down under the headlands in the lower abyss" ("niðer under nessas in ðone neowlan grund," 31). Where the King of heaven is adored and praised by his loyal troops, Satan as a faithless lord receives spirited abuse from his enraged followers. The devils' outburst, that they loathe the sight of the one who has misled them ("Atol is þin onseon!" 61b), parallels Adam's comment in Genesis B (819b–820) when he tells Eve he wishes he had never seen her. The dryht of heaven, as we have observed, is symbolized by a vision of an indivisible and harmonious divine body (the heavenly troops are "limbs about the dear One," Christ and Satan, 154a); this corporate source now cannot be reached by Satan's hands or seen by his eyes, nor can the sound of its brightest trumpet be heard by his ears (168–171). Satan's acute sense of himself and the other wretched monsters around him as stained and wounded parts (129–130, 155–156) of a dismembered body is supported by other images of monstrosity, the dragons at hell's door and the venomous adders, serpents, and naked men striving with them (132–135). (In the hall of Hel in the Voluspá the walls are covered with coiling snakes and the dragon Níthhogg and the Fenris-Wolf gnaw and rend human corpses.) In its defiance of narrative chronology, the inclusion of the image of human bodies at this point in Christ *and Satan* indicates the poet's rhetorical stance; in the linear sequence of the informing mythology man has not yet been created but, so far as the readers or listeners who are being instructed in the horrors of the satanic condition are concerned, this markedly hortatory and evangelistic poem is, so to speak, set in a timeless present. The homilist in the poet does not forgo the opportunity to make a didactic point with his reader or listener even in defiance of the logic of chronology.

It has frequently been noted that the extended lamentations of Satan in hell involve a massing of the formulas of Old English elegy. Without question, certain elements normally found in elegiac passages are here—lament for a past glory, images of exile and of bondage, and a sense in the one who laments of the perversion of all that is desirable—but the poem is not elegiac. The poet, in line with his homiletic purpose, does not leave Satan's elegiac perspective unchallenged; we are constantly reminded, by expressions like *se alda* (the old one), *feonda aldor* (prince of devils), *fah wið god* (hostile to God), and *atol æglæca* (horrid monster), that the satanic rebel, who in the midst of exile and misery longs for the glory of the Lord, is the archetype of all torment (*yfeles ordfruma,* 373a)[10] in God's universe. He reappears, either as himself, or as a demon emissary, or as the spirit that possesses a human being in the throes of presumptuous pride, in numerous Old English poetic contexts.

3. THE COSMOGONIC MYTH

The story of the Creation of middle-earth and of man in *Genesis A* (92–234) is not at all, as sometimes is claimed, a lifeless paraphrase of the first two chapters of the biblical

---

10. In the Jewish apocalyptic Book of Enoch, in the part called the Apocalypse of Noah, the Flood is related directly to the sin of the angels who have had intercourse with the daughters of men and so are thrust into the abyss to await the Judgment (10:6). As Jean Daniélou has pointed out, this material about the angels initiating evil in the antediluvian world makes its way into the common Christian typology of the Flood; see *Sacramentum Futuri* (Paris, 1950); English trans. by Don Wulstan Hibberd, *From Shadows to Reality* (Westminster, Md., 1960), pp. 74 ff.

Genesis. Once the Prince of the heavenly dryht has sent the rebel troops to the *wræcstowe* (place of exile, place of punishment, hell), he decides to reestablish the dwellings and bright thrones of his kingdom—by creating the earth, sky, and wide waters. The Creation of the world is at once a restoration of an original divine pattern and an extension of the celestial dryht into another part of the universe. We shall see later how fundamental this concept is in Old English poetry and how it relates logically to the concept of what is real or divinely sanctioned in human actions. God the Creator is depicted in a rich profusion of words or formulas—*drihten* (Lord), *stiðfrihþ cining* (strong-minded King), *wuldorcyning* (King of glory), *helm eallwihta* (Protector of all creatures), *frea ælmihtig* (almighty Prince), *heofonweardes gast* (Spirit of heaven's Guardian), *metod engla* (God of angels), *lifes brytta* (Dispenser of life), *heahcining* (great King), *se wyrhta* (the Maker), *sigora waldend* (Ruler of victories), *scippend ure* (our Creator), *se þeoden self* (the Prince himself), *nergend ure* (our Savior), *lifes weard* (Keeper of life), *waldend ure* (our Master), *se rica* (the mighty One), *frea engla* (Prince of angels), *se halga* (the holy One), *dugoða hyrde* (Keeper of glory), *lifes leohtfruma* (Source of light and life), *healdend* (Guardian), *brego engla* (Lord of angels), *god* (God), *bliðheort cyning* (joyful King), *metod alwihta* (God of all creatures), *se alwalda engelcynna* (the All-Ruler of the race of angels), *halig drihten* (holy Lord)—there seems to be an inexhaustible supply of epithets, each with its own special variant of meaning in depicting the attributes of the Deity who dominates the poem.

Although the manuscript lacuna (beginning at 168b) deprives us of part of the account of the successive days of Creation, what remains is a vivid and, in its way, splendid reworking of an ancient myth. The poet writes from an earthly perspective and at a point in time from which he looks back to the beginnings (*ærest*), but still there is an immediacy in what he describes that makes his poetic creation in a sense contemporary with the acts of God in shaping the world. His poem reactualizes one by one the events that took place *in geardagum* (in days of yore, once upon a time).

In the beginning God looks out on a wide land, deep and

dark, alien to himself, empty and useless (103 ff.). This waste place is joyless, covered with dark mist, and brooding in endless night, until the divine Word or "Dispenser of life" (122) moves over the waters, bringing radiance and constructive power into the former shapeless darkness. The account of Creation on the first three days, before the manuscript break, involves three motifs: the bringing of light into the darkness (119b ff.); the formation in the midst of the *mereflod* (flood of waters) of a *hyhtlic heofontimber* (pleasing heavenly structure) whose roof still remains above men, says the poet (144b ff.); and the quelling of the primordial waters as the Spirit of God moves over them (155b ff.). These acts of creation are explained, quite unnaturalistically, as taking place so that the empty and useless void that precedes Creation need not remain *græs ungrene* (112 ff., ungreen grass). As in Cædmon's *Hymn*,[11] the metaphor functioning here is that of the newly built middangeard as a great, light-filled hall in the midst of the *garsecg* (ocean) or surrounding waters, a hall whose roof is the heavens, whose dryhten is the Creator, and whose inhabitants, now to be created, are the earthly dryht composed of Adam and his progeny. The image of the middangeard as a hall or *fæsten* (153, fortress) has major metaphorical significance in Old English poetry and appears to have a distinctively Germanic character. Huppé's allegorical reading of Cædmon's *Hymn* is detailed in its correlating of the Old English formulas with explanations of the Creation in commentaries, but he misses the basic metaphor.[12] N. F. Blake has found close parallels between the *Hymn* and the "hymns of praise" toward the end of the Psalter but has also noted that Cædmon's image of a "roof" over the children of men is not in the psalms, although the idea may be implied in the establishing of heaven, the home of God, above earth, the home of men.[13]

There is a delicacy, almost fragility, in the account of the

11. *PR* 6.106.1–9.

12. B. F. Huppé, *Doctrine and Poetry: Augustine's Influence on Old English Poetry* (Albany, N.Y., 1959), pp. 114–15.

13. N. F. Blake, "Cædmon's *Hymn*," *Notes and Queries*, n.s. 9 (1962): 243–46, especially 245.

creation of the "lovely woman," Eve (184), from the rib of the softly sleeping Adam, the latter knowing no pain and feeling no wound, and there is a pronounced sense of the divine charity at work as we are told of the youth and innocence of the human pair—"Heo wæron englum gelice" (185b, "They were like angels")—of their burning love for God, and of the joy of the *bliðheort cyning* (joyful King) as he blesses his new creatures and gives all living things into their hands. As God contemplates his works, he finds his new world "excellent and ready for guests, filled with gifts, with enduring benefits" (209–210a). Metaphorically, it would seem, Paradise is the dryhtsele whose treasures symbolize the lasting favor of heaven. It is also a broad land, rich in produce and containing gold and jewels (218 ff.). It knows nothing of dark rain clouds or wind and is irrigated by four noble rivers (210b ff.).

Whether we are to see typological symbolism of the Church in the *Genesis A* account of the Creator beholding in love his new creatures, I am not sure. Traditionally the special mystery of Adam is his sleep, the Church having been born from the pierced side of Christ by the sacraments of water and blood, as Eve was born from the side of Adam. At the beginning of his *Treatise on the Mysteries*,[14] Hilary of Poitiers saw Adam's sleep as one of the great sacraments of the Old Testament. For him it was a type of the death of Christ, who had (as the poet of *The Dream of the Rood* also tells us) "slept" in death and by this sleep brought into being the Church. The relation between Adam and Eve, then, is a figure of the relation between Christ and his Church, the Church having been born of the Word made flesh.[15] In favor of such a reading it could be noted that God is more than once designated as the *nergend* (Savior) in this poem, and there certainly seems to be typological symbolism working in other episodes. Against the reading is the fact that the poet says explicitly (180b–181a) that Adam did not bleed upon removal of his rib. It is largely

14. *Traité des Mystères* (Latin and French texts), ed. Jean-Paul Brisson (Paris, 1947), 1.5.82–84.

15. See Daniélou's discussion of this symbolism: *From Shadows to Reality*, pp. 48–56.

through the symbolism of the shed blood of Adam that Hilary's allegory was possible.

It seems likely, in view of this comment by the poet,

> Flod wæs adæled
> under heahrodore   halgum mihtum,
> wæter of wætrum,   þam þe wuniað gyt
> under fæstenne   folca hrofes.   [150b–153]

[Flowing water was divided beneath the high heavens by holy power, water from water, for those who still remain beneath the bulwark of the roof for the people.]

that he has in mind not only the hall as a metaphorical *imago mundi* (image of the world) but also as a figure of the Church. From the days of the ancient Church onward, a normal part of the liturgy of Baptism involved the idea that the division of the waters in the primordial act of Creation, so that life might emerge, was an Old Testament type of the division of the waters of Baptism by which the new Christian was born. In its fundamental significance Baptism was seen to be in line with the great works of Creation and redemption performed by God throughout the Old Testament. This would suggest that the Anglo-Saxon poet's comment on the separation of the waters by God "for those who still remain beneath the bulwark" is an allusion to the waters of Baptism and to the Church as the new Creation called into being by the *lifes weard* (Guardian of life) in the midst of the *mereflode* (sea flood) of middle-earth. In Christian symbolism water has always, of course, existed in a double aspect: on the one hand, as a principle of destruction and instrument of judgment, it destroys the sinful world, as well as symbolizing primordial chaos; on the other hand, it represents the principle of creation itself, the element from which all life emerges. If these connotations, at once traditionally Christian and archetypal, are working in the passage, it would seem likely also that the four noble rivers of Paradise are the antithetical image for the waters of chaos in the *westen* (waste) described at the beginning of the myth.

4. THE FALL OF MAN

The story of the Fall of Adam and Eve (*Genesis A*, 442–851; *Genesis B*, 852–964), like that of the Creation of the world, points back to events mythically anterior to itself, even as it brings new elements into the overall narrative. The earthly creation, as we have seen, has its model in the heavenly dryht. The ruin of Paradise through the disobedience of Adam and Eve parallels the earlier disruption in heaven, caused by the defection of Satan and his troops. This means that the poet or scribe responsible for inserting a translation of an Old Saxon account of the Fall of Man (442–851), having also included a 195-line résumé of Satan's rebellion (246–441), was acting with a precise sense of the connections between the two myths. The student of Milton's *Paradise Lost* cannot fail to notice the great difference in the weight of guilt put on the human pair in the Anglo-Saxon and the seventeenth-century poems. In the Old English, the satanic initiative is far more decisive in causing the Fall than Milton makes it in his work. Milton insists on his man and woman's adequate rational capacity to resist temptation and on their sufficient forewarning, in accord with his stressing of a doctrine of free will, but the Old English and Old Saxon texts go out of their way almost to excuse the human sin.[16] The titanic rage of the bound Satan in

16. J. M. Evans—"*Genesis B* and Its Background," *Review of English Studies*, n.s. 14 (1963): 1–16, 113–23—has traced the orthodox interpretation of the Fall of Man through Augustine (*De civitate Dei* and *De Genesi ad Litteram*), Bede (*Hexæmeron*), Alcuin (*Interrogationes et responsiones in Genesim*), and Rabanus (*Commentarium in Genesim libri quattuor*) and has pointed out the unorthodoxy, also previously noted by other critics, of the *Genesis B* version. This unorthodoxy he explains in the light of the influence of certain Latin Christian poems: Cyprianus Gallus, in his *Heptateuchos*; Avitus, *Vita Adæ et Evæ*; Claudius Marius Victor, *Alethia*. Evans also comments incisively on the unusual (in Old English) emphasis on "the human aspect of the Fall story" (p. 113). Daniélou (*From Shadows to Reality*, pp. 30–47) has described a tradition of the Fall in the Eastern Fathers Irenæus, Athanasius, and Gregory of Nyssa which, in its great leniency, is strikingly analogous to *Genesis B*. In sharp reaction to Gnostic pessimism, this tradition held that Adam and Eve were created as innocent children, their fault lay in negligence,

Genesis B, after he has failed in his attempt to be God—"Ic mæg wesan god swa he" (283b, "I can be God as well as he can")—impels him to remind his thanes of the princely treasures he has dispensed to them and of their obligation now to render him service. He promises an eternal reward, a place beside himself, to anyone who can seduce into hell Adam and Eve, new beings now known by him to be living "on eorðrice / mid welan bewunden" (419b–420, "in earth's kingdom wrapped round with riches"). The result is the donning of "war gear" by one of the devils, a denizen of hell suggestively described by the tripartite word *laþwendemod* (of hateful, twisted mind); the putting on of a *hæleðhelm* (a helmet making the wearer invisible); and the journey to Paradise (442 ff.). Although the poet, while describing the tree of life and the tree of death, indicates that the two trees represent God's gift of human freedom to choose good or evil (460 ff.), the emphasis throughout is on the skill of the demonic tempter and on the good intentions of Adam and Eve.

The first assault is on Adam. Having disguised himself as a serpent and twined round the tree of death to procure the deadly fruit (491–494), the hellish emissary, apparently now in the form of an angel (515, 518), offers Adam the forbidden apple; his first words address heroic, unfallen man's most essential characteristic, his deep loyalty to his Dryhten: "Langað þe awuht, / Adam, up to gode?" (496b–497a, "Adam, do you desire anything from God?"). Then the strategy changes to the suggestion that Adam will be able to glorify himself; he will have a greater mind, a brighter and fairer body, and no lack of wealth in the world (pride, vaingloriousness, and avarice?).[17] Adam is not deluded and the serpent transfers his

the chief culprit was the serpent, and the redemption was a liberation rather than an expiation. Adam and Eve in this tradition, as in *Genesis B,* repented immediately. The expulsion from Paradise, accordingly, was a means of salvation rather than a punishment.

17. If it is these three sins alluded to—in Old English the sins would be *ofermod, idel wuldor,* and *gitsung*—three things would be worthy of note. First, prior to his fall, Lucifer has demonstrated all of these sins: in his attempt to put himself above God, in his fascination with his own radiant form, and in his desire for a great throne and kingdom, as

attentions to Eve (547 ff.) who, as the poet explains, has been assigned a "more pliant or timid" (*wacran*) mind than Adam. This makes possible a take-over by the *wyrmes geþeaht* (590, serpent's counsel) and prompts the poet's comment, "It is a great marvel that eternal God, the Prince, ever was willing that so many of his thanes be tricked by lies coming as good counsel" (595b–598). It takes Eve a whole day, with the serpent standing by, to turn Adam slowly to *hire willan* (to her desire), to the point where he takes from her hand *hell and hinnsið* (hell and a journey hence) and *deaðes swefn* (a sleep of death) (715 ff.). Throughout the temptation sequence, Eve's mind is dominated by a false vision of heavenly joys, and she is presented as quite innocent of what the future will hold for her and Adam. (See especially 708 ff.) Once the serpent has succeeded and Adam, believing that it is his Lord's will, has eaten, the demon capers and laughs for a while and then returns to his lord in hell, to Satan, "the captive fastened in rings" (762).

The images describing Adam and Eve as they become aware of their fallen condition (765 ff.) show a characteristic Old English emphasis on demonic influences that is entirely lacking in the biblical Genesis. As they come to realize their nakedness and Adam begins to upbraid Eve, the blackness and the raging of hell immediately are known to them, so that they gloomily anticipate the imminent replacement of "the best of lands" by a world of hunger and thirst, wind, clouds, hailstorms, frost, burning heat, nakedness, lack of shelter and of food. Above all, they foresee the wrath of God. With this

---

well as in his envy of the riches given Adam in Paradise. Secondly, although this is the story of Adam's fall, Adam in *Genesis* in fact does not fall to these sins when he is tempted but to Eve's conviction, later, that the angel-demon actually has been sent by God. And thirdly, the threefold pattern of temptation may, consciously or otherwise on the part of the poet, parallel the three temptations of Christ. For a discussion of the sins in Old English literature, and of the texts in which the Gregorian and Cassianic traditional lists are found, see M. W. Bloomfield, "The Seven Cardinal Sins in English Literature to 1200," *The Seven Deadly Sins* (Ann Arbor, 1952), pp. 105–21. On pp. 251–52 Bloomfield provides a table of Latin and Old English equivalent terms for the sins.

anticipative vision of the fallen world, experienced mentally even before God has cursed them, Adam is led to repent of his original prayer for a companion (816–820). Eve meekly accepts her husband's recriminations while he goes on to describe his penitential mood in terms that reach out widely into the canon of Old English poetry. He vows that he would gladly go sea-faring through the vastness and the depths of the ocean, could he but work the will of God. He imagines himself as an exiled thane with no lord he would serve anywhere in the world, now that he has lost God's favor (827 ff). He and Eve, aware for the first time of the sin of concupiscence, separate and go into the green wood to hide their nakedness. There, each morning, they pray that God will not forget them and that he will show them "how to live in the light" (851).

The epithets for God as he arrives in Paradise are significant. This is not the Hebrew Old Testament Yahweh or the Vulgate *Dominus Deus* but the Anglo-Saxon Dryhten or Prince, who here is also the Christian God of mercy—*frea ælmihtig* (almighty Lord), *mære þeoden* (famous Prince), *nergend usser* (our Savior), *bilwit fæder* (merciful Father)—and he addresses Adam as *sunu min* (my son). The formulas depicting the loss of Paradise are also richly connotative in the way they connect with other texts in the poetic records. In its fallen condition, human life now, according to *Genesis A*, is to be subject to three major influences, each of these implicit in the three-fold curse on the serpent (the devil), on Eve (the flesh), and on Adam (the worldly exile). The Adam who, just after the Fall, had indicated his readiness to become a seafarer for God is now the archetypal wanderer-exile figure who, "deprived of the joys of Paradise," must seek in "a sorrowful land" for "another homeland." The Old English poetic image of man as an exiled wanderer on earth is undoubtedly biblical. This has been recognized by numerous Anglo-Saxonists but has probably been demonstrated most adequately by G. V. Smithers.[18] The author of Hebrews 11 (believed in medieval times to be

18. "The Meaning of *The Seafarer* and *The Wanderer*," *Medium Ævum* 26 (1957): 147 (complete three-part article *Medium Ævum* 26 [1957]: 137–53; 28 [1959]: 1–22, 99–104).

Saint Paul) was working, ultimately, under Alexandrian and
Platonic influence, as he develops his memorable meditation
on the text, "Now faith is the substance of things hoped for,
the evidence of things unseen." In so doing he recounts the
great Old Testament examples of faith in *invisibilia:* Abel's
sacrifice, Enoch's bodily translation, Noah's deliverance, Abraham's exile in strange lands as he sought a city built by God,
Sarah's conception of Isaac, the offering of Isaac, and seven-
teen other *exempla.* In the midst of this spiritual history of the
Old Testament, he uses and defines the archetypal Christian
metaphor of the *peregrinus:*

> These all . . . confessed that they were strangers and
> pilgrims on the earth. For they that say such things de-
> clare plainly that they seek a country. And truly, if they
> had been mindful of that country from whence they came
> out, they might have had opportunity to have returned.
> But now they desire a better country, that is, an heavenly;
> wherefore God is not ashamed to be called their God: for
> he hath prepared for them a city. [13–16]

As Smithers has shown, the widespread currency of the
peregrinus image was largely due to Augustine's elaboration
of it in the *De civitate Dei* [19] in terms of the two cities, composed of two kinds of men, one (like Abel) born *peregrini* in
this world and belonging to the city of God, the other (like
Cain) born *cives* of this world. The former are predestined to
reign eternally with God, the latter to suffer lasting punishment with the devil. Augustine also extended the *peregrinus*
figure to all men: "Homo ciuis est Ierusalem, sed uenditus sub
peccato, factus est peregrinus" ("Man is a citizen of Jerusalem,
but having come under sin, he was made an alien.") [20] In
Adam, then, we have the origin of the two cities. The *Genesis
A* conclusion of the Fall of Man story seems clearly to be based
on this traditional symbolism. Also not in the biblical Genesis

19. *De civitate Dei* 15.1–2.
20. *Enarratio in Psalmum CXXV* 1, 3 [ed. *Corpus Christianorum,
Series Latina XL Aurelii Augustini Opera, Pars X*] (Turnhout, 1956).

but Pauline,[21] and part of early medieval understanding of it,
is God's statement to Adam that from now on there will be
a cleavage between his body and his soul: "þe is gedal witod
lices and sawle" (930b–931a). The soul and body *topos* is
common throughout medieval literature, its two most notable
Old English poetic uses being the vivid, even grisly *Soul and
Body I* and *II*,[22] in which a damned soul energetically de-
nounces the body in which it lived and the poet, in gory details, describes the body disintegrating. But the story of the
loss of Paradise in *Genesis A* ends on a theme of divine love,
barely suggested—in the clothing by God of the human pair—
in the biblical original. Although Paradise is now barred to
Adam and Eve, the poet explains, they may still enjoy the sky
bright with stars, the abundance of the earth, and the pro-
ductivity of both water and land.

5. THE FIRST MURDER

In the next episode of the story of God and man (*Genesis
A*, 965–1262), the judgment of God, this time on Cain, is more
stringent. As the first fratricide or murderer of kinsmen, he is
driven far into the path of exile, "accursed forever," and loathsome to his kinsmen. The blood of Abel is swallowed by the
middangeard and a tree of murder and crime springs up, its
branches symbolizing every dire happening in human life.
Cain is represented as eternally without grace, as the figure
who continues the *wælgrimme wyrd* (cruel fate) begun for man
in Eve's sin. The green earth withdraws its delights from him,
and he goes to live in an eastern land, far from his father's
dwelling.

The appropriation by the Anglo-Saxon poet of the biblical
myth of the brother-slayer can be appreciated by recognizing
the way in which he interprets the twigs of sorrow on the
demonic tree as still affecting human lives in his own day (993).
It is not difficult to imagine the fascination of the archetypal
story of the brother-slayer for a society maintained by laws of

---

21. "So then they that are in the flesh cannot please God" (Rom. 8:8).
This is a recurrent theme in many parts of the Pauline Epistles.
    22. *PR* 2.54–59.1–166; 3.174–78.1–121.

kinship but threatened continually by fratricide and murder. The Cain cycle continues in *Genesis A* up to the slaying of Cain by Lamech, at which point the dead Abel, who was the good son of Adam and Eve, is replaced by Seth. The race of Seth is dear to the Lord, and its splendid princes exercise their *drihtscipe* by the lavish dispensing of treasure. Finally, however, the cycle of benevolence is again broken when the sons of Seth choose wives from the race of Cain, thus giving birth to *gigantmæcgas* (giant offspring) loathsome to the Creator. Here again, in the story of Cain and Abel, we have for the third time in *Genesis* the theme of exile: Lucifer, exiled from the dryht of heaven, Adam from the dryht of Paradise, and now Cain from both God and man. In the Old English terms *awyrged* (accursed) and *leof gode* (beloved by God) we can see, moreover, the traditional antithesis and basic metaphor underlying Augustine's concept of the "two cities." From Cain's offspring rise up the citizens of the world, hateful to God. From Abel comes the favored race of Seth predestined for divine blessings. The typology here, moreover, would seem to be the traditional one of Abel as a foreshadowing of the faithful of the Church, the children of grace, his sacrifice being an Old Testament figure of the Passion of Christ and of the deaths of the martyrs. Similarly, Cain represents the society of the impious whose cupidity attaches them to the things of this world, thereby making them children of Satan.

6. The Deluge

In line with the idea of a "blood-feud" (1351) between those loyal and those disloyal to God, the Deluge (*Genesis A,* 1263–1610) is the Creator's vengeance on the society of Cain who have polluted or made monstrous the life of man and have also filled the "wide fertile plains" with unrighteousness. Noah, singled out for his fidelity, is instructed by the "Savior" (1295) to fashion the ark—variously described as "a mighty sea-house" ("merehus micel," 1303), "the greatest of sea-houses" ("geofonhusa mæst, 1321), and the "sea-hall" ("sundreced," 1335)—in which a small dryht of loyal creatures, remnants of the original created order, may survive. The poem includes a good deal about the excellence of the ark and its "seafaring" inmates; at line 1439 it is described as a "hoard," a treasure ship under divine protection from which a new creation at one with God eventually emerges.

The description of the Flood itself is vividly handled, in terms of a vast, overwhelming torrent of black waters grimly slaughtering the doomed enemies of God by "exiling lives devoid of grace from their bodies" (1385–1386a). The heroic seafarers in the ark, guided by their pilot Noah, become weary of their long voyaging but wait patiently until "the Guardian of life" gives them a clear sign that the green earth is ready to receive them. The black raven, symbol of Cain and the fleshly society destroyed in the Deluge and called "the enemy" (1447),[23] perches exultant on the floating corpses of the Flood's victims and does not return to the holy vessel. The grey dove, in a justifiably admired passage of poetry, seeks far and wide for a leaf of a tree on which to rest but returns, weary and hungry, over the dark waves to Noah's hand. Finally the wild culver, buoyant and free, brings back to the ark an olive twig, symbolizing joy and the return of God's favor, and then flies away a last time to the green hills, never again to show herself under the dark boards in the wooden fortress.

The amplification which now follows of the biblical account of God's command to Noah, as the latter emerges from the ark, indicates clearly the thematic purpose at work throughout the passage. Noah, successfully having completed that seafaring in the Lord's favor which the newly fallen Adam had longed for, offers a sacrifice and thanksgiving to the "Prince of glory" (1511), who in turn gives into his lasting possession the "all-green earth" (1517) and its creatures, with the command, formerly also issued to Adam, to be fruitful and multiply (1512–1514a). In the divine prohibition of murder which follows (1518 ff.), the Old English is more detailed and more focused thematically than Genesis is, probably because of Germanic

23. Here I follow the MS *se feond* (the enemy) rather than the emendation *se feonde* (the exulting one) of Krapp and others. See also Huppé, *Doctrine and Poetry*, pp. 174–76, where he cites Bede, *Pentateuch*, 223, and *Hexæmeron*, 100–102.

cultural influence, and once again indicates how the story of Cain continues to be relevant throughout the story of Noah. Noah is told that everyone who with the spear's point takes the life of another destroys his own soul, because God zealously seeks out killers and brother-murderers. Man was created in the likeness of God and, by adherence to holy customs, still has the form of the Creator and his angels. He thus is able to enjoy heavenly grace while still on earth. The overall force in the poem, then, of the myth of Noah is to recall the restoration of that primal unity between God and man which existed in Paradise but was disrupted by Adam and Eve and, subsequently, by their murderous son and his offspring.

The interconnections of the Flood myth in *Genesis A* with the establishment earlier in the poem of the motifs of the Creation as a hall in the midst of the waters, of seafaring and exile, of rebellion against God, and of fratricide point not only to the carefully executed structure of the poem but also to the presence of traditional typological symbolism. One of the most ubiquitous themes in patristic literature is that of the Flood as a type of Baptism and of Judgment. The Deluge experienced by Noah, in *Genesis A,* like the primeval waters in Creation, is chaotic and antithetical to the created order, a symbol of the absence of divine love; it is also creative or redemptive, a figure of that new life which comes to the individual Christian through baptismal immersion and emersion. It is also a foreshadowing, in its destruction of evil and its preservation of the good elements in the world, of the Last Judgment. From the Christian perspective of the poet, the Deluge is at once past and future event, symbolically identifiable with Creation, Baptism, and Judgment (this last traditionally being the baptism by fire). The vivid description, dwelt on by the poet, of the inmates of the ark longing for release and for the reappearance of the green world symbolizes the Christian's longing for Paradise and for heaven.

The second main typological meaning involved in the myth of the Deluge is that of the ark as a figure of the Church and Noah as an Old Testament type of Christ. At God's command Noah establishes the ark and takes into it the faithful rem-

nant of the original Creation. He preaches to a sinful world—
"He told men that a dire event [or judgment, *þing* being the
Judgment in certain contexts], a terrible punishment, was
coming to the people. They did not care!" (1317b–1319)—but
succeeds in saving only the few who are to become the nucleus
of a new order. The ark in which they are saved, the poet tells
us, "is an exceptional creation, a people set apart" ("syndrig
cynn," 1324b), that becomes more powerful the more fiercely
stormy waters and dark sea-streams beat against it (1325–1326).
It is filled with treasure and sacred to God. On it the *selfa
drihten* (the Lord himself) places a sign and raises it up from
the earth, with *þa æðelo* (that excellence, that nobility) in it,
when he closes or locks up the ship prior to its experience of
the terrible waters (1388b–1390). In the midst of the new postdiluvian Creation, Noah makes sacrifice to God and becomes
the recipient of a convenant with him, thus prefiguring Christ
who descends into earth and hell but is resurrected to become
founder of a new humanity through a new covenant by which,
in Old English terms, the ancient *fæhðe* (blood-feud) is canceled (1351).

7. THE TOWER OF BABEL

The replacement of the unfallen Adam in his Paradise by
Noah in his vineyard, eagerly surveying the green earth and
waiting for its produce, is temporary. Noah's drunkenness—
"swæf symbelwerig" (1564, he slept, banquet-weary)—and
his lying naked, (1566), symbolizing irrationality (*heafodswima*,
1568) and the related abuse of the flesh, are linked by the poet
with the sin of Adam and Eve, by a contrapuntal reference to
the angel with the sword of fire at the gate of Paradise (1573b–
1576). This new "fall of man" in turn is succeeded by the sin
of Ham (1577–1597) and the beginning of another cycle of
peoples at war with God and his chosen ones. Ham's descendants include the wicked and tyrannical kings of Babylon,
commencing with Nimrod. Japheth and Shem, however, represent the faithful Abel-element in human society, each beget-
ting sons and daughters favored by heaven (1602 ff., 1640 ff.)
and living out a life of "joys in the homeland" until their

souls go to God's Judgment (1610). In the briefly but graphic-
ally told myth of the tower of Babel (*Genesis A, 1649–1701*), it
is the former of these societies, the Babylonians, who repeat
the by-now-familiar pattern. Driven by pride *(for wlence and
for wonhygdum, 1673)*, like Lucifer in heaven, they construct
"in their own honor" (1663) in the green plains of Shinar a
mighty fortress that towers up to the stars and serves as a
human challenge to God himself, a challenge made by men
who turn, paradoxically, from God even as they aspire, by
their own devices, toward heaven. Here "the most mighty
chieftains of the people" dwell in pleasure until confusion of
languages and physical dispersal are brought on them by God.
They are called, appropriately at this point, *Adames eaforan*
(1682, Adam's sons). Kinsmen become foreigners to each other,
and the Babylonians are scattered, leaving behind them "the
strong tower and high fortress" (1700) as a ruin emblematic
of human pride and arrogance and of God's judgment on the
folly of the citizens of the worldly city.

8. The Faith of Abraham

The *Genesis A* reworking of the story of Noah and its sequel
is, as we have seen, a symbolic amplification of the newly
fallen Adam's desire, earlier in the poem, to prove his true
thaneship to his Dryhten by becoming a faithful seafarer.
Noah, with God's grace, at first succeeds splendidly but eventually repeats Adam's sin. Now, in the story of the wanderer-exile
Abraham (1702–2936), the theme of Adam as an exile from
Paradise searching for a true homeland is picked up and explored in considerable detail (almost half of the total poem
directly concerns Abraham). Abraham and his brother Haran
are born in Babylon but are *hæleð higerofe* (warriors brave
of heart), friends of the Prince of angels singled out for special
grace (1706 ff.). The theme of the quest for the Promised
Land, already abortively anticipated in the account of Noah's
vineyard, now emerges, in God's command to Abraham to go
to Canaan, the "all-green land" (1751, 1787), and there live
in peace and heaven's favor. Here again we are involved in traditional typology. In early Christianity, as in Judaism, Abra-

ham is the patriarchal man of faith. In the Church he is also the model of "going forth" from the world, Babylon, to seek a better, an "all-green," homeland.

Before he is permitted to claim his ideal homeland in any permanent sense, he is tested in several ways. Famine in Canaan sends him and his company to the glittering halls and fortresses of the proud Egyptians and then back to Bethlehem (1811–1879). They prosper greatly in terms of worldly wealth to the point where Abraham's nephew Lot is given a separate kingdom, the land of Sodom and Gomorrah by the Jordan River (1890–1931a). The poet underlines the symbolic meaning of his narrative by explicitly comparing Lot's *grene eorðan* (green earth) to Eden: "It was refreshed by waters, bright in its streams, covered with the fruit of the earth, and like God's Paradise, until God the Savior, because of human sin, delivered Sodom and Gomorrah to dark, surging flame" (1922–1926). In the midst of the perversities of the Sodomites, Lot lives as if in Eden, wealthy in his possession of rings and twisted gold (1935–1944), until Orlahomor with his "war wolves," the Elamites, lays siege and captures him with his household (1960–1981). This latter event provides the poet with an opportunity for a bravura performance of battle poetry (1982), beginning with the image of carrion birds singing happily and designed thematically to exalt Abraham as God's mighty warrior triumphantly active in a world where the murderous spirit of Cain and of the fleshly society has taken over. As the panegyric concludes, Abraham is praised directly by the poet, then by the priest Melchizedech, and finally by God himself, this last involving the first direct mention of the Covenant between Abraham and God out of which emerges Israel, the major Old Testament type or figure of the Christian Church.

In this context the encounter of the victorious Abraham with Melchizedech is also symbolic. The King of Salem, called by the poet "bishop of the people" (2103) and "God's bishop" (2123), comes bringing an offering (*lacum,* 2103) and greets Abraham "fairly" and "with honor," thus recalling the traditional Christian interpretation, based on Hebrews 7, of Melchizedech as a figure of Christ. In his offering of bread and wine and in his priestly actions, he was traditionally interpreted according to three aspects: as prefiguring the oblation of Christ, as an Old Testament author of the sacraments, and as high priest of the Covenant with Noah, now about to be renewed with Abraham.

The remainder of *Genesis* elaborates the idea of this Covenant, in the context of further descriptions of peoples outside the faith—the Sodomites, the Moabites and Ammonites (descended from the incest of Lot and his daughters), and Abimelech, the lecherous, *wine druncen* (wine-drunk) king who conceives a passion for Sarah. Through his adventures with these people Abraham finally is prepared for his supreme test, the necessity of displaying complete obedience to God's command by sacrificing *his agen bearn* (his own son).

In traditional symbolism Isaac is important because of two factors, his *ortus* (birth) and his *immolatio* (sacrifice), both commented on continuously throughout the catechetical tradition of the Church.[24] His birth was miraculous, that is, by divine intervention and in spite of Sarah's barrenness and the advanced age of both parents. His birth, moreover, heralded by an angel, indicated a child of promise, and his name in Hebrew meant "laughter" or "rejoicing." According to Saint Paul (Gal. 3:16), Isaac as the seed of Abraham was a type of Christ. Because he was born of the free woman Sarah and not, like his half-brother Ishmael, of a bondwoman, he received his father's inheritance, even as the Christian people, laughing and rejoicing, escape the bondage of the Law of the old Covenant and receive the freedom of those born according to the Spirit (Gal. 4:22–28). Isaac's sacrifice, for which, like Christ, he himself carried the wood, is the paramount trial of Abraham's faith (Heb. 11:17–19) and foreshadows the immolation of Christ, both in the willingness of the f(F)ather to make the sacrifice and in the divine intervention by which the s(S)on is rescued from death.

As a poem, *Genesis* has been treated with contempt by more than one critic, although the part of it commonly known as

24. Daniélou, *From Shadows to Reality*, pp. 121–22.

Genesis B has often been praised. One can understand how the gaps in the manuscript, the inclusion of the stylistically different *Genesis B,* the highly selective following of the Vulgate Genesis, the addition of extrabiblical materials, the exclusion of much of the original, and the sudden termination at verse 13 of Genesis 22 might seem, on one level, to add up to a hodgepodge or to a failure to demonstrate any overall controlling purpose. Even Bernard Huppé's detailed search for thematic unity in the poem by resort to early commentaries,[25] although it is convincing on the whole in its interpretation of the doctrinal content of the work, leaves the question of imaginative unity largely unaddressed.

At several points in this essay it has been noted that *Genesis,* in its successive episodes or myths, repeats images from earlier in the text in such a way as to suggest a constant returning to beginnings. After the initial description of the ideal dryht of heaven, of the heavenly Prince with his thanes in glory, and of the subsequent rebellion, through pride, of Lucifer and his troop, the pattern is simply repeated with variations. Paradise is an extension of heaven and appears vestigially throughout, in the "green-earth" and the "gold-hall" motifs found whenever those human figures faithful to the Dryhten are temporarily victorious. The pride and rebellion of Lucifer and the establishment of the demonic dryht are continued in the fallen Adam and Eve, in Cain and his progeny, in Ham and the Babylonians, in the Elamites, the Sodomites, the Moabites, and the Ammonites. Ranged against the demonic figures and societies are the unfallen and the penitent Adam, as well as Abel, Seth, the victorious seafarer Noah, Lot, and Abraham.

The poem begins with a doxology in praise of the power of God and ends, after Isaac's miraculous "resurrection," with the patriarch Abraham praising his Dryhten for all the blessings shown him. *Genesis* is, to some extent, an epic or narrative of heroic action and is a coherent, intelligible poem on the level of literal narrative, but it cannot be understood on this level alone. It is myth and like all true myth has its unity in its interlocking structure of metaphorical identities, consoli-

25. *Doctrine and Poetry,* pp. 131–210.

dated by means of traditional typological connotations attached to the human figures and events. The source of all
real action is God. There is no one human protagonist, although the recurrent nature of the symbolism invites us to see
the various human figures as extensions of Adam, in either his
unfallen or fallen aspects. The final episode, the sacrifice of
Isaac, as we have seen, manifestly exploits the traditional view
of Abraham as an earthly type of God the Father, willing to
sacrifice his only son; at the same time the related symbolism of
the Old Testament Israel as a type of the Church appears to be
functioning. The frequent use throughout of *nergend* (Savior)
for God is simply the most obvious indication of the fundamental metaphor that gives shape to the poem. The power
and love of the Christian God are revealed in each creative
act and are the very substance of the poem. Whether or not
there is any direct lineal connection between the composer(s)
of *Genesis* and the monk called Cædmon, it is clear that the
tradition is the same, for *Genesis* is, on the whole, a skillful
poetic re-creation of the biblical vision of man's relation to
God in the formulas and trappings of the world of Old English
dryht poetry. It is at once an Anglo-Saxon reworking of the
archetypal quest theme of the Bible (Paradise lost and Paradise
regained) and a poetic articulation of basic Christian doctrines.

9. THE EGYPTIAN CAPTIVITY AND THE EXODUS

Where the latter half of the first poem of the Junius MS
recounts the birth of the Israelite people, through Abraham's
exile, the Covenant, and the sacrificial foreshadowing of the
Passion of Christ, *Exodus* explores, more extensively, the
symbolic meaning of "Israel," in terms of the leading by God,
through Moses, of a "homeless" (139, 534) people of wandering
exiles, "Abraham's sons" (18), into a "homeland" (18). The
action of the poem is conceived as an apocalyptic battle between Israel, the *drihtfolca mæst* (greatest of dryht peoples)
favored by the Prince of heaven, and *godes andsacan* (God's
adversaries), the demonic dryht of Pharaoh. The formula
drihtfolca mæst appears at three climactic points and is used
of both sides in the conflict: first, it describes (34) the rich,

worldly society of Egypt at that moment when their "hall-joys"
enter the sleep of death and their treasures are snatched away
during the Israelite flight from Egypt; secondly, it is used (322)
of the fearless tribe of Judah in full battle array beneath the
standard of the golden lion, as Moses leads them through the
Red Sea; and thirdly, as the last two words of the poem, the
formula describes with grim irony the Egyptians lying dead
on the shore while the Israelites exult that they have won
back "Joseph's treasure." As in the case of Abraham and his
quest in *Genesis A,* so for Moses it is the Lord of heaven who
initiates the action (8 ff.) by selecting a champion and giving
into his hands the lives of his enemies as well as land and
power of weapons. In return, it is the heroic mission of Moses
(through wasteland wandering along "narrow, lone paths and
an unknown road," through seafaring successfully in another
deluge, and through a violent battle between God and Egypt)
to lead Israel, by the "green token" or "symbol" (281) he bears,
along the dry roads and through the shining fields that now
open up, reminiscent of the primal Creation in the depths of
the miraculously suspended sea waters (282–289a), until the
Israelites arrive at the Promised Land.

That "all the many marvels" (10) described here signify the
salvation of the Christian community or Church through
miraculous rescue from hell can hardly be doubted. The poem
begins with a reference to reward in heaven for the blessed,
after the baleful experience or journey of death (1–7), and ends
with Moses' explanation of his "deep" or "profound message"
(519) to the Israelites of the distinction between the order of
fleeting joys in the "guest-hall" (535) of the world and the
lasting bliss prepared for them, if they "obey holy doctrine"
(561). In the wordly hall where they are "homeless" the Israelites know sorrow and lamenting, and they know also that the
pit with fire and the worm are beneath them. If, however, as
Moses instructs them, they are willing to let their souls interpret or "unlock" (523) the great mysteries of scripture, they
will be led by God to heaven and need not fear the Judgment.

Like the race of Cain, the Babylonians, the Sodomites, and
the Elamites in *Genesis A,* the Egyptians are presented primarily as those who "fought against God" and thus have their

archetype in the dryht of hell. They break their oaths with God's people (147), and they worship devils. In their pursuit of the fleeing Israelites they are closely associated with carrion birds and wolves and are metaphorically identified as *heorowulfas* (sword-wolves) thirsty for battle, probably recalling the traditional biblical figure of Satan as the wolf preying on God's flock. They are "landmen" (179) or worldlings (35, 512, "keepers of treasure") compared with the "seafaring" Israelites, and they are a "proud" dryht, associated with a "captivity" (49) "accursed of old" (50), and with tyranny and darkness. When the Israelites flee and idols in Egypt fall down, not only are the Egyptians "reft of treasure" (36) but the "devil" and the "hosts of hell" are robbed (45–46a) of their treasure, the souls of the Israelites. Like the perverse race destroyed in Noah's Deluge, they are fated by God to die, and it is God himself who prepares "an ancient sword" (495) of judgment with which to smite them in the midst of the stormy, bloodstained *mere* (300, 495), the Red Sea.

As the poem, through a process of symbolic metaphor—and a relatively thin, frequently broken line of literal narrative—establishes the demonic character of Pharaoh's dryht, so it also demonstrates that Moses and his troop are to be identified with other Old Testament exiles for God, with the seafarer Noah who took "the greatest of treasure hoards" through the Flood (362 ff.), and with Abraham who was willing to slay his son in obedience to God (380 ff.). The reference to Solomon who built the temple on Mount Zion in Jerusalem involves a metaphorical identification of this mountain with the one on which Isaac is sacrificed, each of these events depicting major points in the Covenant (*wære, treowe*, 387, 388, 422, 423) relationship between God and his people.

Whether or not this kind of symbolism justifies a reading of *Exodus* in terms of the ritual of the Baptism of catechumens on Holy Saturday, as J. W. Bright suggested,[26] it seems abundantly clear that the themes of rescue from hell through the Cross of Christ, and of a new Creation emerging from the watery depths into the Promised Land, are fundamental to any

26. "The Relation of the Cædmonian *Exodus* to the Liturgy," *Modern Language Notes* 27 (1912): 97–103.

Christian account of spiritual rebirth, the evident major concern of the poem. In his very valuable edition of *Exodus,*
Edward B. Irving, Jr., says flatly, "no sane reader would be
likely to call *Exodus* a poem about baptism." [27] J. E. Cross and
S. I. Tucker agree, to a point—they accept that the poem is not
symbolically about Baptism—but emphasize that *Exodus* gives
considerable indication of having been decisively influenced by
the allegorical tradition of reading scripture and that the
commentaries should be used to help with lines and phrases
that do not respond to a realistic interpretation.[28] B. F. Huppé
says that Bright was moving in the right direction by consider-
ing the liturgy but was hampered by examining only modern
liturgical practice. Huppé suggests that what is needed is re-
course to the commentators on the biblical Exodus if "the conceptual source" of both the liturgy and the poem is to be
recognized.[29] It is clear from the few interpretative suggestions
Huppé makes that he considers *Exodus* an allegorical poem.

It will be evident, in terms of the main thesis of this book—
that Old English poetry should be approached primarily as
an environment of images, many of them with symbolic meanings derived from traditional typology and all of them
contributing to the establishment of an Old English poetic
mythology—that my reading of *Exodus* will not be determined
by a search for the poem's conceptual source. But it is necessary to know the traditional symbolic use of the Exodus story
in the Christian initiatory rite of Baptism. Jean Daniélou's
brilliant and detailed account of the biblical and patristic
development of the rich, coherent symbolism of Baptism [30]
should be read by anyone seeking to learn what was involved

27. *The Old English Exodus,* Yale Studies in English, 122 (New Haven,
1953), p. 15.
28. "Allegorical Tradition and the Old English *Exodus*," *Neophilologus*
44 (1960): 122–27.
29. *Doctrine and Poetry,* pp. 217–23.
30. Jean Daniélou, *Bible et liturgie,* rev. ed. (Paris, 1951); Eng. trans.,
The Bible and the Liturgy (Notre Dame, Ind., 1956), pp. 19–126. Further
useful information can be found in Dorothy Bethurum's notes on Wulfstan's catechetical sermons in her edition, *The Homilies of Wulfstan*
(Oxford, 1957), pp. 299–339.

in the ancient and early medieval liturgy of Baptism and by anyone attempting to understand the Old English *Exodus*. This is not to say, in a simplistic way, that the poem is *about* the liturgy of Baptism. It is to say that the poem—in one of the Old English poetic canon's most intricate uses, for Christian purposes, of the verbal resources of the ancestral Germanic tradition—exploits with extraordinary effectiveness many of the typological meanings traditionally incorporated in the rite of Baptism. Whether the poet learned these first as a catechumen, perhaps in a monastic community where his initiatory instruction would be more complete than it would be for an ordinary lay Christian, or later, through hearing, perhaps even composing, catechetical sermons with the help of commentaries, is a subject for conjecture. At the very least it is evident that he knew the traditional typology of the Exodus so well that he could recast it in the aristocratic heroic diction of the scops. It is not possible within the confines of this essay to develop a detailed exegesis of *Exodus,* but I should like to illustrate briefly the statement just made.

Huppé has identified the theme of *Exodus* as "escape from the world through Christ." [31] This concept is fundamental, certainly—it is also fundamental to many other Old English poems, probably to the majority of them—but its identification does not take us very far into the poem. Huppé's brief summary of Exodus typology and Bright's interest in the connection with Baptism indicate the area to be investigated.

Of the many functions of the sacraments in the life of the Church throughout history, one of the most central was their task of defining the essential events of Christian experience in terms of the great works of God in the Old and New Testaments. The ongoing sacramental life of the Church is the prolongation in historical time of the creating, redeeming, and judging acts of God recorded in the Bible. In the rite of Baptism, ideally preceded by forty days of instruction by the priest in the literal and spiritual meanings of the Bible from Genesis to the Apocalypse,[32] the candidate engages in two

31. Huppé, *Doctrine and Poetry*, p. 218.
32. Daniélou, *The Bible and the Liturgy*, p. 25.

essential acts: the *apotaxis* or renunciation of "the pomps,
the service and the works of Satan," to whom until now
(through the sin of Adam) he has belonged; and the *syntaxis*
or adherence to Christ, who now receives him as a new creature. Through this crucial experience the Christian undertakes
to consider his life as a pilgrimage during which he will hence-
forth move toward that ultimate union with Christ which is
prefigured in the rite. Each stage in the process of the baptismal ritual is thought of as part of a drama in which the candidate, who until now has been in the possession of the devil,
struggles to escape his power. As the catechumen approaches
the refreshing waters, the devil pursues him, hoping to retrieve
the soul (the "treasure," in the language of *Exodus*) now
escaping from his bondage. But the initiate goes down into the
waters, is healed and saved, and emerges a new creature, ready
to sing the song of salvation. When the devil and the rulers of
the world arrive at the waters, they are conquered and destroyed.

This ritual experience, when understood by an Anglo-Saxon
poet skilled in the military formulas and themes of the heroic
tradition, must have seemed a "gift" wonderfully suited to his
abilities, especially since the biblical account of the Exodus
used in the liturgy was already formulated, to some extent, in
terms of a story of war. Appropriately, then, he begins his
poem with the promise of the salvation that will emerge after
the bitter conflict: "in heaven above for everyone of the
blessed, after the deadly journey, a cure for the evils of life, an
eternal benefit, for each of the living ones" (4–6). Only after
this does he describe the journey of death through the wilderness and the chaotic sea, that "wandering" and "seafaring"
requisite for emergence into the Promised Land or heaven.
Only after he has indicated the cure or reward, the "booty"
(5), does he describe the necessary acts of war by which it will
be achieved. The poem ends with Israel in possession of that
booty, the ancient treasure of Joseph (585), "a heavenly
treasure for men" (588), and singing the song of the elect who
have triumphed over sin and death, as these latter are symbolized in the course of the poem by Egypt, the wilderness, and

the stormy sea. The "laughtersmiths" (43), "treasure" (35, 143, 512) and "idols" (47) of the worldly kingdom, the "wilderness terror of the gray heath-monster" (117–118), and the "mere-death" (465, 513) of the Red Sea must all be conquered before the new life is possible.

The fusion of Anglo-Saxon formula and typological symbol is detailed and impressive. Moses, the brave, wise, and powerful prince of the people, is the traditional recipient of the Old Law (2) and of the knowledge, from God, of both Creation and the name of the Deity (22b ff.). He is also the preacher and teacher who admonishes and instructs Israel in her moments of peril. He has connotations, by a process of typological symbolism, with the priest catechizing the would-be initiates into the way of salvation and then administering the baptismal rite itself. In his various symbolic aspects he is, moreover, a traditional Old Testament figure or type of Christ in the following aspects: in the New Testament on a mountain in Galilee Christ brings to the twelve apostles the New Law which transforms the Old Law of Sinai, given to the twelve tribes of Israel; he fulfills the mysteries of Creation by restoring the green fields of Paradise; he completes the meaning of the rod of Moses by the reality of the cross; in his Passion he is the antitype or reality of which Isaac in his sacrifice is the shadow; he himself is the Temple of God prefigured in Solomon's temple; he conquers the stormy sea of Galilee and rescues its intended victims; he shows a straight path through the wilderness; he enters the abyss and breaks down its walls to defeat Satan; he brings to believers the treasure of the kingdom of heaven. Above all, perhaps, in *Exodus* Moses is the guide, under instructions from heaven, who leads "the sons of Abraham" (18)—Israel, the Church, the individual soul—along "enge anpaðas uncuð gelad"; that is, along the difficult, lonely, and unfamiliar road of the exiled wanderer-pilgrim which leads down to the sea [33] whose waters, through which

33. Of the many biblical recollections of the Exodus, one is especially striking in connection with the much-discussed Old English words *enge anpaðas uncuð gelad*. In Psalm 76 (Vulgate numbering; 77 in King James version) the poet tells how God in his greatness has with his

he must fare, simultaneously are the great destroying and re-
newing experience of death to the world and hell and of
rebirth into the fellowship of Christ. The *beamas twegen*
(two pillars), the guiding cloud by day and the fire by night,
are explicitly identified by the poet with the Holy Ghost
(93–97). They are the visible signs of the presence of God by
which the exiles are led as they attempt to shake off their
terror of the demonic forces pursuing them so that they may
enter the healing waters. The Red Sea metaphorically becomes
a great armed fortress—with *foreweallas* (bulwarks) reaching
up to the roof of heaven—within which Israel (like the chosen
ones in the ark in the myth of Noah) is saved by God from
the judgment of the waters. The Holy Ghost, now metaphorically a sail (105), is the "guide of life marking the way of
life" (*lifweg*, 104) which, in this context of journeying
forth toward the sea, is the *forðweg* (way forth), the *flodweg*
(129, 106, floodway, way of the sea).

A full commentary on *Exodus* would reveal more of the
poem's extraordinary fusion of heroic diction and biblical
symbol. For our purposes in this essay, it will be sufficient to
have recognized the poem's highly metaphorical qualities, its
main images and structure, and its place in the Old English
scripture-based poetic mythology.

10. The Assyrian Captivity

Judith,[34] although probably composed considerably later
than the Cædmonian poems, takes its place in the biblical
narrative of the story of Israel after *Exodus*, with its account
of the escape from Egypt, and before *Daniel*, with its depiction
of the Babylonian captivity. Built, like *Exodus*, around one

---

arm redeemed his people in the Deluge, concluding (19–20), "In mari
via tua, et semitae tuae in aquis multis, et vestigia tua non cognoscentur.
Deduxisti sicut oves populum tuum in manu Moysi et Aaron" ("Your
way is in the sea, and your path in the great waters, and your footsteps
are not known. You have led your people like a flock by the hand
of Moses and Aaron").

34. *PR* 4.99–109.1–349. For discussion of date, see ibid., pp. lxiii–lxiv.

dramatic and crucial episode of Israelite history, *Judith* describes how the Creator enables his champion, Judith, to deliver the Hebrews from the hands of the Assyrians. The conventional depiction of the heroine owes a good deal to the traditions of hagiography, that early literary antecedent of what we now call melodrama. She is an exemplar of faith (89, 344), wisdom (13, 14, 41, 55, 125, and others), beauty (14, 58, 128), spiritual power, and bravery (109, 146), and she emerges as the beloved leader and deliverer of her enslaved people. She is described as a "blessed maid . . . adorned with rings and laden with circlets" (35–37a) who commits her being into the hands of God at each moment of peril or triumph (80 ff., 151b ff., 185–186, 341b ff.).

Her would-be molester, Holofernes, also is described in terms of the absolute categories of hagiography. He is an exemplar of all that is wicked in the worldly dryht, as seen by evangelical Anglo-Saxon Christians. He is a heathen devil worshiper (61), proud, lecherous (26, 62), tyrannical (26, 46b ff., 55b, 257 ff.), and bestial (110), and he is depicted in the midst of wild, tumultuous banqueting (15 ff.), surrounded by "companions in evil" (16). His planned rape of the fair Judith is the climax of his irrational (68b–69a), carousing nature; unmanned by drunkenness, he is "fated" (19, 104) for destruction. Like Nebuchadnezzar in *Daniel,* Holofernes, in his role as tyrant in relation to his followers, is probably determined in part by the traditional Germanic type of the "bad king," seen in Old English in Eormenric in *Deor* and Heremod in *Beowulf.* The poet lavishes expressions of contempt on his villain, to the point where we begin almost to favor this man described as "hateful to the Savior" (45), "the foul one" (76), and a "heathen dog" (110). Holofernes' beheading by Judith is meant, however, to seem the proper nemesis, both poetically and theologically, for the man who has utterly abandoned his reason and has tried to violate one of those who seek "God's help in a right mind and true faith" (96–97a).

It is not in terms of subtle characterization or of credible description of the clash of two peoples that *Judith* has a claim on modern critical attention. Its interest lies in the poet's spirited and colorful [35] but highly stylized depiction of a sharply polarized conflict between a woman of God and a creature of Satan. Judith, like the other champions of the Old English poetic mythology, although she operates ostensibly in the context of a beleaguered kingdom of middle-earth, is a radiant exemplar of divine wisdom and power. Her people have fallen into the grip of an earthly dryht whose metaphorical affinities are all with the dryht of hell and whose dryhten at death goes down "under the deep headland to be bound in torment forever and twisted round with serpents" (111b ff.). Both in life and in death Holofernes is a spiritual inhabitant of the *wyrmsele* (119, hall of serpents) of the joyless ones. Once "the evil one" (28, 48) is dead, Judith returns to the "sacred stronghold" or "holy city" (203) of Bethulia and leads her people to triumph over the Assyrians. The poem ends with her ascription of all the glory to the Lord who created the wind and the air, the skies and broad regions of the earth, the fierce streams, and the delights of heaven. It is evident that on the level of metaphor, where the poem's structure is most clearly visible, *Judith* is an account of the restoration of one part of God's Creation to its primal state of unity with heaven. It is probable, also, that the basic symbolism of the two societies antithetical to each other implies in the poem a Church-versus-the-world contrast of the kind we have seen in *Genesis* and *Exodus*.

11. THE BABYLONIAN CAPTIVITY

Daniel [36] can be read as both lineal continuation of the narratives of *Genesis A* and *B* and *Exodus* and as a symbolic recapitulation of motifs established in them. Where *Genesis A* shows the beginning of Israel, on the basis of Abraham's fidel-

---

35. Alain Renoir has defined the narrative method of *Judith* by analogy with modern cinematographic technique, "which follows a given action from beginning to end without interruption and changes the point of view by either enlarging or narrowing the field of vision." See *"Judith* and the Limits of Poetry," *English Studies* 43 (1962): 145–55.

36. *PR* 1.111–32.1–764.

ity, and *Exodus* describes the same Israelite faith in one of its most decisive tests, *Daniel* picks up the story and reverses the order of the narrative. In *Genesis A* and *B, Exodus,* and *Judith* we have observed what might be called a dialectical patterning in the handling of human desire. Each champion chosen by the Dryhten—Adam, Noah, Abraham, Moses, Judith—has to work out his or her destiny in relation to two societies, the celestial dryht shown at the beginning of *Genesis A* and the dryht of hell first made manifest when the satanic society is established. When the champion is obedient to the Lord, there appears on the level of middle-earth one or both of two images of desire fulfilled, the idealized dryhtsele, where treasures are dispensed generously, and the *grene wong,* both serving as images of the original Creation temporarily restored. The ideal earthly dryht and the green plain have their mythical antecedent or paradigm in Paradise, as described in *Genesis A,* and are at the same time prefigurations of the Christian dryht or Church.

Genesis A and *B, Exodus,* and *Judith* (at least the fragment we have) move toward high points in their respective actions—Abraham's triumph of obedient faith, Israel's arrival on the far shore of the Red Sea, and the deliverance of the Bethulians. *Daniel,* on the other hand, begins with the vision of the transformed Israelite dryht in the midst of hall-joys in Jerusalem and shows this society, first, seized by *wlenco* (pride) and devilish deeds at the wine-drinking, and then driven into the exile of the Babylonian captivity. Although the manuscript text apparently is fragmentary and we cannot know, therefore, the complete poem, it is unlikely that there was more in the missing part than Daniel's interpretation of the writing on the wall and the account of the slaying of Belshazzar.[37] Israel as a unified society does not reappear after the beginning of the poem. Instead, the attention is focused on the condition into which the former people of God have fallen, a condition symbolized by Babylon and its two successive kings, Nebuchadnezzar and Belshazzar. Above all, Babylon is an image of Lucifer's sin, *superbia,* or the unwillingness to recognize the

37. Ibid., p. xxxi.

divinity of God, accompanied by the desire to set up a splendid kingdom as a rival to that of heaven. *Daniel,* in brief, is a poem about insolence and worldly pride, symbolically imagined as devil worship.

The three boys, Ananias, Azarias, and Misael, are "Abraham's sons" (193); like the patriarch, whose Covenant with God Azarias remembers in the furnace (309 ff.), they are exiles for God, the faithful "remnant of the weapons" (74) who survive after the intricately constructed fortress of Salem on the high hill of Zion has been sacked by "the race of ancient enemies" (57) and her treasures strewn "under the rocky slopes" (61) while her people are taken "on the long journey" (68) into Babylon. Their captor Nebuchadnezzar—repeatedly described as "wolf-hearted" (116, 135, 246) and a king who listens to *deofolwitgan* (128, devil-prophets or wizards) for counsel—gives orders that the Hebrew youths are to lack nothing *in woruldlife* (103, in life in this world) indicating, in the larger myth which structures the poem, that he has the role of Satan who offers all worldly pleasures and security in return for worship of the false god or idol set up in the plain of Dura. Their temptation, moreover, goes beyond the world and the flesh to include marvelous deliverance from a fiery inferno, that is, from the devil himself.

The architect of the action in this sharply stylized poetic myth is God. Daniel's function is that of an angelic intelligence commissioned to explain the mind of God to worldlings. The Hebrew youths, like the saintly champions in hagiographies, have only to remain obedient to *drihtnes domas* (32, commandments of the Lord) and loyal to *eces rædes* (30, lasting benefit) even to the brink of death, and their triumph is assured. The hymn they sing (362–408) prior to their miraculous rescue from the furnace is a doxology to God by the order of all created things. Nature is described as completely harmonious in all its parts and as caught up in praise of God, thus symbolizing the order of reality in which true obedience has meaning and recalling, by association, the world as God originally fashioned it.

Nebuchadnezzar for a time recognizes that the miracle of

the inferno is "a clear sign from God" (488). The temporary result is that in his dream his kingdom becomes, metaphorically, a *wudubeam wlitig* (498, beautiful forest tree), towering up, like the fortress of Babel in *Genesis,* to the stars in heaven and extending its protective branches over the various regions of the earth. But the proud king reverts to his normal role, that of an *eorðlic æðeling* (524, earthly or worldly prince), and even as the tree in the dream has been cut down, so by an act of divine judgment Nebuchadnezzar's kingdom is "cut" away from him. At this point in *Daniel,* a symbolic wasteland (621) succeeds the earlier paradisal harmonies celebrated by the three boys, and Nebuchadnezzar's descent in the chain of being is completed by his metamorphosis into a beast. As such, he learns humility and the necessity for giving alms and protection to the wretched. The stripping of the proud king (almost as in *King Lear*), until he is a *nacod nydgenga* (832, one who must go naked by necessity), is a stripping away of the "old man" and a despoiling of the worldly powers of evil of the dominion they exercise over men by means of this old man. Typologically the king's nakedness and exile recall the phrase *nacod niedwædla* (naked, needy person), applied by God to the fallen Adam when he too is being driven into exile and deprived of his former joys (cf. *Genesis,* 926 ff., and *Daniel,* 631 ff.). Nebuchadnezzar is restored to his kingdom only to be succeeded in due course by his son Belshazzar, another exemplar of pride who carouses at a banquet at which the holy vessels stolen from the temple in Jerusalem are defiled by pagan riotousness.

Daniel has reference to time in three aspects: it recalls the past time of the literal story of the Old Testament book of Daniel on which the poem ultimately is based; it concerns the Church in that period of sacred history between the First Coming of Christ and the Parousia, during which the faithful elect are to continue their witness, even risking martyrdom, and during which repentance, as for the Babylonian king, is still possible; finally, especially in the symbol of Nebuchadnezzar's great image in the plain of Dura (a traditional figure for the coming of Antichrist), *Daniel* has an eschatological

time reference, to those events associated with the separation
of the two cities during the Last Judgment. In the context of
the Junius MS, the poem describes a "Baptism by fire" which
is also a judgment, so that we can see a balance with the accounts of Baptism by water in the Deluge and the Red Sea
crossing. It recapitulates, in its story of the sanctity and
loyalty of the three children and of Daniel, all sanctity and
loyalty from the time of Creation—Adam repentant and serving his Lord; Abel; the race of Seth in its gold-halls; the
faithful remnant in Noah's ark; the man of faith and of exile,
Abraham; and the Israelites in their Exodus and achievement
of the halls of Canaan—to the time of the Babylonian captivity. At the same time *Daniel*, in its apocalyptic reference, can
be read as anticipating the conflict of the poem following it
in the manuscript, the undisplaced mythical account of the
war between Christ and Satan. The hall-joys and feasting of
Israel at the beginning of *Daniel* are, moreover, traditional
eucharistic symbols of union with divinity, an enactment of
God's instruction to Israel to eat and make merry in Jerusalem
(Deut. 12:4–7, 17–18), thus adumbrating or anticipating figura-
tively the sacred banquet and messianic blessings of the Apocalypse.

Similarly, the demonic connotations of those images antithetical to those applied to the faithful remnant can be read
as symbolic recapitulation of the Junius MS images for the
fleshly or worldly society which has its archetype in the dryht
of hell. The proud, presumptuous figures of Nebuchadnezzar
and Belshazzar look back to Lucifer, Cain, the builders of the
tower of Babel, and the proud, tyrannical Pharaoh, even as
they anticipate Satan in *Christ and Satan*. The parallel exists
in two ways: the Babylonian kings in their rebellion have, like
Lucifer, an initial splendor and brilliance; like Lucifer also,
they are shown ultimately as contemptible, as easily defeated
by God. As Augustine says of those who oppose God's rule,
"They can do no damage to Him, but only to themselves; their
enmity is not a power to harm, but merely a velleity to oppose
Him" (*De civitate Dei* 12.3).

Judith and the four texts of the Junius MS, then, are (each poem in its own way) a treatment of the myth of the war between heaven and hell. Dryhts on earth triumph or fail, both in the middangeard and in relation to the eternal society of God, in direct correspondence to whether they are obedient to the heavenly Gift-dispenser or not. Each earthly society takes its metaphorical significance from either the demonic or the apocalyptic dryht, and each lord or thane, if he serves Christ rather than Satan, is part of the work of restoring Paradise. But Paradise is never regained for long; Noah's vineyard is corrupted by his own sin, and the wine-halls of Salem become the scene of pride and devilish deeds. On the whole, those who would serve the Dryhten must do so as exiles in a world dominated by tyrants who serve Satan and live as Cain does. The banqueting in Jerusalem at the beginning of *Daniel* turns to pride; carousing and the sacrilegious feast of Belshazzar, with its parody of the Eucharist and of the joys of hall dwellers at one with God, are the inevitable results. In terms of the major organizing metaphors of the mythology used in the Junius MS and in *Judith,* the captivities in Egypt, Assyria, and Babylon are all one, that spiritual condition of sin traditionally depicted as bondage to the world, the flesh, and the devil. The community or brotherhood that comes into being or is rescued through the conquest of sin, death, and hell is the Church, the remnant of the original Creation or of the original Israel now in exile. This community's enmity is toward the wolflike tyrants, Pharaoh, Holofernes, Nebuchadnezzar, and Belshazzar, and its unifying totem or sign is the *wuldres tacen* (sign of glory, cross).

12. THE ADVENT OF CHRIST

The Advent lyrics of *Christ I,*[38] through antithetical but related emotions of joyful expectation (over the imminent coming of Christ) and sorrow (over the evil of the world) and also by means of traditional Old English images of human life without God or Christ, look forward to the most decisive event in human history as presented in the Christian mythology. In the rich, associative language of liturgical and exegetical tra-

38. *PR* 3.3–15.1–439.

dition, here serving the needs of lyrical form, Christ is presented as the Head of "that great hall" now in ruins (an *imago
mundi?*) whose workers rejected him (2 ff. and Ps. 117:22) and
as the skilled "Craftsman" (12) who now will come again, both
to bring together the vast walls of the hall and to restore the
ruined house of the human body which he once created from
clay (14–15).[39] Those who pray for his coming are bound and
doomed men, sorrowing in prison as they wait for the joyous
journey of the Sun who is the Lord of life (25b ff.). They are
also wanderers in the "narrow" world (31–32), seeking a homeland but scattered by the "accursed wolf" (256) and pressed
hard in their exile by "hateful hell-fiends" (364–365) to the
point of "feuding" (368) against God.

As R. B. Burlin has shown, [40] the lyrical voice of these anti-
phons speaks for all mankind and, accordingly, changes to
represent different persons or groups. At times it is personal
and contemporary (or "metahistorical"), the voice of someone
looking for a spiritual advent and relying on the season's
liturgy for inspiration. Again it is placed in a quasi-historical
context in which the actual Advent is still only a historical
expectation; the patriarchs and the prophets who dwelt in
darkness but recognized the coming of Christ are given a
privileged position. The citizens of Jerusalem, introduced as
allegorical *personae*, are linked with the patriarchs and the
prophets. There is no attempt to establish and maintain a
consistent point of view in time throughout the sequence.
Instead, the poet proceeds by means of mythical statement or
symbolic metaphor, so that the reader receives a sense of a
single simultaneous pattern in which past, present, and future
all converge in a series of moments of apprehension describing
the Advent of Christ into Judaism, into the individual Christian soul, into the Church each Advent season, and into the
world at the time of the Parousia.

In terms reminiscent of the symbolism of the Junius MS,

39. Robert B. Burlin's *The Old English Advent: A Typological Commentary* (New Haven, 1968) presents the most complete and incisive
critical commentary on this poem now available.
40. Ibid., pp. 76–77.

with its fusion of biblical myth and Anglo-Saxon formulaic
language, human life before the Advent of Christ is depicted
in terms of exile and in the images of a ruined dryht extending back to Adam's original lament and even beyond to the
mythical account of the angels who first feuded against God.
The biblical figure of the rejected cornerstone fuses with Old
English symbolism of the dryht. The designation of the temple
and the world as the "great hall" now about to be restored by
Christ recalls the metaphor used in Cædmon's *Hymn*: the
order of Creation, especially Paradise, is, as we have seen, a
splendid dryhtsele beneath the roof of the heavens, filled with
God's gifts but ruined by the disastrous banquet of Adam and
Eve. As a result of the Fall, Creation has become both a wasteland in which Adam wanders and a hall or prison enveloped
in darkness. The *banhus* (bone-house, body) of man must be
restored to its pristine state, and Jerusalem stands waiting
for her heavenly King. The Lord whose coming is prayed for
knows how those wretched ones in the ruined dryht of the
world have to wait for grace or mercy, "hu se earma sceal are
gebidan" (70)—cf. the beginning of *The Wanderer*—and he
will loosen their bonds. In terms of the poetic mythology with
which this essay is concerned, *Christ I* gathers up, symbolically,
all those exiles and ruins of middle-earth located between the
time of the fall of Adam with the consequent ruin of the hall
of Eden, on the one hand, and the coming of Christ, on the
other, and then demonstrates how Christ by exiling himself
from heaven puts an end to man's separation from that dryht
which is his proper spiritual home. Through the mysterious
miracle of the virgin birth, Christ, who metaphorically is described in *Christ II* or *The Ascension* as a *mægna goldhord*
(788, golden Treasure of glory) coming to a dryht with no true
treasure, enables "a bride laden with rings" (292) to unlock the
door of man's captivity (147, 154, 260, 360 ff.) and thus begin
to cancel the blood-feud (368) begun on earth by the guilt
of Eve (96 ff.). Mary thus becomes, we may observe, though
the poet does not use the exact expression, the "peace weaver"
par excellence of Old English poetry.

  In reading a poem like *Christ,* with its highly wrought,

poetic Christology, we have a good example of how little interest Anglo-Saxon poets had in what modern scholars and churchmen call "the historical Jesus." In this, of course, they are like the creators of the late medieval cycle plays, probably, in fact, like most medieval people. Since these early Anglo-Saxon craftsmen of words work within the framework of a theology that assumes God and heaven to be reality and middle-earth to be important only as the scene in which Christ and Satan battle for the human soul, they have little sense of a need to make Christ and his life comprehensible in terms of historical categories of time and space. Normally, any mention of Christ's deeds on earth is accompanied by some suggestion of the whole pattern of his work, in heaven, hell, and middle-earth, thus preserving in each poetic context what we might call the full mythological resonance of the Christian story told in the poetry as a whole. Those events in the life of Jesus of Nazareth recorded in the synoptic Gospels that show him as teacher, preacher, healer, and friend to man—precisely the materials of primary concern to "liberal" theologians—get scant attention in Old English poetry, probably because they do not readily accord with an idea of a cosmic, timeless Christ who reveals a spiritual reality which, apart from the Incarnation and other such decisive divine acts, is only vestigially or inadequately present in what we would call the existential world. *Andreas,* probably more than any other Old English poem—in the conversation between the seafaring Andrew and his unrecognized pilot—refers to various events of the earthly life of Christ but always with a heightened sense of the Christ figure as a worker of marvels. In *Christ II* the deeds of the Savior are described largely in terms of movements throughout the three-tiered universe. In *Christ and Satan,* Part 2, Christ himself presents, in the context of the Harrowing, an account of his work from Creation to the present moment of the poem's action. The important "facts" about Christ for the Anglo-Saxon poet are those miraculous happenings that underly the credal formulations of the Church —Creation, Advent, temptation by the devil, Crucifixion, descent into hell, Resurrection, Ascension, and Judgment.

13. The Temptations of Christ

The account in *Christ and Satan* (663–729) [41] of the temptation of the "Creator and King of all creatures" (583–584) by the "accursed one" (674, 690, 698) unfortunately is incomplete because of a gap in the manuscript, beginning at line 675, but there is no reason to suppose that the traditional threefold pattern was not adhered to by the poet. The temptation of the loaves, traditionally connected with the apple in Paradise and representing the submission of the spirit to the flesh through gluttony (*gifernes*)—"Man shall not live by bread alone"— is mentioned briefly. Satan's offer to give Christ all the kingdoms of the world—"Ic þe geselle on þines seolfes dom / folc and foldan" ("I shall give into your own sway the people and the world")—is also here, this temptation being the invitation to give way to avarice (*gitsung*), as did Adam and Eve when they desired to know good and evil and thus improve their worldly state. Satan's suggestion that Christ exhibit his divinity by throwing himself from the pinnacle of the temple—paralleling the promise to Adam and Eve that they will be "as gods" and signifying the temptation for Christ to deny his nature by abusing it through vaingloriousness (*idel wuldor*)—is missing.

The account of Christ's temptations in the last poem of the Junius MS is brief, and it is the only one in the extant poetic records dealing with this part of the biblical story, possibly because of that relative underemphasis, already noticed, on the "humanity" of Jesus in Old English poetry. Christ's rejection of Satan's temptations does appear to parallel the threefold pattern of the temptation of Adam in *Genesis B*, although as we mentioned earlier the unorthodoxy of the treatment of the Fall in that poem shows Adam not, in fact, falling to those particular sins. [42] They do seem to be implicit, however, in the

41. *PR* 1.156–58.

42. In the Anglo-Saxon period two of the most influential statements on the various sins are Cassian, *Collationes* 5.vi (*Patrologiae Latinae, cursus completus*, ed. J.-P. Migne [Paris, 1878–90] 49.615) and Gregory the Great, *Homilia XVI in Evangelia*, 2, 3 (*PL* 76.1136).

threefold curse on the serpent, Eve, and Adam after the *Genesis A* text resumes. If this is the case, the *Christ and Satan* account of Christ's temptations would provide another piece of evidence for the poetic and symbolic (not authorial, or even editorial) unity of the whole manuscript. Significantly, the Junius codex has as one of its very first events the rebellion of Lucifer. The defeat of Lucifer, through Christ's successful rejection of the temptations in the wilderness, appropriately, then, is the concluding theme of the manuscript. The initial brilliance and "superb" qualities of Lucifer in *Genesis,* like those of Babel, Egypt, and Babylon, are now replaced by the cringing, whining Satan completely defeated by Christ triumphant.

14. The Crucifixion of Christ

The Crucifixion, mentioned frequently in Old English poetry, receives memorable and extended treatment in *The Dream of the Rood.*[43] The conventional figure of the lamenting thane whose lord is lost to him here becomes that of the rood on which the Dryhten is killed; the rood, in turn, metaphorically is a living body adorned with garments, gold, and jewels, a heroic being that in the course of devotion to its Lord has both been laden with treasure and wounded with the gore of battle (22b–23). Its personal tragedy and triumph are depicted in terms of submission and obedience, of bowing to the necessity of being the shameful but, paradoxically, willing instrument on which its beloved Dryhten dies, because the Lord wills it. This submission is at once a gross travesty of a thane's loyalty to his lord and a supreme vindication of it. The warrior-rood has power in war but dares not use it: "Ealle ic mihte / feondas gefyllan, hwæðre ic fæste stod" (37b–38, "I could have killed all the enemies, yet I stood firm"). The striking paradox of the thane's loyalty which is also heinous treachery is not very different from the knotted paradoxes of John Donne: "Batter my heart, three-person'd God . . . That I may rise, and stand, o'erthrow mee, and bend / Your force,

43. *PR* 2.61–65.1–156.

to break, blowe, burn, and make me new." [44] The details of the Crucifixion in *The Dream of the Rood* are metaphorically conceived, so that the rood trembles when embraced by *se beorn* (42, the Man, Prince, Warrior); its body, wounded cruelly by dark nails and shafts, is identified with the wounded body of the "Prince of mankind" (33) to the point where it is covered both with its own blood and with that of Christ. It remains, after the deposition, as the visible representative of the crucified Christ.

This pattern of images, often commented on admiringly, is a triumphant and moving fusion of heroic diction and Christian story. What has been largely ignored in discussions of the poem is the way it serves as an imaginative climax to the kind of symbolic metaphor observed so far in this essay. The description of the Crucifixion in *The Dream of the Rood* is another "curiously inwrought" variation of the war between the demonic dryht and the Lord of Creation. The setting is earth, and the malefactors who violate the rood and crucify Christ are designated as *beornas* (men, princes, warriors), but the repetition of the word *feondas* (30, 33, 38), meaning both "enemies" and "fiends," and the divine nature of the protagonist keep very much alive the apocalyptic reference, even in the midst of a high degree of concreteness in the imagery. The *geong hæleð* (young Man, Warrior, Hero), Christ, is supported not only by the rood as faithful thane but by those who sing a "sorrowful lay" (67b–68a) while preparing the tomb in which their "limb-weary" (63) Lord is to rest after the battle and also by the *dryhtnes þegnas* (75, Lord's retainers) who deck the cross with gold and silver. As in the poems of the Junius MS and *Judith,* the war between heaven and hell involves two kinds of earthly society, one in league with hell, the other faithful to heaven.

What gives *The Dream of the Rood* its extraordinary imaginative force is a markedly greater degree of humanity in the figure of Christ than we find in any other Old English poem, as well as an extraordinary lyric intensity in the description of

44. *The Divine Poems of John Donne,* ed. Helen Gardner (Oxford, 1952), p. 11.

the dreamer and the speaking rood. The heroic Christ who is crucified is the God of heaven—*wealdend* (Ruler), *heofona hlaford* (Prince of heaven), *weruda god* (God of hosts), *ælmihtig god* (almighty God), and so on—but he is also "the Savior," "the Prince of mankind," "the young Hero," "the Son," "the Man of God," "a fair Life-dwelling," or simply "the Man," "strong and brave in the sight of many." Christ, in *The Dream of the Rood*, then, is human. But he is also remote. He is ideal heroic Man, and he is God. In his act of voluntary dying, he is as independently powerful as in his Resurrection later.[45] He is the true form of the human race once revealed in the newly created Adam, a form visible to earth dwellers since the Fall only as a ruined shape. His act of stripping himself before the battle of the cross is richly symbolic, in two contexts. His struggle in the Passion is located in the world of warriors, spears, and earthly heroism, but it is essentially spiritual and requires no physical armor for him to triumph. In the context of biblical typology—this context being relevant throughout the poem, especially in lines 95 ff., where the poet correlates the Crucifixion just described with the Fall of man, the Resurrection, the Ascension, and the Last Judgment—the heroic Christ's divesting himself of his garments has both retrospective and anticipative symbolic content. It is at once a stripping away for mankind of the "old man" Adam, a restoring of the human form to that primitive innocence enjoyed before Adam and Eve wore clothing as the mark of their shame, and it is also an anticipation of the individual Christian's necessary dying to the "old man" through being stripped naked in Baptism, in order to be resurrected in Christ.

The mythical or apocalyptic nature of *The Dream of the Rood* is also evident in the way the obedience of the rood, a tree from the forest, effects a brief restoration of the primal Creation to unity with its Creator (55b–56), even though the foreground action of the Crucifixion is obviously set in the fallen world where rebellion against God by *strange feondas* (30, powerful enemies) reaches a climax. The theme of the

45. J. A. Burrow, in "An Approach to the *Dream of the Rood*," *Neophilologus* 43 (1959): 123–33, has defined very skillfully the relation of the natural and the supernatural in this poem.

laying waste of the created order, through the slaying of the Lord of Creation, is depicted in the language of pure myth. As the rood sees "the God of hosts violently stretched out" (51b–52a), the "bright radiance" is enveloped by shadows, dark beneath the heavens, and the whole Creation weeps (54–56).

In such a passage we encounter poetry that is quintessential Christian elegy. In the mythical mode of imagining violence to the Creator is violence to the body of the whole world fashioned by him. When the divinely established pattern is disrupted by demonic men, hell's shadow passes over middle-earth, and nature laments the death of her King. This is not an example of what Ruskin called "pathetic fallacy"; at least from the perspective of an Anglo-Saxon poet it is not, for there is no fallacy, imaginative or doctrinal, in demonstrating poetically the ideally unified nature of heaven and earth. There are no Adonis appearances in Old English poetry, but in a poem like *The Dream of the Rood* one can easily see analogies with the gods of vegetation and nature. Unlike the fertility gods, however, Christ as presented here does not have to wait for a cyclical rebirth according to the revolving seasons. Instead he rises in glory and passes out of the created order altogether, leaving behind the jeweled rood as a symbol of how he has consummated the union of the faithful on earth with the saints in heaven. By "tasting death" (101) and thus erasing "the ancient works of Adam" (100), he has revealed the *lifes weg* (88, way of life) to those, like the visionary poet, willing to leave behind worldly joys.

In *Christ III* (1081–1203), in the midst of a description of the whole race of Adam lamenting the arrival of Doomsday, the red rood of the Crucifixion reappears, shining brightly in the place of the sun. Here, on an unmistakably mythical level of expression, Christ, the Lord of all Creation, again is presented as the god whose death gives rise to violent upheavals in the world he has made. The poem tells, in greater detail than *The Dream of the Rood,* of the wounds and sufferings of Christ in the Crucifixion and of how the "all-green earth and the heavens above" (1128) fearfully experienced the suffering of their Prince. The sun was darkened, the veil of the temple was rent, as if cut through by a sword's edge, the earth quaked, walls and stones collapsed, the sea rose up, the stars gave up their brightness, the earth disgorged its dead, and the trees made known who had created them by weeping and turning their sap to blood (1132b ff.). Again, as in *The Dream of the Rood,* there is present here an imaginative sense of the whole of biblical history from Creation to Doomsday coming to a symbolic focus in one climactic event. The foreground narrative is set in the eschatological context of the Judgment, but the events of the Judgment have meaning only as they simultaneously embrace the myths of Creation, Fall, and Crucifixion, especially the last of these, as it tells of the human perversity that caused the Passion of Christ. The same total *mythos* or narrative structure is explicit in *The Dream of the Rood,* but there the myth given foreground treatment is that of the Crucifixion, not the Judgment, and the didactic focus is on the dreamer and his life from that moment in which the vision of the rood comes to him, thus transforming his existence into an eager seeking after the eschatological banquet and *dream* (joy) of heaven (140–141).

15. The Harrowing of Hell

The myth of the Harrowing of hell comes, ultimately, from the apocryphal Gospel of Nicodemus.[46] By the time Old English poetry takes shape, this narrative is as integral a part of Christian mythology and doctrine as is the myth of the Fall of the Angels, the latter also being an early apocryphal accretion to biblical writings. In the sixth Advent lyric of *Christ I,* there is mention (145–163) of how the captives of the earth, hard pressed by the hosts of hell, have long awaited the coming of Christ, in the expectation that he not only will cleanse the peoples of the earth but also will make his way into the infernal depths. The description of this journey appears both in *The Descent into Hell* [47] and in *Christ and Satan,*[48] but the treatments differ considerably in the two poems.

46. S. J. Crawford, ed., *The Gospel of Nicodemus* (Edinburgh, 1927).
47. *PR* 3.219–23.1–137.
48. *PR* 1.147–51.378b–511.

The Descent into Hell assumes a knowledge in the reader
or listener of the linear narrative of the events of the Crucifixion, burial, descent into hell, and Resurrection of Christ and
then goes on, through a process of lyrical, associative verse not
unlike that of *Christ I,* to express in an almost liturgical manner certain emotional reactions to these redemptive acts of
God. Where the account of the Harrowing in *Christ and Satan*
maintains the traditional ordering, with the Harrowing preceding the Resurrection, the more lyrical poem commences at
dawn on Easter morning. Mary and her companion are somewhat muted elegiac figures, going to lament at a cold tomb the
death of their Prince. Their response, on finding the grave
empty, is not described; instead the poet tells how a splendid
troop of angels earlier has come to surround the *beorg* (8, sep-
ulcher). The grave is now open, and the body of the young
warrior-Prince has been given back the spirit of life, while
the earth shook and hell dwellers exulted. The scene then
shifts to hell and the pre-Resurrection happenings there
(17 ff.).

The significance of the advent of Christ into hell is expressed in the lyrical praises of John the Baptist and, possibly,
of Adam. Whether it is Adam or John who is designated as the
burgwarena ord (origin, or chief of city dwellers) in line 56
and who speaks from there to the end of the poem (or to some
point prior to the end, line 75 or line 106 or elsewhere [49]), it
is clear that the spiritual condition described is that of the
exiles of Adam's race, long penitent and awaiting release from
the bonds of sin and hell. There is mention too of the demonic
inhabitants of the dryht of hell, but the emphasis is on those
faithful to God in the course of Israelite history, from Adam
through the patriarchs and prophets up to the time of John.
Now, in imagery strongly reminiscent of the Christ of *The*

49. For the view that John is the speaker not only of lines 50–55 but
of the long speech addressed to Christ, beginning at line 59 and con-
tinuing to the end of the poem, see Genevieve Crotty, "The Exeter
Harrowing of Hell," *PMLA* 54 (June, 1939): 349–58. This article is useful
also for information on other versions of the Harrowing and their possible
relation to the Exeter Book poem.

Dream of the Rood, "God himself" (52), a figure of warlike splendor and heroic ferocity, comes to hell, determined to break down its walls and plunder its strength. The poet uses military imagery, however, only to show its irrelevance to a triumph entirely spiritual in import. God, as "helm of the heavens" (34), the poet explains, does not need wearers of helmets or byrnied warriors in this battle; at his approach the bolts and bars simply fall away from hell's fortress (37–42a), and the ancient shadows of hell vanish into the radiance of heaven's victory (53–55).

The exuberant welcome of Christ by his loyal servants from the Old Testament stories is described as a termination of their tragic condition of lordlessness. The speaker at lines 59 ff. uses the language of thaneship—*dryhten min se dyra* (my beloved Dryhten)—as he welcomes Christ and as he recalls how, from old time, he has retained the sword, byrnie, helmet, and armor given him by his Lord. In antiphonal lyrics addressed in turn to Gabriel, Mary, Jerusalem, the Jordan River, and finally to Christ the Creator himself, the poem builds to its climax in the symbolism of Baptism and cleansing. The miraculous work of Christ, in his coming to Bethlehem, to Jerusalem, and to the Jordan, now must be extended to include hell itself. Christ is urged, with *blipe mode* (joyful spirit) to sprinkle with Jordan's water the inhabitants of hell's fortress, even as earlier he has baptized the middangeard (133–137).

Traditionally the Jordan is the stream which pours out the grace of Baptism on the whole world because Christ descended into its waters and quelled the dragon hidden there: [50] "You, Jordan in the land of the Jews," says the Old English poem, "you remain undisturbed in that place! Not at all did you flow over earth's inhabitants; they were able to enjoy your water in happiness" (103–106). The Jordan is traditionally exalted, also, because the Holy Spirit descended on its waters at Jesus' Baptism, thus regenerating men through Baptism and planting them in the Paradise of God and in so doing fulfilling the baptismal figure of the original streams of the earthly Paradise. The poem follows in a well-established tra-

50. Daniélou, *The Bible and the Liturgy,* pp. 41–42.

dition in its close association of the myth of the descent into hell with the rite of Baptism, in that Baptism was normally administered on Resurrection Sunday. Then, too, the parallel of the descent into the baptismal waters and the descent into hell accords with the idea that both are burials of the sinful self that a new creature may emerge. Christ's descent, as a pattern for the Christian, represents the victory over death in its own domain and the deliverance of man from his bondage to demonic powers. Hence, too, it is appropriate that the central position in a poem on the Harrowing of hell be given to John the Baptist who baptized Christ.

Once again, in this poetic account of the journey into hell by the Lord of Creation and of the presence in hell of a faithful dryht waiting to be reunited with its Lord, we can see how extraordinarily persistent is the Old English poetic sense of redemption and heroic activity as a restoration of an originally ideal order of Creation. As with the emergence of a new Creation out of Noah's Deluge or of the green fields in the depths of the Red Sea, so here, less elaborately, heroic deeds in the abyss make visible again the order of the world as God intended it to be.

The dryht of hell is given more extended treatment in the account of the Harrowing in *Christ and Satan* than in the shorter poem, *The Descent into Hell*. The clamorous terror of the devils as Christ comes at dawn to extend the ancient "feud" to hell is preceded, logically, by a brief restatement of the Fall of the Angels and the work of Lucifer, the *yfeles ordfruma* (373, originator, or leader, of evil). Where *The Descent into Hell* shows John exulting at the penetration of heavenly light into the murky fortress, *Christ and Satan* presents Christ's coming as seen from the perspective of the devils, aware that now their humiliations will be intensified. Even when Eve speaks (407–434), it is mainly to recall her own and Adam's primordial sin under the influence of Satan, who now, "about three nights" (424) before the Harrowing, has returned from earth to hell (indicating his presence among the *strange feondas* (powerful foes) of the middangeard while they crucified Christ). After releasing the many thousands of

hell's faithful, Christ fastens the bonds of torment more se-
curely on the devils and thrusts them further into the darkness
(441 ff.). Before leaving hell in triumph, however, he sits down
among his loyal troop and recounts the story of his dealings
with man from the time of Adam to the end of his thirty-
three years as a man on earth (468–511). He explains how he
has now fixed his hearers' destiny—"Ic eow þingade" (507, "I
have made terms" or "a settlement for you")—by permitting
spears to pierce him on the gallows. By submitting to death
through the physical warfare of this world, he now may lead
his thanes to the eternal joys of the doughty with the heavenly
Dryhten.

16. The Resurrection and Ascension of Christ

The Dream of the Rood achieves one of its most telling
effects by presenting Christ, at the moment of his deposition
from the cross, as a wounded, "limb-weary" warrior resting
awhile after a great battle as his comrades stand round him.
The metaphor is deftly used and then permitted to recede
into the background, as the poem moves on to the account of
the lamenting friends of Christ burying him in the evening-
tide. Another suggestion of the same complex of dryht images
perhaps can be seen, referring back to the "ancient deeds of
Adam" and forward to eucharistic participation in the death
of Christ's body, in the glancing use of the idea of banqueting
on the night after the battle. The Lord "tasted death," the
poem says, but rose again "as a help to men with his mighty
power" and ascended into heaven, from where, at Doomsday,
he will come to seek out that man "who for the name of the
Lord was willing to taste bitter death" (101 ff.). The dread
banquet of Adam and Eve in the dryhtsele of Eden caused that
death which now in the Resurrection is swallowed up in
victory. As Christ's body receives life again at dawn on Easter
morning, so we are told in *The Descent into Hell* (17–23a), a
troop of angels looks on, the ground shakes, hell dwellers
laugh, and the young Warrior rises in power from the earth.
There is no stone fastened strongly enough, as *Christ and*

Satan expresses it (515–591a), even though clasped with iron, to resist the mighty strength of the Lord of angels.

In two poems, the post-Resurrection appearances of Christ lead up to accounts of his Ascension. In *Christ and Satan,* angels sent by him tell the disciples that they will be able to look on "God in Galilee" (529). When he appears to them on the road, they fall to the earth, giving thanks that they have been permitted to see the "Creator of angels" (533). The incident of "doubting Thomas" follows, culminating in a sacramental interpretation of the blood from the side of Christ as the "bath of Baptism" (544); once Didymus touches it with his hands, he recognizes *se deora . . . hælend* (541–542, the dear . . . Savior). At the end of forty days, the hand of God appears in the sky in the midst of thousands of angels and takes the "Prince of heaven" home (557–573a).

The line, "Siteð nu on þa swiðran hond   sunu his fæderes" (579, "The Son now sits on the right hand of his Father"—recalling credal statements about Christ's Ascension—indicates where we are in terms of typological symbolism. Traditionally the feast of the Ascension is the liturgical celebration of the royal enthronement of Christ. Whereas in the Nativity and the Crucifixion Christ's divine kingship is humiliated on behalf of man, in the Resurrection and the Ascension it is exalted, so that human nature, both Christ's and mankind's, is restored to its rightful place in the presence of God. The seating of Christ on the right hand of the Father has both a retrospective significance and an anticipative one. It recalls one of the messianic psalms used liturgically in the feast of the Ascension from very early times: "The Lord said unto my lord, 'Sit thou at my right hand, until I make thine enemies thy footstool' " (Vulg., Ps. 109). Similarly it looks forward to the Judgment, narrated a few lines further on in *Christ and Satan,* beginning at line 597.

Christ II, based largely on Gregory the Great's Ascension sermon [51], also shows a traditional connection with the Ascension liturgy in the angels' hymn to the newly ascended Christ,

51. *PL* 76.1218–1219.

with its echo of another messianic psalm: the angels' "Geatu, ontynað! / Wile in to eow ealles waldend / cyning on ceastre" (557–585, "Open, O gates! The Ruler of all things will come in to you, the King into his city") recalls the verse repeated by the psalmist, "Life up your heads, O ye gates: and be ye lifted up, ye everlasting doors; and the King of glory shall come in" (Vulg., Ps. 23).

In *Christ II*, while the disciples listen to "their Giver of treasure" (460) and in so doing are initiated into sacred mysteries, the emphasis is on their readiness to enter the heavenly city, even though their apostolic work on earth has yet to be done (461b–467). Before ascending to heaven through the roof of the temple, Christ commissions his thanes to proclaim to all men "the bright faith" (483), to break down idols, and to sow peace in the hearts of men by abolishing hatred (481–484). Despite the promise of their Dryhten that spiritually he will be with them (476 ff.), the Ascension is followed by elegiac lamentation (499b–505), until once again heaven acts on behalf of mankind. The band of the apostles, described in terms of a lordless dryht, waits sorrowfully in Jerusalem (533–540a).

Cynewulf does not tell of the experience of Pentecost, but *Christ and Satan* mentions it briefly (568b–571), followed by a short account of the damnation of Judas who has sold the Son of God for "silver treasure" but is rewarded for his dark deed by the "wretched monster in hell" (578), an interesting demonic modulation of the ubiquitous treasure symbolism of dryht poetry. The account, in *Christ II*, of heaven's welcome of her ascended Lord to the "gift-throne of souls" (572) "after the war play" (573) shows him receiving the "greatest of banquets" (550). Christ in triumph takes his "high seat" (555) in the midst of a radiant troop of thanes who sing a hymn of praise, telling how in the Harrowing he has despoiled hell of all the tribute wrongly swallowed by it in former days and has taken from hell's captivity as booty to his throne in the heavenly dryht the souls of the elect.

The champions of the devil with their weapon thrusts could do nothing against the strength of the one who now has made war "against his ancient foes" (557–585). The result, for man, of this war, as Cynewulf explains, is the settlement of the "greatest of feuds" (617); now the curse on man—by which he had to endure misery and exile and finally to chant a death song as he returned to the earth, there to be overwhelmed by worms (621–626)—is destroyed, and a choice is possible for all men. The myth of the Ascension in *Christ II* and *Christ and Satan* is handled on a level of considerable abstraction, but the images used exploit the associations of traditional dryht poetry—feuding, exile, sacred obligations of vengeance, war, the rewards of victory, and, especially, the panegyrics and banqueting rituals in the hall after the battle. The treasure dispensed by the triumphant Christ, as he sits by the Father in heaven, is help and salvation to the sons of men who still live on earth *(Christ and Satan, 579–597)*.

One of the most persistent themes running through *Christ II* is that of the human obligations and responsive loyalties exacted by the miracle of the Ascension. The culmination of this theme is the poet's own personal resolve not to neglect the need of the soul while living in this world (815–820a), followed by the penitential metaphor of life as seafaring through stormy seas toward the heavenly harbor (850–866). But the basis for this conclusion to the poem has already been well established, primarily in the account of the great "leaping" acts of the cosmic Christ on behalf of a lost humanity (712–743), the most notable of these acts in this poem being the Ascension. Cynewulf's close association (600 ff.) of Christ's gift of *hælo* (salvation) with the benefits of nature provided by God in the Creation—food, riches, gentle weather, the sun and moon, dew and rain, and all good things for the nourishing of life—provides further grounds for this conclusion.

The theme of the "gifts of men" a little further on in the poem (659 ff.) continues the emphasis on God's goodness in his role as Gift-dispenser to mankind. J. E. Cross has convincingly shown [52] that this theme, found here and also in the Exeter Book *Gifts of Men* and *Fortunes of Men,* is to be under-

52. "The Old English Poetic Theme of 'The Gifts of Men' ", *Neophilologus* 44 (1962): 66–70.

stood in two contexts. The first of these is the parable of the talents in Matthew 25:14–30. The second is Gregory the Great's correlation of the man in the parable—who went into a far country leaving behind gifts or talents with his servants— with Christ ascending to heaven but later returning to judge the respective uses of the talents he has earlier dispersed. Cross also has cited in this connection the Pauline text, "When he ascended up on high, he led captivity captive, and gave gifts unto men" (Eph. 4:8). He does not mention the Old Testament source of the Pauline text, Psalm 67:18, this psalm also being one of those used in the liturgy for the feast of the Ascension: "Thou hast ascended on high, thou hast led captivity captive: thou hast received gifts for men." The Pauline version, in its reference to the gifts given by Christ rather than to those received by Yahweh, is a Christological reading of a messianic psalm.[53] It is this latter version of the "gifts of men" theme that Cynewulf utilizes in his homiletic-poetic attempt to combat the "stony heart" (641) of the man unmindful of divine goodness. His poem demonstrates, more-over, a keen sense of the traditional theological and liturgical connection between the myth of the Ascension and the com-mission to Christ's followers to evangelize while time still remains to them in this "fleeting" life.

Christ's victories over a sinful world and over the dark abyss of hell and his return to heaven are described by Cyne-wulf in two symbolic figures of animation and exuberant life: Christ is a soaring bird, whose flights between earth and heaven are not comprehensible to those of darkened under-standing and hearts of stone (633–653); he is also a "leaping" stag (744–755), a figure taken from Gregory the Great but going back ultimately to the Song of Solomon: "The voice of my beloved! Behold, he comes, leaping upon the mountains, bounding over the hills" (Song of Sol. 2:8). The energetic joy of the bird and the bounding stag, neither creature capable of being impeded for long by those influences that would bind it to the earth, recalls other creatures in Old English poetry—

53. Daniélou, *The Bible and the Liturgy*, p. 312.

Noah's wild culver, the phoenix, and the hart in *Beowulf* that risks death itself rather than be taken captive by the hellish mere.

Cynewulf's Ascension poem includes a passage (691 ff.) that can be taken as a typically Old English symbolic statement of the connection between heaven and middle-earth once Christ has disappeared into the order of eternity. In a development of Habakkuk 3:11—"Sol et luna steterunt in suo" ("the sun and the moon stood still")—and Gregory's use of it, attention is appropriately focused on the sun and the moon, the two heavenly bodies that most obviously transcend the purely earthly context even at the same time as they profoundly influence its condition. In a fusion of solar myth and lapidarian metaphor (691b–701a), the sun and the moon, "sacred jewels" in the sky, are presented as God himself; as the Sun the Deity is "a glorious radiance to angels and to earth dwellers," and as the Moon he is "a spiritual star," the Church, brilliant in its union of truth and righteousness. This myth-based identification of spiritual reality on earth with that in heaven is, however, an as yet incompletely realized ideal, and Cynewulf goes on to describe (701b ff.) the Church of the faithful suffering persecution under heathen shepherds. The coming trials of the faithful in the world, now that Christ has ascended, are appropriately described in images reminiscent of the mutilation of Christ's body in the Crucifixion and, at the same time, anticipative of the shedding of the blood of the martyrs (706–709a). It is out of this imagery that a poem like *The Fates of the Apostles* takes its rise as the next episode of early medieval Christian mythology. Also, as will be shown in Essay Two, it is in this part of the total mythology that hagiographic symbolism has its genesis.

17. THE ACTS OF THE APOSTLES

The Fates of the Apostles,[54] as a poem, has been abused mightily by critics. We are told that it "would hardly have attracted attention if Cynewulf's acrostic had not been attached

54. *PR* 2.51–54.1–122.

to it," [55] that it is nothing but a signature and a list, and that the dullness and lack of inspiration characteristic of it are not found in the other writings of Cynewulf.[56] A recent editor says bluntly that "the poem has no literary merit" and that it is to be delegated, ignominiously, it is clear, to the class of memorial verse.[57] An earlier critic found the poem's material too diversified and its structure too compressed to give any great opportunity for poetic imagery or design but reserved a little praise for "the personal passage" in which Cynewulf, according to his custom, reflects on death and appeals for sympathy and prayer.[58] Now I would not want to defend *The Fates of the Apostles* as a great or complex and rich poem, but the nature of the strictures on it leads one to wonder if it is not being censured with the help of criteria not necessarily relevant to it or, in fact, relevant to the bulk of Old English poetry.

The concern with individual authorship and genius, with "inspiration," with "literary merit," and with "personal" lyrical expression strikes one as increasingly bizarre in a generation in which Anglo-Saxon scholarship and criticism, on a fairly massive scale, have demonstrated that traditionalism, individual artistic anonymity, and fidelity to tried and true formulas and themes, rather than individualistic personal expression, were thought by the Anglo-Saxons to be the important matters. In fact, a significant number of relatively neglected Old English poems are waiting for attention from critics of a taste or historical sympathy sufficiently catholic that they will not be impeded by modern prejudices against medieval Christian concerns. To scant any Old English poem because it is "memorial verse" or a "catalogue" of saints is mentally to cripple oneself for understanding and interpret-

55. Claes Schaar, *Critical Studies in the Cynewulf Group* (Lund, 1949), p. 34.

56. Rosemary Woolf, ed., *Juliana* (London, 1955), p. 7.

57. Kenneth R. Brooks, ed., *Andreas and the Fates of the Apostles* (Oxford, 1961), p. xxxi.

58. Charles W. Kennedy, *The Earliest English Poetry* (London, 1943), p. 230.

ing a poetic corpus whose main cultural purpose is perhaps best indicated in the formulas *We gefrugnon* (We have heard) and *Ic gefrægn* (I have heard). The much admired *Beowulf*, as well as the hagiographic poems, is memorial verse.

Cynewulf's description of how, weary with wandering and sick at heart, he finally discovered his song about the apostolic heroes (1–4a) may have some connection with a personal or autobiographical quest for the "long home" (92) he aspires toward. It may not have. What is beyond question is that the poem is a vehicle for passing on a tradition thought to be both glorious and of decisive importance for all Christians whose lives are made significant only insofar as they accept the exemplary roles of Christ and his saints. As champions of the Lord who is the Sun, the apostles' taking of the gospel into a heathen land is a "dawning of day" and a "cleansing" of the newly converted land (65b–67). The complete absence of any irony or realism in the treatment of "the twelve noble-minded ones" (86) does not indicate a lack of poetic ability on Cynewulf's part, since the poem clearly is one of several Old English panegyrics about those heroes whose merit lies in their triumphant choice of eternal reality rather than fleeting joy on earth.

W. B. Yeats, in *A Vision*, praised the culture of sixth-century Byzantium for the way its artists "were almost impersonal, almost perhaps without the consciousness of individual design, absorbed in their subject matter and that the vision of a whole people." [59] One wonders whether such a concept of the transpersonal nature and function of art, in a certain kind of society, is not more germane to any consideration of hieratic Old English poetry than the well-worn questions about authorship and sources. (In any case it is clear that the dominant ideological assumptions underlying this early Christian poetic tradition would treat the later Yeatsian return to "the rag-and-bone shop of the heart" as pitiful, or tragic, or simply as irrationally self-destructive.)

59. **W. B. Yeats,** *A Vision* (a reissue with the author's final revisions, New York, 1961), pp. 279–80.

18. The Last Judgment

Two myths, those of Creation and Doomsday, from the over-all narrative pattern of Christian mythology, appear more frequently in Old English poetry, often in brief mentions, than all the others. We have noticed how the mythical poems have a pronounced tendency to hearken back to primordial Creation for much of their significance. To describe the tragedy of the Fall, whether of man or angel, one needs a sense of an earlier ideal pattern, and to depict the demonic nature of life in Egypt, Sodom, or Babylon it is necessary to remember the antithesis of the demonic way of life, the earthly Paradise and the heavenly dryht beyond.

The poets' powerful nostalgia for a return to their begin-nings, however, is accompanied by an equally pervasive and shaping eschatological myth. Without the awesome visions associated with the Doomsday story and the descriptions of a final *telos* toward which all actions in the three-tiered universe move, the great bulk of Old English poetry would lose its main basis of narrative movement and progression as well as its didactic and often homiletic *raison d'être*. The Doomsday vision, moreover, is not something that appears only as the final climax of the overall mythology; a sense of the *eschaton* and the accompanying theme of divine judgment appears in nearly all accounts of those particular battles of the dryhts of heaven and hell, fought out on any level of the cosmos, in-cluding the earthly one, that have been considered in this essay. The creation of hell for Lucifer and his fellow rebels is itself an act of judgment; the presentation of it involves imagery that is part of the Doomsday myth. So it is also with the flaming sword exiling Adam from the dryhtsele of Eden, the mark placed on Cain's forehead as he is driven into the wilderness, the confusing of the builders of Babel, the divine wrath directed toward Abimelech, the smiting of Sodom and Gomorrah, the ancient sword of the Deluge with which God smites Pharaoh's troops, the decapitation of Holofernes, the cutting down of the great tree of Nebuchadnezzar's kingdom, and the consigning of the damned in hell to a deeper part of their gloomy hall in the Harrowing myth—all these configurations illustrate heaven's constant cleansing and redeeming of the created universe.

In four particular works the Doomsday myth is given extended treatment: *Christ*,[60] *Christ and Satan*,[61] *The Judgment Day I*,[62] and *The Judgment Day II*.[63] The conclusion of *Christ II* prepares for Part III (on the subject of the Judgment) by introducing a vision of the end of things. Symbols of the green plain and the ideal fortress or hall have been central in descriptions of the divinely sanctioned order that appears intermittently throughout the mythical poems; so now it is these same creations that are annihilated in the final terror: "Wongas hreosað, / burgstede berstað" (810b–811a, "Plains shall fall in ruins, cities disintegrate"). What earlier has been revealed as good and desirable, within the limits of an all-demanding loyalty to heaven, is now simply part of "eall þeos læne gesceaft" (842, "all this fleeting Creation") and is to be swept away. Hence, as Cynewulf points out, the only way to avoid panic and terror in that great day is "to think eagerly in this barren time on the beauty of the soul" (848–849). Then follows the great metaphor, derived by Cynewulf from Gregory and important in many Old English poems, of life in the middangeard as dangerous seafaring through wild waves toward a harbor that can be reached only through the grace of God's holy Son. Christ's own earthly voyage, at the end of *Christ II*, has ended in the triumph of the Ascension. Earlier he has been designated *mægna goldhord* (787, golden Treasure of glory), but now, in the Doomsday context, his judgment flame, like a wrathful warrior (cf. the Red Sea deluge in *Exodus*), strides forth over the whole Creation, consuming "the ancient treasures that man, while his pride remained with him on earth, once clung to" (812–814).

Christ III, through vigorous, apocalyptic description does two things. It presents a splendid vision of Doomsday events,

60. *PR* 3.27–49.867–1664.
61. *PR* 1.154–56.597–664.
62. *PR* 3.212–15.1–119.
63. *PR* 6.58–67.1–306.

and it explores the intimate, decisive connection of these events with the earthly sufferings and death of Christ. Old English elegiac poetry, as Essay Three will show more fully, has its archetype in lamentation over the loss of Paradise. The universal lament, as the whole of Adam's race now is summoned to the last "doom" or "reckoning" (to þinge, 926), is the ultimate mythical extension of the elegiac utterances but lacks entirely the sense of pitiful waste appropriate to elegy. Sympathetic handling of the frustration of human desires now gives way to a totally renunciatory attitude toward all human goals except the teleological one, that is, the acceptance of the soul of the faithful thane into the heavenly dryht. The beauties of the order of Creation—the seas with their fish, the earth with her mountains, the high heaven radiant with stars —all disintegrate as the Son of God appears above the vaults of heaven, surrounded in solar brilliance and drawing near to the stronghold of Zion. The vision is not of a new heaven and a new earth but of an eternal, unchanging heaven at that point in mythological time when "all the ancient treasures of the kings are swallowed by flame" (995b–996) and the earth disappears forever.

Throughout Christ III there runs a recurrent emphasis on the two completely separate groups of souls arraigned before the Judge, the "onhælo gelac engla ond deofla, / beorhtra ond blacra . . . hwitra ond sweartra" (895–897, "a hidden host of angels and devils, of shining ones and dark ones . . . of white and of black"). No subtle distinctions are made. As each individual soul is rejoined to its body, the image of that person's former works and the memory of all his words and thoughts are brought to light in a spiritual anatomizing that is presented as the unlocking of the hoarded treasures of the heart before the Son of God (1047–1073a), who himself is "the Ornament of life" (1073). Judgment is through the red Rood of the Crucifixion which, as the final apocalypse unfolds, appears and blots out the sun (1081 ff.). The cosmic violence and turbulence surrounding the Crucifixion, described here retrospectively and in detail, were a symbolic foreshadowing of the final annihilation of earthly corruption now taking place in the Judgment.

The account of Doomsday in *Christ and Satan*, beginning at line 597, has a less cosmic range in its choice of images than *Christ III*. As God approaches the world, archangels with mighty voices sound their trumpets above the fortresses of men, summoning both the living and the dead to rise up and be divided into two groups, the *wlitige* (beautiful ones) and the *unclæne* (corrupt ones) (608–609).

The Judgment Day I is an apocalypse in little. It resorts to a kind of mythological shorthand, mentioning briefly familiar symbolic episodes of the Christian story—the bright Creation (11, 58), Adam's sons (101), fallen man flushed with banqueting and oblivious to the care of his soul (77b–80), the Crucifixion (67–67a), a vision of hell (18b–29), a vision of heaven in which the "Lord of victories constructs and decorates a bright hall" for his faithful followers (92–93a)—all now converging for their meaning "on that great day" (6) of the Judgment. The theme is monitory, the mood homiletic.

The Judgment Day II, in the same mood, presents the same theme and warns the reader or listener about the coming righteous destruction of the world as well as about the necessity of seeking the healing arts of the one great Physician (46, 66). The passages describing the terrible portents and events are powerfully done (92 ff.). In a cumulative massing of images the order of Creation is shown as caught up in a vast, annihilating wrath—the earth shakes, the hills fall, graves collapse, the sea roars, stars fall, the sun grows dark in the morning, and the moon has no strength to chase the night shadows. The multitude of Adam's race come to stand in terror before their Judge. From this account of the destruction of the world, the poem moves on to the horrors of hell (187–246), where worms tear the hearts of the guilty and wretches wander forever in the midst of a lasting night filled with heat, cold, and an immense stench, these torments being the rewards for drunkenness at feasts, for laughter, lust, sloth, and other vices. Finally and necessarily, the Doomsday Apocalypse culminates in a vision of heaven (247–306) and in so doing completes the articulation of the meaning of the Judgment for each level of the three-tiered universe. It is consonant with the hortatory tone and the imperious rhetoric, aimed at the conviction of individual sin—"Ic acsige þe, la,   earme geþanc" (65, "I ask you now, troubled spirit"); "Ic bidde, man, þæt þu gemune" (123a, "I urge you, man, that you remember"); "Hwæt dest þu, la, flæsc?" (176a, "What are you doing, flesh?")—and with the poet's description of his poem as "these gloomy verses" (11) that the depiction of heaven proceeds for a time in terms of negation, of saying what undesirable aspects of earthly life are absent in heaven. Eventually, however, the poem does open up for its climax, in a splendid, transcendental vision of the inhabitants of the heavenly dryht receiving exalted gifts from the Giver of victories. All the nations, the patriarchs, and the prophets shine there forever, we are told, amidst a multitude of red roses, while a virgin band led by Mary, purest of maidens, circles about between the Father and the Son.

The main intellectual stance of the one who speaks in *The Judgment Day II* is that of an evangelist alternately urging repentance and thundering warnings about the destruction to come; the rsult is a strong, sinewy handling of the Doomsday myth. There is, however, another perspective present in the poem, discernible briefly at the beginning in the lyrical account of a paradisal setting—calm woods, musical streams, and plants, all in the midst of an *ænlicum wonge* (incomparable plain) (the same adjective is used to describe the paradisal plain in *The Phoenix*, 8–10). Seated in this benevolent spot, the poet, like Adam in Eden, is overwhelmed by a sense of personal sin; the tumult of his spirit is closely associated with the violent wind and storm which now engulf the formerly harmonious setting. This short recollection of the myth of Paradise lost, joined with mentions of Christ's unbinding of prisoners (48), of the thief on the cross (57–64), and of the traditional visions of heaven and hell, indicates that once again we are concerned with a poem that assumes knowledge of, and exploits, the overall Christian mythology. With the myth of Doomsday, the process begun in the "green plain" of Eden is complete, and the human story has wound itself back into the society of heaven whence it came.

The Flames Cool into Life
Old English Narrative Romances as Displaced Myths

The poems discussed in Essay One are all based, more or less directly, on myths with widespread traditional status in the early medieval Church. As I have arranged them, in the linear sequence of the traditional Christian story of God and his universe, they can be thought of not simply as a collection of poems based on biblical and apocryphal stories but as a coherent Old English poetic mythology with a beginning, a middle, and an end. Each individual myth is an episode in a total narrative and is capable of revealing certain basic truths about the nature of God and Christ—in relation to man, to other heavenly beings, and to the devils in hell. Essay Two is primarily concerned with those narrative romances—*Andreas, Juliana, Elene, Guthlac A, Guthlac B,* and *The Phoenix*—that focus on protagonists (heroic or saintlike) presented as somewhat "human" rather than as fully mythical beings capable of moving at will throughout the three-tiered cosmos. *The Phoenix* is included here in a rather special sense, which will become clear in the discussion of Christian heroism that concludes the essay.

In several important ways these narrative poems are almost as much involved in the concept of myth as symbolic metaphor as the poems in the previous configuration are. It will be a major purpose of this essay to demonstrate that fact. Still, certain distinctions can profitably be drawn between the two groups. The texts in the Junius MS, along with *Judith, Christ I, The Dream of the Rood, The Descent into Hell, Christ II, The Fates of the Apostles, Christ III,* and *The Judgment Day I* and *II,* together form an imaginative unity that parallels the literary shape of the Bible and points fairly directly, therefore, to the major organizing mythological force at work in Anglo-Saxon culture. The six narrative romances, on the other hand, however intimately they are involved in biblical symbolism, have a more derivative relationship to that mythology. Their concern is with the world after the Ascension and before Doomsday, that world sketched briefly in Cynewulf's *Fates of the Apostles* where demonic forces still operate and therefore make necessary, from the champions of Christ's Church, heroic or saint-like actions. The mythical poems of our first essay also have a good deal to say about the life of the Church in the world but tend, finally, in their dominantly apocalyptic symbolism, to present the prevailing extraterrestrial view of reality, to the point where even the modicum of this-worldly realism found in the romances is abandoned in favor of almost unimpeded mythopoeia. What is fundamentally involved in both groupings of poems, either directly or in a somewhat displaced form,[1] is an Anglo-Saxon concept of the Bible as the living Word of God, still working through the compositions of poets like Cædmon and Cynewulf. According to this idea, God or Christ is not only the principal actor in the biblical story but also the chief interpreter of it.

Bishop Ælfric, in his "Catholic Homily I, xii, on John 6:9,"[2]

1. The critical term *displacement,* derived from psychoanalytical writings, is used in this and the following two essays in the sense defined by Northrop Frye: "The adaptation of myth and metaphor to canons of morality or plausibility" (*Anatomy of Criticism: Four Essays* [Princeton, 1957], p. 365). The term *romance,* as used in my book, also is derived from Frye's theoretical criticism. It is not primarily a generic term, the one often used in literary histories to describe texts in such categories as "The Matter of Britain" or "The Matter of France." It designates that mythos of literature concerned primarily with an idealized world. It normally has close affinities with myths, the kind of verbal statements I have discussed in Essay One, but is distinguishable from them in that the protagonist of romance is not primarily a god or divine being but a man. At the same time he has powers of action beyond those of ordinary men and inhabits an imagined world in which marvelous events are commonplace. Romance is a society's idealized fiction, in which the dominant cultural values or ideology of that society are represented, often naïvely, as unavoidably triumphing.

2. Benjamin Thorpe, ed., *The Homilies of the Anglo-Saxon Church* (London, 1844), 1: 181–92.

although speaking specifically of the five books of the Pentateuch and their symbolic connection with the five loaves in
the New Testament, articulates the traditional view of Christ
as both the author and the final interpreter of the Old Testament Law:

> Þa bec wæron awritene be Criste, ac þæt gastlice andgit
> wæs þam folce digle, oð þæt Crist sylf com to mannum,
> and geopenede þæra boca digelnysse, æfter gastlicum
> andgite.

> [These books were written concerning Christ but the
> spiritual meaning was hidden from the people until
> Christ himself came to man and revealed the mystery of
> the books, according to a spiritual sense.]

Further on in his sermon Ælfric makes essentially the same
point about Christ in relation to the prophetic books:

> He is witega, and he is ealra witegana witegung, forðan
> ðe ealle witegan be him witegodon, and Crist gefylde
> heora ealra witegunga.

> [He is a prophet, and he is the prophecy of all prophets,
> because all prophets prophesied about (or "through")
> him, and Christ fulfilled all their prophecies.]

In relation to this traditional idea the mythical poems of
Essay One are God's reshaping of his Word so that it can more
firmly establish his kingdom in one of the lands of northern
Europe. The six poetic romances depict actions of post-
Ascension Christian champions in widely scattered geographical settings, actions analogous to those of the patriarchs, the
prophets, and the apostles. One of the six poems, *Andreas,*
does actually concern two of the apostles, Andrew and
Matthew, but the poem about them, like the others in this
group, is not as immediately based on biblical materials as
are most of the poems discussed in Essay One.

In *Andreas,*[3] possibly the most abstract and, in some ways,
the most bizarre of all the Old English narrative romances, we
find working in oddly compelling ways several of the mythical

3. *PR* 2.3–51.1–1722.

structures and symbolic motifs of Essay One. Andrew is introduced as one of the twelve *tireadige hæleð* (2, glorious heroes)
listed in *The Fates of the Apostles* and recalled again at the
beginning of *Andreas,* whose splendor, the *Andreas* poet tells
us (3b–6), did not fail in the battle when, taught by their
Prince, they went eagerly over the earth, each to his "fated
place." Andrew, like the other apostolic thanes, is presented
as ostensibly human—with an initial sluggishness and a Jonah-
like unwillingness in the face of heaven's demands (189 ff.),
with his share of fears and rebelliousness, and with a good
deal of curiosity. The poem in which he appears concerns a
series of actions set, rather precariously, in an earthly context.
Compared with the high degree of abstraction from observable laws of nature or credible narrative encountered in the
description of Christ's movements throughout the cosmos in
Christ I, II, and *III,* what we find in *Andreas* is only slightly
more realistic. Still, one can proceed only so far in understanding the special qualities of this poem by resorting to a study
of the "sources"⁴ or of the actual geographical places and
events that may conceivably at some point in history have
given rise to the traditions out of which *Andreas* eventually
came.⁵ As a poem it is decisively cast in the "romance" mode,
and its canons of plausibility are very wide. Much of the time
its fiction works close to the level of undisplaced myth, and the
structure of its images is pronouncedly and pervasively antithetical. That its literal meaning frequently is absurd, and has

4. The usual view of the source of *Andreas* is that it was a Latin
version of the Greek Πράξεις 'Ανδρέου καὶ Ματθεία εἰς τὴν πόλιν τῶν
ἀνθρωποφάγων ("Acts of Andrew and Matthew in the City of the
Anthropophagi"), available in M. Bonnet, ed., *Acta apostolorum apocrypha,*
vol. 1 (Darmstadt, 1959), pp. 65–116. The main point about the source
in relation to *Andreas* is that practically all the major incidents, though
not necessarily the poetic elaborations of them (e.g., the storm at sea is
not described), are also in the Greek text. See *PR* 2. xxxvi–xxxvii; also
Kenneth R. Brooks, ed., *Andreas and the Fates of the Apostles* (Oxford,
1961), pp. xv–xviii; and Leonard J. Peters, "The Relationship of the
Old English *Andreas* to *Beowulf,*" *PMLA* 44 (1951): 844–63.

5. For the origin and development of the legend of Saint Andrew, see
G. P. Krapp, ed., *Andreas and the Fates of the Apostles* (Boston, 1906),
pp. lix ff.

often been thought so, can be seen from the impatient, even exasperated comments that creep into editions or discussions of the poem.[6]

What is needed, it seems, if *Andreas* is not to go on being considered a poem so fantastic and freakish as not really to merit serious attention of any other than a linguistic or historical sort, is a critical theory capable of handling its highly wrought, "fabulous" qualities. The assumption in this essay is that *Andreas* is a serious, sometimes almost witty poem on the subject of spiritual blindness and tyranny and that its memorial handling of the life of Andrew as an exemplary life is a sustained, complex display of Old English poetic craftsmanship. In its marvelous or highly fictional aspects, it has much in common with the other romances to be described in this essay and also with the mythical poems of Essay One.

Andreas, Elene, Juliana, Guthlac A, and *Guthlac B* fall into the broad area of literature that Northrop Frye calls "romance." [7] More precisely, they are very near to the uppermost limit of the romance mode, where fictionalism is extreme and where the structures of myth are easily discernible. To suggest that such poems had a major liberating and educative role in Anglo-Saxon culture is not to imply that the Anglo-Saxons were incredibly naïve compared to ourselves, with our more sophisticated ideas of plausible cause and effect, but to invite consideration of the mode of imagining of an earlier period, a mode that in several of its essentials and for a variety of reasons has been revived in some of the most important literature of our own time. The harking back to traditional stories and then reshaping them in terms of contemporary

6. See, for example, Brooks's ed., p. xxvi, where he uses these expressions: "sometimes tasteless and inapposite use of this material"; "somewhat lacking in invention"; "a vigorous if misplaced enthusiasm." In the notes to the text in this edition there are a considerable number of such strictures. S. B. Greenfield is less severe but still somewhat apologetic for the poem, mixing praise and blame; see his admirable *Critical History of Old English Literature* (New York, 1965), pp. 105–7. For an enthusiastic but also perceptive account of *Andreas*, see C. W. Kennedy, *Early English Christian Poetry* (London, 1952), pp. 113–21.

7. See the partial explanation of this term in note 1, this essay.

significance, the reliance on a sense of implicit connections between individual works within a poetic tradition, the sense that deeds done *on fyrndagum* (in days of old, in ancient days) are simultaneous with the poet's own time, discontinuity in the handling of space and time so as to create an imaginative point of vantage free from both these human categories, the generally nonrepresentational nature of most Old English poetry—in all these things we are confronted with poetic phenomena familiar from the writings of major artists like Yeats, Joyce, and Eliot, to name three of the most obvious, in our own century. The ideology and the cultural trappings of Old English are remote in many ways, but several of their imaginative techniques and preoccupations are not.

Most of the poems in the canon are presented as "remembered" by the poet. This appears to mean not just a matter of oral or written transmission of materials from the past but also that memory is the faculty by which the poet recalls for his people the archetypes or models of behavior to be imitated and those to be shunned. The mnemonic process by which Widsith [8] tells his audience of his travels through centuries of time and in many hundreds of miles of space does not point to a memory by which he analyzes the past and carefully learns from it historical lessons. Rather it designates an imaginative means of identifying with the ahistorical, of vesting the life of a wandering scop with a significance it could not have in the meaningless flux of history. By associating his own life with those of kings and queens of exemplary generosity in the royal centers of power throughout the ancient world, his existence assumes reality and importance. By singing of the deeds of noble or stingy kings, Widsith, who identifies himself as one of a typical band of "gleemen of men" (136), gains for himself *heahfæstne dom* (143, lasting glory under heaven). His clearly unbelievable (at least to us, possibly also to learned Anglo-Saxons) claim that he has literally been in the places and has associated with the peoples he lists is not a flagrant and dishonest attempt to defy "facts" but the consequence of a kind of memory that has little to do with the scientific, lineal

8. *PR* 3.149–53.1–143.

ordering of historical events. The tradition-minded scop, who says that "Every prince must live according to the customs" (11), selects and characterizes notable rulers according to that gnomic wisdom which decrees that they "must first be generous in gifts" *(Maxims I, 82–83)*.[9] Even the annalistic writers of the *Anglo-Saxon Chronicle* display little interest in reducing the data of history to meaningful or plausible chronological order. Their function is to memorialize significant people and events so that those who are part of the society will remember why a certain year is important, for themselves and for others.

The task of the poets of the romances is, in this sense, not essentially different from that of the *Widsith* poet or the chroniclers. Whoever composed *Andreas* obviously was little concerned with what actually happened to the apostle Andrew when he dropped out of sight in the New Testament. The important thing, since he was one of the thanes of Christ, was to see that his memory lived on as an extension into the life of the Church of the miraculous work of Christ himself. It is this purpose that we see taking shape in *Andreas,* with its marvel-filled account of the bringing of spiritual vision and salvation to a formerly heathen people.

Structurally, as well as in the mode of its imagining, *Andreas* is a romance and has much in common with narrative romances of other periods of literature. Despite the disruptions of space and time because of heavenly and hellish influences, its dominant organizing principle is sequential, and its plot involves a series of adventures leading up to a major one in which the hero almost dies, followed by his recognition as an agent of heaven and his success in converting the Mermedonians. Using Frye's terms,[10] we can recognize the basic pattern of the successful quest divided into three main stages. First there is the perilous journey and the preliminary minor adventures, the *agon;* then the major struggle and near death of the protagonist, the *pathos;* and finally the recognition or *anagnorisis* of the hero. The first of these involves Andrew's

9. *PR* 3.156–63.
10. *Anatomy of Criticism,* pp. 186–203.

reluctant receiving of his divine commission, followed by the seafaring in stormy waters with Christ as his unrecognized pilot. While at sea, Andrew undergoes a kind of ritualized instruction in divine mysteries, in the form of a long dialogue in which both he and Christ "unlock their word-hoards" (316, 470, 601) and the hero proves to be admirably *wis on gewitte* (316, wise in understanding). Two essential elements dominate the seafaring episode (ending at 828): Andrew's learning how to handle a ship in stormy waters; and the recounting by both Christ and the hero of the events of Christ's earthly life, especially those involving the persecutions that came as a result of the Jews not recognizing him. In this failure of the Jews, although it is not spelled out, there seems to be an oblique comment on Andrew's own protracted failure to recognize the identity of his comrade.

After Christ disappears into heaven, other adventures follow: the miraculous translation of Andrew to Mermedonia (829b–840a); the carrying of his thanes over the sea by eagles surrounded by a host of angels (857–891); the hero's belated recognition that his garrulousness on board ship has been directed toward his heavenly Dryhten (851–856, 897–909); and the second appearance of Christ to him (910–980). This last is significant in that Christ, whom Andrew this time knows immediately, now has the form of a "boy" or "youth" (*cniht*), suggesting to me, perhaps a little fancifully, that Andrew, whose heroic function is to emulate the life of Christ, is still at a youthful or inexperienced stage of development, in terms of the agonies now looming up, but is at last ready to begin in earnest his imitation of the life of Christ. The boy commands Andrew to enter the city but first recalls his own Crucifixion and wounding with the spear. He tells the hero that he, Andrew, must now go in *gramra gripe* (951, the grip of the enemy) and that he will be wounded and bleed but that he is to maintain his heroic integrity: "Wes a domes georn" (959, "Always be eager for glory"). The account of the agon concludes at line 1057, after Andrew's entry into the Mermedonian dungeon—variously described as a *deaðwang* (death-plain, field of death), a *morðorcofa* (room of torment), and a *gnornhof* (house of trouble)—from which, with the help of the Holy Ghost, he rescues Matthew and 240 other prisoners. Matthew leads this throng "into God's keeping," by covering them with clouds to protect them against the enemies' arrows.

Andrew's pathos or death struggle follows logically from his disruption of the cannibalistic rites of the Mermedonians. Here there is a demonic parody of that divine sacrifice of the Son which underlies the Eucharist, when an old chieftain of the cannibalistic Mermedonians offers his son as food (1108 ff.). The boy's cry of dereliction (1125–1128) moves Andrew to pity, and he melts the enemies' weapons like wax, thus rescuing the boy (1135–1154). Deprived—first by the rescue of Matthew and the others and now by the saving of the boy—of their food supply, the Mermedonians are plunged into lamentation, their wine-halls are desolate, and their counselors, like the Scyldings enslaved by the cannibalistic Grendel in *Beowulf,* sit lost in futile deliberations. At this point (1167), appropriately enough, Satan appears to them and informs them that Andrew is the cause of the crisis and should be killed. For three days the hero is subjected to grotesque physical tortures and mutilation; his nights are passed in an icy dungeon where he has to endure the taunts of Satan. His cry of dereliction and his prayer for deliverance on the third day evoke a heavenly reassurance in which God says, in effect, "Don't carry on about your troubles, dear fellow, they're not too bad. I have everything under control" (1431–1433). God's speech here includes an almost direct quotation from Christ's sermon on the signs of the coming Apocalypse in Matthew 24: "heofon ond eorðe, hreosaþ togadore, / ær awæged sie worda ænig / þe ic þurh minne muð / meðlan onginne" ("heaven and earth together shall pass away before any word which I speak by my mouth shall be brought to nothing"). At this point Andrew looks behind him and sees springing up "blossoming groves bright with flowers," wherever his blood has dropped on the rocky slopes (1446–1449). Praising his Creator he is returned to the "dark night" of prison, and there is completely restored bodily, thus concluding his pathos (1450–1477).

Following his "resurrection"—"Aras þa mægene rof, sægde meotude þanc" (1496, "Then brave in strength he rose up, gave thanks to God")—Andrew receives a strange vision of the Decalogue inscribed on two great, storm-beaten pillars of stone, "the ancient work of giants," standing in his prison (1492 ff.). By the Old Testament Law thus symbolized, he brings down judgment on the Mermedonians in the form of a destructive deluge or *mereflod* (1526, sea-flood) which first gives rise to wide lamentations on the part of the enemy (1547 ff.), then to their prayer to Andrew to still the waters (1555b ff.). At this point he steps forth from prison, and a street or "pleasant plain of victory" (1580–1581) opens up for him in the depths of the waters, as it did for Moses and Israel in the Exodus. The fourteen worst of the Mermedonians disappear into an abyss that also swallows the receding flood waters (1587b ff.). A little later, in return for a general conversion of the Mermedonians, the fourteen dead are restored and baptized, the pagan altars are torn down, a church is established, and a bishop appointed. The poem ends with the expected exaltation of the hero, with the Mermedonians sadly bidding farewell to their warrior-saint as he takes his ship over the waves (1695 ff.). It is not, however, the elegiac note that remains. The pattern of Christian triumph is completed, with the newly transformed community praising the Creator whose *blæd* (glory) shines over all holy ones of earth and heaven: "Þæt is æðele cyning!" ("He is a noble King!").

Read on a purely literal level, in terms of narrative plot, *Andreas* like many romances is naïve and credulous, as the foregoing statement of its structure will have indicated. This kind of reading, however, sees only the skeleton or abstract shape. The fabric of the highly wrought, associative imagery characteristic of *Andreas* raises it to the level of a complex and rich symbolic poem, where many of the apparent absurdities disappear. To demonstrate this claim fully would require a lengthy study of the imagery and language of the poem, in the context of Old English poetry as a whole and also in the wider context of hagiographic literature. Still, one can proceed some considerable way by recognizing the typological nature of the symbolism involved and also the peculiarly Anglo-Saxon method of adapting biblical matters.

I have suggested that structurally *Andreas* is a successfully completed quest and that thematically it has to do with the overcoming of spiritual blindness and demonic tyranny. The enemy defeated by Andrew is, in line with the mythical shape of the poem, not just a group of cannibals living in some remote geographical area. With very little abstracting we can see that metaphorically they are the dryht of hell and their kingdom is the place of damnation. An abundance of images makes these identities clear. The Mermedonians inhabit a "wasteland" bound in crimes and enveloped in "the treachery of the fiend" (19–21a). As in hell, where monsters tear on naked corpses, so here all newcomers are cannibalistically devoured; before consuming their victims, the Mermedonians blind them and, through sorcery, administer a poisonous drink that destroys the *gewit* (reason) so that, like Nebuchadnezzar in his exile, they become bestial, desiring hay and grass to eat (21b ff.). Such a process is obviously a figurative account of the plunging of the human soul into a state of brutish irrationality so that it may be devoured by hell. Matthew, who precedes Andrew in his visit to this demonic place, is symbolic of the Christian soul integrated through loyalty to Christ—"Him wæs cristes lofe / on fyrhðlocan fæste bewunden" (57b–58, "The love of Christ was firmly locked in his breast")—and therefore finally victorious, although first he must go through a battle with the enemy host. The city of the Mermedonians is a scene of Babylonian confusion, filled with tumultuous multitudes of the "devil's thanes" (48), "men ready for hell" who rush toward the apostle to bind him "by the craft of the fiend" (50–51a). They tear out his eyes and give him the same poisonous drink that other victims receive, but he continues steadfastly praising his Lord. A holy light shines in his prison, and God tells him that after twenty-seven days of suffering the *neorxnawong* (102, paradisal plain) will be revealed to him. Meanwhile the *wælwulfas* (149, war

wolves)—the Egyptians in *Exodus* are called *heorowulfas*
(battle-wolves)—continue their plans for a demonic banquet
at which Matthew and his companions are to be eaten.

It is in relation to this activity of the dryht of hell that
God begins the counteraction involving Andrew's mission. The
apostolic champion is no more an ordinary human being than
his enemy is. The mythical associations are established from
the beginning. Just before the hero is mentioned we are told
that he who established middle-earth remembers how he
himself once voluntarily lived in bondage and misery, only to
have the love he showed the Jews returned with darkest sorcery
(161–167a). This memory leads him to "unlock his mind-
hoard" to Andrew, who is busily instructing the Achaians in
"the way of life" (172), and to tell the potential hero that he
is to go and rescue Matthew before the latter is killed and
eaten by the Mermedonians. From this point on, the poet
surrounds the deeds of Andrew with numerous Christlike
associations so that the mission of rescue is made to seem
closely analogous to Christ's mission to the Jews.

First, however, the Dryhten has to overcome Andrew's initial
sluggishness about heroic exploits (189–234). Andrew pleads
ignorance about seafaring, claiming that the mighty errand
given him would require an angel's knowledge in crossing sea
and land. The result of this reluctance is that he is described
by the word *sæne* (204, 211, slow, dull, sluggish), a term also
applied to one of the sea beasts in Grendel's mere (*Beowulf*,
1436). Heaven brooks no such objections, and God points out
that he can move whole cities at will. Andrew is to embark at
dawn next day and does so, no longer a timid soul but *heard
ond higerof* (233, brave and stout of heart), ready for the
battle. "Heaven's candle" (243) shines above the cold sea, and
three glorious thanes, Christ and two angels, come dressed as
seafarers (244b–249), bringing a "high-necked ship" (266)
for the hero's use.

Immediately Andrew is subjected to temptation, with the
disguised Christ playing the role of tempter, to see that the
hero's basic loyalties are the right ones before he takes up his
work of deliverance. The suggestion that Andrew should not

be setting forth without rich treasure with which to pay the pilot and without adequate food and drink elicits the proper response (290–342). Having recollected Christ's commission to himself and his fellow apostles, that they should go into all the world taking no gold or silver and knowing that he would provide for them, Andrew "unlocks his word-hoard" in such a way as to show clearly that he is rich in the spiritual treasure that really counts. The poet comments, "I have never heard of a fairer ship laden with rich treasures" (360b–362a), thus making very clear the symbolic level on which the sea voyage is described.

The human temptations to rely on the world and the flesh are thus set aside by the hero. Next follows a violent storm (369b ff.), during which Andrew's thanes are terrified but refuse to leave their lord; Andrew tells them that he knows, because of Christ's stilling of the storm on the Sea of Galilee, that it is God who is master of the flood (427 ff.). That the chaotic waters symbolize, in the traditional way, the hell that threatens unwary seafarers and that the ship, moving forward "most like a bird" (497) is the human soul, secure and fearless against hell's onslaughts because Christ is its pilot (*Christo gubernante*), can hardly be doubted. The subsiding of the storm (in recognition by the waters that Andrew has the grace of the Holy Ghost) shows the hero's oneness with the Creator "who binds the waves and the dark billows, and who suppresses and chastens the force of their power" (519–520a). The union of Andrew's soul with Christ is elaborately documented in the long passage that follows; each shares his "treasure" with the other, treasure here meaning, specifically, knowledge of the many miracles worked by Christ while he was on earth.

The experiences of Andrew among the Mermedonians begin with him sitting beside "a brazen column" (1062) thinking holy thoughts and waiting for "war deeds" (1063–1066). Around him raven a people who have "no joy of treasure" (1159–1160). His ensuing persecution (1219–1428) involves a dialectical motif of images which makes the structural design clear: the mutilation of his body is associated with rocks, winter storms, and dark nights in prison, during which he is constantly harassed by a taunting, gloating Satan; his spiritual triumphs are linked with the rising sun. Finally, when his body fibers are destroyed and his blood and locks scattered over the whole region so that he prays "the One who gives banquets to souls" (1416–1417) to release him by means of death, he is ready to serve as the redemptive agent through whom God constructs a sacred place in one of hell's kingdoms. The extended use of the theme of *sparagmos* (rending, tearing, mutilation) here is one of the poem's most vivid metaphorical means of identifying its hero with Christ's sufferings and Passion and also, typologically, with the eucharistic sacrifice. Where Christ actually dies, however, and then is resurrected, the protagonist of hagiography frequently, as here, engages in a mimesis or *similitudo* of the death of Christ, illustrating the kind of concession to realism, albeit slight, that one expects in romance or displaced myth. The immediate result of the hero's struggle, once again in Old English poetry, is the appearance of a green, blossoming plain, part of the original Paradise. Before the sacred place can be extended to include the whole of Mermedonia, there has to be a deluge that both judges and cleanses or baptizes. By the end of the poem the land rescued from confusion is the "pleasant plain of victory" (1581), the site of "bright halls of ring giving" (1657).

It is not difficult to see why, in a traditional, religious society, the moment in which a church is founded implies the Creation or recalls the cosmogonic moment when God's Word began to shape (in Anglo-Saxon terms) the *westen* (wasteland, wilderness) into a *goldsele* (gold-hall). At that point in which Andrew's experiences transcend the cyclical images of day and night, of summer and winter, he is an agent of absolute reality entering middle-earth, making orientation possible for those caught in Babylonian confusion. What is to become part of the Christian world, freed from the Heraclitean flux of the *læne* (fleeting, transitory) world, has first to be "created." This poem (and most others in Old English) assumes a total opposition between the territory occupied by the people of God and that of those bound in devil worship. It describes how one of Christ's "glorious heroes," through complete and exemplary willingness to accept the life of Christ as a paradigm for his own, extends the gift-throne of the Dryhten to a place of darkness. It is the account of a human figure initiated into the society of heaven through total identification of his life with that of a god.

Elene,[11] like *Andreas,* is a quest romance involving a series of adventures culminating in one major event, the triumphant finding of the true cross and the establishment of the Christian Church in Jerusalem. The poem is also, less obviously, a thoroughly "baptized" reworking of the archetypal quest for buried treasure and the freeing of a people enslaved by a monster. In its connections with biblical typology, *Elene* centers on the rood as the "most famed of trees pushing forth its leaves from the earth" (1224b–1226a), a symbol of the triumph of the Creator over those demonic forces laying waste his earthly kingdom. As a champion of the faith, Helena, so far as any development through testing and major conflict is concerned, is a more static figure than Andrew. She is a "radiant war queen covered with gold" (331), a rather stylized, Byzantine creation whose function is to be the agent of the miraculous invention of the cross. The sea voyage she experiences can hardly be called a perilous one. It is exuberantly described but at no point poses any threat or severe testing for the heroine or for anyone else. The waters into which her troop of "wave-stallions" (236) move are called the *fifelwæg* (237, the sea monster or sea beast's home), indicating that the traditional iconography of the sea as potentially damnatory for the unwary soul is latent here, but Helena's spiritual condition is secure and her mission divinely sanctioned. Similarly, the three conferences with the *witena gemot* (assembly of wise ones) of Jerusalem, organized by the managerial empress, are in no way a palpable physical trial for her. The agon or conflict proceeds on a more mental or spiritual level and involves powerful resolution on Helena's part to find what she seeks, despite a prolonged series of obstacles and disappointments. The anti-Christian Jewish society against which she is pitted

11. *PR* 2.66–102.1–1321.

is given, in accord with the quite staggering intolerance toward
all other religions characteristic of this poetry, numerous connotations of the dryht of hell. The Jews are "stiff necked and
stonyhearted" (565), they are unfaithful to the Covenant of old
(288 ff.), and they are caught in a spiritual blindness that will
deliver them into hell's bondage (293 ff.), so that Helena must
"cleanse" (678) Calvary hill on which they have polluted the
rood. The climax comes when the newly converted Judas
prays to God that the long hidden "golden treasure" (790) be
revealed. Then follows the anagnorisis or recognition of the
new order of reality made possible by the triumph of Helena
and the cross over the enchantment which for many years has
enslaved Jerusalem. In her joy at finding the cross, and also
the nails of the Crucifixion, Helena displays that "gift of
wisdom" (1143) which, more than any physical goal, has
been the object of her quest.

Although it is not deficient in miracles, *Elene* does not
work consistently as close to the boundary of pure myth as
does *Andreas,* with the result that the striking metaphorical
identifications that stud the other poem are, in the main,
absent. It does, however, make considerable use of biblical
materials, especially of passages from the Old and New Testaments to do with the perversity of the Jews, a perversity that
comes to its climax in the Crucifixion of Christ. The references
to these parts of scripture take the form of analogies between
the acts of the Jews in the foreground narrative of the poem
and those of their biblical predecessors. Further evidence of
the greater degree of displacement in *Elene* than in *Andreas*
lies in the large amount of attention given to the mental and
emotional processes of the Jews, especially of Judas, who at
one point, having been called an *anhaga* (solitary one) by the
poet (604), compares himself to someone walking hungry in
a wilderness and finding both a stone and a loaf (611–618).
In due course, we are to understand, as Helena's persuasion
of him becomes more effective, Judas, like the man in the
parable and like Israel wandering in the wilderness needing
manna, will accept the loaf of real food for the soul and reject
the useless stone. The fullness of Cynewulf's treatment of

Judas and the care exercised in presenting the Jewish side of
the conflict are unusual in Old English poetry. There is never
any doubt that, thematically, the Jewish attitudes are meant to
be condemned, but they are given expression to a degree not
permitted any other devil-worshipping dryht in the poetic
canon.

The *hoptasia* or vision of Constantine near the beginning
of *Elene* (69–98) introduces a double symbolic pattern—of
miraculous treasure, and of heavenly light dispelling the
spiritual darkness of the fallen world—a pattern that continues its identification of light and treasure throughout the
poem. The setting is the frontier of the "kingdom of Rome"
(59), where Huns and Goths have gathered by the surging
waters of the Danube (35–39) to attack Constantine and his
tiny dryht. The Romans, because of the very unequal odds,
are plunged in gloom, until heaven intervenes by sending to
the emperor in his sleep (69) a vision of a "lovely weaver of
peace" who reveals a gold-covered cross that is now to become Constantine's "symbol of triumph." This visionary
treasure is immediately efficacious in the defeat of the pagan
enemy and in dispersing the carrion beasts conventionally
associated, we remember, with the warring, destructive society
of Cain. The cross also brings about the conversion of Constantine who, on his return to Rome (148 ff.), is instructed by
Roman Christians in the story of the Incarnation, the Crucifixion, the Harrowing, the Resurrection, and the Ascension.
Only after this catechesis, when he is, so to speak, in mental
possession of the whole structure of Christ's life, does the
rood-treasure become the object of his mother Helena's quest.

Later, when the prayer of Judas (725–801), involving the
whole created order and urging the Ruler of victories to reveal
the *goldhord* (790), is answered (832b ff.), the cross begins to
work miracles (887b ff.). At this point, the dryht-of-hell symbolism emerges into the foreground, and we can see the
essentially apocalyptic-demonic antithesis which gives the
poem its shape. The devil, rather like an enraged dragon and
described as *synna brytta* (957, dispenser of sins), appears in
Jerusalem (888b ff.) to complain loudly that Christ has always

plundered his possessions and that now that the rood-treasure has been stolen, with the help of a second Judas, he, Satan, will not be able to hold sway over the souls of sinners. Undeterred, Helena has the rood overlaid with gold and gems and enshrined in a splendid church on Calvary hill (1017 ff.) and then goes to discover the miraculous nails (1091–1092, "hidden treasure") of the Crucifixion. These are unearthed when a brilliant flame brighter than the sun reveals them, deep in the ground, gleaming like the stars of heaven or like gems of gold (1109 ff.). Appropriately, they are sent to Constantine, "the ring giver of men" (100, 1198), who by the time of Cynewulf's poem was widely revered as the emperor who altered the whole course of Church history by putting the weight of the Roman Empire behind the Christian religion.

The light-and-treasure motif comes to its conclusion in the epilogue (1236–1321), where the poet represents himself as a man who once received treasures in the mead-hall but was in spiritual anguish because he could not understand the truth about the cross until God revealed it to him. Now, however, heaven has guided him to a position of clear vision and understanding, in which the "fleeting" world of earthly joys is revealed as illusory. The life of middle-earth now for him is seen as caught up in flux and impermanence and is symbolized by a smoldering torch, declining youth, water flowing away, the rise and fall of the wind, the nature of clouds, and time itself. This explicit statement of the main spiritual themes of the whole romance, the difference between true and false treasure and the dispelling of spiritual darkness through the glory of the rood, terminates in a vision of the Judgment in which sinners from earth are purged and taken as "pure gold" (1309) into the dryht of heaven.

It is evident that the quest-for-treasure archetype has combined in this poem with the basic Christian quest for spiritual resurrection and ascension. The climax of *Elene,* then, true to the Word that shapes it, has its model in the Resurrection and Ascension of Christ. The true cross is first recognized by the empress through its power to raise the dead (887b–889a). In a very real sense, *Elene* is a poetic sequel to *The Dream of*

the Rood; it is an account of the victory of the cross (later in
Church history than the main action of the earlier poem) over
the same *strange feondas* (powerful enemies) in Jerusalem
who were responsible for the Crucifixion. Three lines of *The
Dream of the Rood* (which has survived in the same manuscript as *Elene,* though separated by four sermons from it) are
both an integral part of *The Dream of the Rood* and also encompass, by anticipation, the main action of *Elene:*

> Bedealf us man on deopan seaþe. Hwæðre me þær dryht-
>   nes þegnas,
> freondas gefrunon,
> ond gyredon me   golde ond seolfre.

> [They buried us in a deep pit. Nevertheless, servants of the
> Lord, friends, found (? the line is defective) me there,
> adorned me with gold and silver.]

Juliana [12] is composed in the same broad mode of romance
as *Elene* and *Andreas.* Like them it is episodic and sequential
in its narrative, involving the trials and testing of a holy
person, as preparation for a final glorious vindication of the
supernatural order of reality which that person represents.
Juliana's quest is for the "city of glory," and the account of
her earthly life is one of *gewindagas* (days of struggle), ending
in her bodily death. The social context of her vita is evident
in the descriptions of the persecuted Church and of the Church
triumphant at the beginning and end respectively of the narrative. On the level of myth the poem is held together by a
sharply diagrammatic and stylized set of vertically organized
images which make clear that, here again, we are faced with a
poem about the war between the lords of heaven and hell
for the soul of an earthly warrior.

The spatial structure of images against which the action of
Juliana is set is important, since in its essentials it is characteristic of hagiographic literature in general, not only in Old
English. The middangeard in this poem is a grassy plain on
which there is an eastern city, Commedia; nearby is the sea.

12. *PR* 3.113–33.1–731.

Above this level of the immediate action are the true God and his angels. Below is the pit of hell, with the king of hell dwellers and his devils. In its literal aspect, *Juliana* is a narrative of the conflict between Eleusius, a wealthy prefect who has power and *hordgestreon* (22, hoarded wealth) in a pagan world, and Juliana, the daughter of one of his prominent subjects. But both the lower and the upper levels constantly penetrate into the middle area, with the result that the main significance of the work derives from the supernatural frame of reference. Juliana and her protective angel look to the heavenly kingdom while the demon (called Belial in the Latin *Vita* but not named by Cynewulf),[13] Eleusius, Affricanus, the Emperor Maximian, and the other persecutors have their spiritual home in hell.

Each character or group of characters is easily recognizable as giving loyalty to either the dryht of heaven or that of hell. Juliana's well-being, like that of the other "champions" (17) of God in this mythopoeic tradition, is intimately connected with the ideal created order. When she refuses marriage with Eleusius because the fear of God is greater in her mind than all the nobleman's treasure (35b ff.), she is keeping her virginity unspotted for the love of Christ (28b–31), in anticipation of an ultimate heavenly union with him. There is no purely individualistic insistence on personal integrity and chastity involved here. Juliana's *gloriosa passio* as a martyr springs from a love of God, and her hostility to the world is not a passionless stance but a suffering that permits her to transcend the world. Her resoluteness, moreover, is the spiritual condition of a soul whose function on earth is to help restore part of the fallen world to its originally created form. Juliana tells her father she will never agree to an alliance with Eleusius unless the prince, "with offerings, shows his love for the One who created light, the heaven and the earth, and the vastness of the seas" (109–110). It is by this divinely created order that she later prays for protection (272 ff.) when a devil disguised

13. *Acta Sanctorum quotquot orbe coluntur*, collected by Ioannes Bollandus, et al. (Antwerp, 1643—Brussels, 1894); for Juliana, see vol. 2, 16 February, pp. 875–79.

as an angel (244, 261) tries to trick her into worshipping the pagan gods. Three times she is associated with the radiant beauty of the sun (166–168, 227b–230, 454); in the last of these references, simile gives way to metaphor, and she is called by the poet "the candle of glory."

The central portion of the narrative describes an extended struggle between Juliana and the devil, who comes to her in prison disguised, like the tempter in *Genesis B,* as an angel. Here the protagonist is involved in a ritual of casting off the devil and his works, one of the rituals of martyrdom very close in its theological significance to the apotaxis or renunciation of Satan in the baptismal rite experienced by all Christians. The essential difference, however, between Juliana's battle with the demon and that of the ordinary Christian is that hers is a confirmation of a loyalty already firm and a suffering on behalf of others, as the end of the poem makes clear, whereas Baptism proper is an initiation into the life of faith. The tempter is eventually forced, by Juliana's fortitude and her resistance to his onslaughts, to confess his own sins (289 ff.). They make an impressive list, especially if we assume, as seems reasonable, that the lacuna in our manuscript would represent the same materials as those included in the *Vita:* the Fall of Adam and Eve; Abel's murder; Job's loss of possessions; the idolatries of Israel; the sufferings of Isaiah; Nebuchadnezzar's fashioning of images; the trial of Daniel and his friends in the furnace; Herod's slaughter of the innocents; Judas's betrayal of Christ and his own suicide; the wounding of Christ on the cross by the soldier's spear; the beheading by Herod of John the Baptist; Simon Magus's attack on the disciples; Nero's executions of Christians; Pilate's order to crucify Christ; and, finally, the hanging of Andrew by Ægeas.

This gathering together of all the achievements of hell throughout human history indicates the tradition to which *Juliana* belongs. The mythology about the war between God and Satan adds new episodes, such as those of the life of a martyr like Juliana, as long as middle-earth continues. But the "thanes of Christ" like Juliana who are loyal to their Lord while still on earth break the seemingly inevitable sequence by their miracles of endurance. From the point of view of the devil, his attacks will go on and on, even though he has to admit defeat with a few rare beings like Juliana who are armed with a holy shield and spiritual armor impenetrable by his spear shafts. His description, however, of the dryht of hell and of the terror and scourgings which are normal there for himself and other emissaries of evil gives the lie to his boasting words to Juliana (321 ff.). His torments, in fact, described in the dungeon sequence with Juliana, involve numerous verbal correspondences with the tortures meted out to Juliana herself, both before and after her imprisonment, showing that, on the level of myth or of complete metaphorical identification, the "human" torturers, Eleusius and Affricanus, are devils too, engaged in the same scourgings and mutilations of victims that Satan administers to his prisoners in hell. Toward the end of the poem we find the completion of the dryht-of-hell metaphor. After Juliana has preached to the multitude—about the strong house of faith founded on the living Stone, impervious to all winds (647–657a)—and after she has then gone triumphantly to her death, Eleusius and his men, terrified, take to the sea where they are buffeted about and finally plunged into hell (671b–682). Cynewulf makes the grimly ironic comment that this band of comrades could not expect in that low den to receive rings and embossed gold from their lord (683–688a).

Juliana is a conventional and very abstract poem—in its use of the images and concepts of the dryht; in its focusing of the whole mythological sequence of Satan's war against Christ on its protagonist; in its use of solar imagery; in its stylized, hieratic presentation of human figures; and in its dependence on a schematic pattern carefully worked out rather than on any realism in the depiction of the conflict. Probably inevitably, this abstraction in *Juliana* makes it alien and unattractive to many modern readers whose values and interests are remote from hagiography. Where *Exodus* as a poem proceeds by vivid figurative imagining and *Christ I* or *The Dream of the Rood* conveys intense lyrical force, to all of which we can in some measure respond, *Juliana* abnegates the world so resolutely that we are left detached from the poem. At the same time it is this very abstraction and asceticism that makes Cynewulf's text an admirably clear example of the way the Anglo-Saxon Christian poet writing romance transforms the pagan quest for *dom* (glory) into the quest for salvation. It is not, however, the poetic structure which has changed but the ideological content. Romance as a narrative mythos or plot is not the prerogative of medieval Christian writers, although in its hagiographic manifestations it was extremely popular. Tales of heroism and successful battles against mighty foes, including supernatural ones, are common in most cultures and are simply verbal structures for projecting ideals in some form of fiction. What has happened in Old English poetry to the earlier pagan tradition is that the old dryht loyalties of lord and thane have been transferred to the sky and made cosmic principles.

Although *Guthlac A* [14] apparently is almost contemporary with the actual life on which it is based, it is as schematic and abstract in its organization of images and shaping of materials as *Juliana*. In fact the otherworldliness of the narrative romances reaches its climax here, in a work that is Old English poetry's fullest and most clearly articulated statement of ascetic ideals as they manifest themselves in the eremitical life. The overall tendency of the poem toward mythical abstraction is so pronounced that, where Andrew, Helena, and Juliana all have "human" enemies with heavily demonic overtones as well as visitants from hell, Guthlac's assailants are all unambiguously devils. Like the other protagonists, he, too, receives massive aid from guardian angels. The episodes from Christian myth that give the poem its structure are primarily the temptations of Christ in the wilderness, his descent into hell, his Resurrection, and his Ascension. Enveloping these myths is another one, that of the Fall of the Angels from the golden dryht of heaven and the subsequent war, unending throughout history, between Christ and Satan. Of major importance also in the informing symbolism of the poem is the myth of the restoration of the "green plain" of Paradise. The battle-

14. *PR* 3.49–72.1–818.

field on which the war described is fought is, of course, the soul and body of man, in this case Guthlac's, whose name etymologically can mean "war battle," "war sacrifice" or "offering," or "war grace," all three meanings being appropriate to the triumphant warrior of the soul whose physical life, like Christ's, is sacrificed to demonic forces in order that it may be revelatory of special divine grace.

Guthlac is shown to be only one, however excellent, of those who learn and teach in middle-earth the law and love of Christ. The introduction to the poem describes a typical wayfaring soul journeying toward God and his dryht, joined en route by an angel.[15] In heaven the *eadge sawl* (blessed soul) is welcomed because of the battles it has fought against "accursed spirits" (25), battles that now merit a reward from the King of all kings who rules the heavenly fortress; the reward is glory unending and a Valhalla-like rest after battle. The opening vision of the golden dryht is succeeded, before any overt mention of the individual whose life ostensibly is the subject of the poem, by another vision of a declining, chaotic world far removed from the vitality of the one God created in the first six days.[16] In this lost order of existence as it moves toward the Judgment, nature's produce has lost its beauty, seeds have diminished power, and most of those who claim to love Christ do so coldheartedly. In such a world, says the poet, there is no hope other than in a life of charity and almsgiving among men or in a life of hermitlike retreat into dark and secret places in which to wait for reception into the heavenly homeland. For those who do the latter, the devil waits with terror-filled fantasies and illusory visions of false joys. A troop of

15. Father L. K. Shook, in an article which gives cogent reasons for seeing lines 1–29 as an integral part of the poem that follows, argues that the soul in the prologue is Guthlac's; see "The Prologue of the Old-English *Guthlac A*," *Mediaeval Studies* 23 (1961): 294–304.

16. For discussion of the tradition involved here, see G. V. Smithers, "The Meaning of the *Seafarer* and the *Wanderer*," *Medium Ævum* 26 (1957), especially pp. 140–46; and J. E. Cross, "Aspects of Microcosm and Macrocosm in Old English Literature," *Studies in Old English Literature in Honor of Arthur G. Brodeur,* ed. S. B. Greenfield (Eugene, Ore., 1963), pp. 1–22.

angel thanes, however, with weapons drawn, stands ready to protect the man who faithfully loves his Dryhten. It is in this imaginative context, of a carefully balanced vision of the heavenly society and the world in the clutches of Satan, that the poet, after ninety-two lines, places his protagonist.

Guthlac is *se bytla* (148, the builder), that is, one who builds a sacred dwelling by expelling from a *westen* (81, 208, wasteland) its demonic inhabitants. The achievement of Guthlac's purpose is temporarily impeded by the relentless onslaughts of the devils. From the moment in which he blesses the ground and establishes Christ's rood (176–181a), the way of near martyrdom (472, 514) begins to open up before him. From the perspective of the devils, Guthlac, as an *eadig oretta* (happy warrior), appears to be favored by God and to have been given privileges in what they consider their territory. They react as Lucifer did when he felt Christ favored above him and as Cain did when Abel's offering was preferred to his own; moved by envy, they initiate a "feud" with God's chosen one. As a result, again like Lucifer and Cain, they are driven away from the green places they desire, "Gewitað nu, awyrgde, werigmode, / from þissum earde þe ge her on stondað, / fleoð on feorweg" (225–257, "Go now, wearily, accursed ones, from this place where you stand, flee somewhere far away")—cf. Matt. 25: 41, a text echoed more directly in *Christ III*, 1519—but only to wait as joyless exiles for future opportunities of attack on the idealized place inhabited by God's servant.

Before the commencement of the temptations of Guthlac we find a passage strongly reminiscent, both in an immediate verbal sense and in a broader structural way, of the description of the westen in *Genesis A* (102 ff.) before the Creator began to fashion the middangeard. We are told that the "secret place" (215) to which Guthlac has come previously "stood empty and desolate, in no way a homeland, waiting for the coming of a better guardian" (215–217). The laborious construction—through intense suffering—of Guthlac's *beorg* (barrow) is a prolonged process of exorcising demonic powers in which one special man resists the lures of the world, the flesh,

and the devil to the point where the Word of God, which
effortlessly creates Paradise in *Genesis,* can work freely through
him to restore Eden in one small part of the wilderness of this
world. There is in the poem, however, little interest in the
redemption of middle-earth as such. What matters in this
strongly theonomous tradition of poetry, as contrasted, for
example, with the myth of Eden restored in William Blake's
poetry, is the perfecting of human souls so that they may attain
the eternal Paradise or heavenly Jerusalem.

The most bitter and decisive clashes between Guthlac and
his tormentors are preceded by a spirited fliting (233 ff.) in
which they accuse him of having the greatest *oferhygdu* (269,
pride, arrogance) of any man they have encountered. They
announce that they will attack with their armies and spread
his blood throughout the region. Guthlac counters, saying that
his powers of defense are not swords or worldly weapons and
that he will not shed any blood in taking the place for God:
"Swa modgade . . . wuldres cempa / engla mægne" (323–325,
"So he exulted . . . the champion of glory, in the strength of
angels"). He emphasizes his absolute separateness from his
enemies—"Ic eom dryhtnes þeow" (314, "I am the Lord's servant")—and often wonders how his body may have least to do
with the joys of the world (336–338). The devils wait, hoping
that some human love will draw him away and cause his joy
in the remote place to lessen, but Guthlac plunges instead into
a meditation on obedience and on the meaning of the death
of the physical body. In his mind, which is not *sæne* (sluggish),
the mortal body becomes an image of the whole "fleeting"
(371) Creation from which he actively seeks to escape. This idea
logically establishes in the poem the idea of the relative un-
importance of the physical suffering he is now ready to undergo.

A vision of monastic corruption (412 ff.) shown Guthlac by
the devils provides him with an opportunity to demonstrate
his sense of balance and forbearance when confronted with
youthful wantonness and sensuality and to explain these human failings not as mortal sins but as marks of immaturity. It
also gives him an opening for pointing out to his foes that

one of their main aims is to keep "secret" the deeds of good men, by concentrating on the sins of other less spiritually dedicated ones (505–507). By implication, this is the poet's way of explaining the *raison d'être* of his poem, the praise of a holy man, as well as his method of setting in antithetical relation to each other a triumphantly righteous warrior of God and the demonic forces that would seduce him. In accord with this contrast, the resolution of the conflict that makes up most of the narrative action consists simply of giving all the triumphs to the hero.

The poet goes on to say (519b ff.) that if it is strange that Christ let Guthlac suffer so it is even more wonderful that he himself sought the world and shed his blood at the hands of murderers. As Christ's Passion was a means of establishing the Church, so Guthlac's is a "cleansing" of his soul (535–536) which ultimately makes possible the erection of the beorg. Taken next on "a terrible journey" (566) down "into the deep abysses under the cliffs" (563) to the door of hell itself, Guthlac is told by the devils that he must enter and must suffer with other hell dwellers. This is the climax of his temptations, the invitation to give way to *orwennysse* (575, despair), that is, to surrender all will for salvation and to worship Satan. But in his extremity Guthlac sings a hymn of praise and thanksgiving to God, for all the gifts God has created for angels and for earth dwellers, and goes on to tell the devils how they "have forsaken the fair Creation long ago, the spiritual joy of heaven," when they rejected the Dryhten (629–631). His faith in "the most radiant power of the Trinity" is unshaken (646–647).

Guthlac's rescue from hell is effected by an angel from heaven (684b ff.), one of the twelve apostles, who terrifies the devils, fetters them, and obliges them to return the hero, "whole of body" (688), to "that pleasant spot of earth" (728) from which he has been taken. The return, Guthlac's anagnorisis, is a jubilant climax to this symbolic tale of the building of a beorg or the perfecting of a human soul: "Sigehreðig cwom / bytla to þam beorge (732–733, "Exulting in victory he came, a builder to his barrow"). The mythical connotations of a return to Paradise surrounding Guthlac's resurrection are unmistakable: the holy man's dwelling is now *se sigewong* (742, the plain of victory) and a *sele niwe* (742, new hall or dwelling) and is filled with the hearty voices of many wild creatures welcoming their friend, with flowers and with the cry of the cuckoo announcing the spring—"Stod se grena wong in godes wære (746, "The green plain remained undisturbed in the keeping of God"). The theme of dominion over the brute creation, like that of the regeneration of vegetable life and the blossoming of sterile places, is a traditional part of the imagery associated with the revival of the life of Paradise, especially as this is depicted in the lives of the desert fathers and, much later than the Guthlac poems, in the life of Saint Francis of Assisi. The realization of Paradise for the individual Christian is brought about in three stages: through Baptism, already experienced by Guthlac before his wilderness sojourn; through the mystical and ascetical life, whereby the soul enters more deeply into Paradise; and finally through death. Throughout *Guthlac A* the protagonist is in the second of these stages, eagerly preparing his beorg so that he may be ready for the third, entry into Paradise. Before going on to tell of his hero's ascension into heaven, the poet asks, concerning this revelation of God's love and grace, "What fairer desire has been fulfilled in the life of man, that our ancestors could remember or that we ourselves could make known" (748b–751). In harmony with the spiritual discipline by which the corporeal world has been transcended, there is no mention at the end of the poem of Guthlac's death itself, simply an account of how his soul is taken, in the embrace of angels, into the presence of God (781 ff.).

The generalized conclusion, about the "communicants" or "partakers of the Eucharist, chosen warriors of Christ" (796–797) who have wisely prepared houses for their souls and who experience the beatific vision as they enter "the joy of the land of the living" (818), emphasizes, as did the beginning of the poem, that the life of the *bytla* Guthlac, whose purified soul has become a garden or paradisal dwelling, is an exemplary but typical one, important more for the general truths it embodies than for anything it has to say about the day-by-day existence of a holy man in the Crowland wastes. The historical monk memorialized in Felix's *vita* [17] has significance, as far as Old English poetry is concerned, only insofar as his life is shaped and interpreted by certain Christian myths—the temptations, Passion, Resurrection, and Ascension of Christ—these myths in turn being placed in the larger context of the archetypal struggle of Christ and Satan, begun in the myth of the Fall of the Angels and terminated when Christ restores Eden in the wilderness, thus making possible the resurrection and ascension of human souls.

Where *Guthlac A* finds its imaginative strength in skillful shaping of the raw materials of a life according to biblical paradigms, and by so doing achieves an effect of sharply abstract patterning, *Guthlac B* [18] takes materials of the same life and displaces them in a more "human" direction, although also using biblical myths. Both poems ultimately make some of the same thematic points about the necessity for freeing the soul of its affections for anything earthly if it is to be admitted into the joys of the heavenly gift-throne. But the imaginative resources and impact are quite different. Where the earlier poem never really focuses on the actual death of the saint, *Guthlac B* is essentially a poem about holy dying. In *Guthlac A* the retreat from the world to build a house for the soul symbolizes, so to speak, a desire to inhabit an objective reality, not to live in illusions as do most men but to break through into a real and effective order of being. The yearning desire in *Guthlac B* to go, through death, beyond the *beorg*, however paradisal, and to live in the golden *dryht* of heaven is the logical extension of the earlier labor of constructing a sacred place in part of middle-earth. The war in heaven was the beginning of all misery in the universe, and consequently all desire or expectation of fulfillment must look to the eternal society that existed before Satan's defection. Death, then, in

17. "Vita Sancti Guthlaci" in Bertram Colgrave, *Felix's Life of St. Guthlac* (Cambridge, 1956).

18. *PR* 3.72–88.819–1379.

Guthlac B becomes the object of desire, because it is the supreme initiation into transcendent reality.

Such a choice of subject matter contains the possibility of
elegiac development, and it is this, along with the extensive
dialogue between Guthlac and his thane, as well as the almost
"naturalistic" description of the holy man's disease and an
underplaying of the role of the demonic visitants, that gives
Guthlac B its more humanized or less abstract quality.[19] But
the elegiac theme, however important to the poem's overall
effect, is nonetheless a subtheme, secondary to that of death
swallowed up in victory.

To say that *Guthlac B* is less abstract than *Guthlac A* is not
to suggest that it does not explore its subject matter and theme
in terms of biblical symbolism. It begins with the myths of
the Creation and the Fall of Adam and Eve and exploits these
throughout, not in any sense as ornament or poetic filigree
but as structural elements in a poem about the ravages of death
experienced by all earth dwellers because of the venomous
drink fermented by Satan and poured of old for Adam by his
"young bride" (868–869) in the dryhtsele of Eden. Because of
this drink, the poem tells us, the *somwiste* (968, 1122, love
union) of man's body and soul has been broken and the body
has become, as in the two extant Old English *Soul and Body*
poems, an impediment, to be abandoned as soon as God permits. The original "joyous Creation" (824) was to allow, after
a life of earthly joy, direct access for man to the golden dryht
of heaven (833b ff.), but, with the entry of death into Eden,
Adam and Eve turned "trembling with shame" into "a world
of conflict" (856–857a). This fallen world is imagined as possessed by demons: "Deað in geþrong / fira cynne, feond
rixade geond middangeard (863b–865a, "Death pressed in on
the race of men, the enemy ruled over middle-earth"). None-

19. I am aware that the expression *more humanized* here means more
recognizably human in a *this*-world context, that is, from the non-
theological perspective of a twentieth-century critic. In the historical
context under consideration the fully human, as we have already noted,
is the fully divine and its location is heaven. When I use the term
abstract, then, it means abstracted from the actual world of men and
events that most of us for all practical purposes call the "real" world.

theless it is in this world of demonic possession that Guthlac
and a few rare souls like him make their *lac* (1111, offering)
of lives perfected by victorious battle against fiends. In *Guthlac
A* we are not told what form the devils take, but in this more
naturalistic composition they come as wild beasts or in human
shapes or as serpents spewing poison (907–912). Once again
Guthlac's place of retreat has paradisal and redemptive significance. It is a "plain of victory" (921) where birds with fer-
vent voices praise the anchorite (916–919a), an idyllic spot in
a wilderness to which eager travelers come to be healed in
body and soul (919b–932a).

The progress of the disease which gradually destroys Guthlac's body is described in an intricate amalgam of conventional
Anglo-Saxon poetic figures of speech. The fever is the result
of the dread drink "that Eve prepared for Adam at the beginning of the world" (980b ff.). Death is both friend and monstrous foe, the one who unlocks the "life-hoard" (1144) and
releases the soul from its "fated flesh-home" (1031) and also a
monstrous assailant, moving in from outer darkness toward
the sick man, to seize him with "greedy clutches" (993b ff.).
Guthlac's soul is "a precious ornament" (1059) or treasure: he
waits eagerly for the figure of death to come stalking nearer, to
batter down his body with showers of spears, to seek an entrance with cunning keys (1139b–1145a), and thus to extricate
or set free the only earthly treasure of lasting worth, that it
may be taken as a splendid offering to the knees of the
heavenly Dryhten, where he sits waiting on his gift-throne.

In response to his disturbed servant's questions (1197 ff.),
Guthlac explains how his soul has come to know itself as ab-
solutely free of any earthly attachment; for a year he has
secretly been visited each night by an angel who has imparted
to him the "gift of wisdom" (1246). The poet astutely underlines the force of this theme of otherworldliness by the presence and the lamenting utterances of the wretched, unhappy
thane who watches his lord dying. The mutual attachment of
lord and thane is treated sympathetically, but it is also relentlessly set aside in the face of the only dryht of genuine,
all-commanding authority.

The actual death, following shortly after Guthlac has rejoiced in the "noble season" (1105) of Easter, is a powerful
and moving account of heavenly glory impinging on middle-
earth (1269b ff.). As Guthlac prays, there comes from his mouth
the sweetest fragrance, like that of honey-scented blossoms in
summer, filling the fields with their sweetness. As the black
northern sky wraps the world in mist, a brilliant light from
heaven shines on the holy man and stays till dawn, when the
time "woven by fate" (1351) finally comes and Guthlac takes
the Eucharist. The poem's association here of the last events
of Guthlac's life with the temporal cycle is highly conventional
but nonetheless effective. As we have seen earlier, the season
of spring and of Easter is typologically the memorial anni-
versary of Creation and is therefore the fitting time, according
to the concept of Providence working through the world of
nature, for the Resurrection of Christ and, in this poem, for
the death of one of his most devoted thanes. Liturgically
Easter is the season commemorating and reenacting the
triumph of the world of grace over that of the earlier, now
ruined, Creation. The Eucharist taken by Guthlac in his last
moments in middle-earth is, in the context of imminent death,
his hastening toward the heavenly banquet sacramentally fore-
shadowed in the ritual. It is also one of the most crucial acts
in the "bloodless martyrdom" or "daily crucifixion" that has
constituted his life as a monk and as a hermit who has re-
nounced the whole world, including possessions and family.[20]
As Guthlac prepares to enter the eternal, unchanging Paradise,
he "opens the sacred jewels of his head" (1301b–1302a) to look
toward heaven, and angels arrive to take his soul while
heavenly troops fill the skies with songs of triumph. Such
transcendent glory is more than earth or human eye can bear,
and Guthlac's thane flees in terror from the holy island which
is now convulsed by an earthquake (1325b ff.). His ensuing
elegiac lament (1346b ff.) reestablishes the earthly perspec-

20. For a careful scrutiny of this aspect of monastic life and its
connections with Old English poems, especially with *The Dream of the
Rood*, see John V. Fleming, "The *Dream of the Rood* and Anglo-Saxon
Monasticism," *Traditio* 22 (1966): 43–72.

tive, with its description of a man who has lost to heaven all he yearns for, in a manner similar to the return to earth at the end of the Middle English *Pearl.*

The five poetic romances we have been discussing are not "epics" on a grand scale like *The Odyssey, The Iliad,* or *Paradise Lost,* even though they are poems of heroic action focused on single protagonists and conceived in a broad enough way culturally to embody many of the values of their society. They are narrative poems, with a good many symbolic overtones, deriving from the adaptation of materials of a hagiographic or legendary nature to the conventions of Old English dryht poetry and to the structures of biblical mythology. Each of the five is, in a sense, an extension of the heroic actions described briefly in *The Fates of the Apostles,* an elaboration of what is present there only in a germinal way. Andrew, Helena, Juliana, and Guthlac are all engaged in extending the dryht of Christ into territories where it has not previously been known. Each of them, by his or her brave deeds, is remembered as playing an exemplary role in the unremitting struggle of the Church against the world, the flesh, and the devil. A closer look at the kind of action each is involved in will make clear something essential and radical in the way the Anglo-Saxon Church projected, by means of poetry, its ideals and its desires.

The most basic fact is the absolute centrality in these compositions of the Anglo-Saxon version of biblical mythology, especially of the quest for the green plain or golden dryht of Paradise through conquest of the demonic forces laying waste middle-earth. In its individual reference, this quest is for personal salvation; in its communal reference, it is the aspiration of Christ's dryht or Church toward the eternal fortress of Jerusalem. It is the same narrative impulse seen at work in the myths of Adam, Noah, and Abraham in *Genesis,* of Moses and Israel in *Exodus,* of Judith, and of Daniel and his companions in *Daniel.* Like their Old Testament counterparts, Andrew, Helena, Juliana, and Guthlac are singled out by God as recipients of special grace. Out of this fact comes the assignment of "a mighty errand" whose execution forwards both the individual and the communal quest.

Each poetic narrative centered on a human champion in the mythical poems of Essay One and in the displaced myths of Essay Two involves a vision of some significant part of middle-earth as fallen into demonry or devil worship. When Adam in *Genesis* vows that he will willingly go seafaring in any sea, however deep, to regain the lost favor of his Dryhten (*Genesis A,* 827 ff.), he expresses that desire which works itself out in the subsequent myths, the desire to cleanse the world of hell's influence and to return to pristine unity of thane and Lord. The ark and voyage of Noah are the answer provided by heaven to the monstrous acts of the race of Cain. The long exile and wanderings of Abraham among hostile peoples lead up to the building of gold-halls and the founding of a kindred who are God's people on earth. The Egyptian enemy overcome by Moses and Israel in *Exodus,* like the Babylonians in *Daniel* and the Assyrians in *Judith,* is proud, tyrannous, and in league with hell. There is no essential difference between the dryht of hell in its earthly manifestations in these poems and the enemies against whom Andrew, Helena, and Juliana do battle. *Guthlac A* returns to the undisplaced myth of the earlier narrative and shows a hero fighting directly against devils and hell.

As we have seen, each champion is chosen by God or Christ to take heaven's part in the struggle begun when Lucifer set himself against God in the dryht of heaven. Human life, as in the influential *De civitate Dei,* is consistently imagined as caught up in a dialectic between the two supernatural societies. As the imagery of hell's darkness threatens to engulf the particular dryht in question, God lets the light of heaven shine on a heroic form who then brings ordered glory into Babylonian confusion.

Before the new redemptive scheme or pattern can be revealed, however, the heroic figure must undergo certain trials or educative experiences. These involve him in counsels coming from two directions, from the society of heaven and from that of hell. The function of such advice—it is comfort or persecution, depending on its origin—is to illuminate the protagonist's situation and to give the particular narrative cosmic significance. Christ appears as a seafarer and instructs Andrew, thus assuring that the apostle's spiritual labors will be in accord with heaven's plan. Satan appears at the right moment to inform the Mermedonians what they must do if they would contravene heaven's plan. Guthlac is instructed nightly for an entire year in spiritual mysteries too precious even to be mentioned to anyone on earth, until the hour of his death. The knowledge of hell and of hell's kingdoms on earth also must be acquired, since Christ took on himself the full experience of these levels of the cosmos: through imprisonment, dreadful experiences in the darkness of night, wilderness loneliness, sea terrors, and persecution by tyrants. Juliana and Guthlac receive indoctrination directly from devils. The acquisition of such knowledge involves the learning by the soul of warcraft through rituals of self-sacrifice, each act of spiritual war or sacrifice having a more or less direct connection with the Passion of Christ. The satanic confusion which must be transcended through identification with the actual physical sufferings of Christ leads to the frequency of the theme of sparagmos. Andrew's body is mutilated, and his blood is spread over rocky wastes. Juliana's body is burned and racked and finally decapitated, all because she will not sacrifice her virginity to a heathen. Guthlac's body (in *Guthlac A*) is laid siege to by hell's legions and finally destroyed. In *Elene*, in an interesting variation of the convention, it is the enemy Judas who has the function of sacrificial victim, so that his people may be freed from Satan.

The polarization of images, the schematic nature of the overall designs, and the relative abstraction of the human figures in these poems all contribute to a kind of formal symmetry like that in Byzantine mosaics. At times the heroic figure engages in actual physical conflict or war, as in the case of Abraham against Orlahomor or Judith against the Assyrians, but this is relatively rare, and even in these two examples the spiritual and theological overtones of the wars are what count thematically. On the whole there is an unmistakably "functionary" quality to these heroes and heroines, intimately connected with the fact that they seldom commit any deed in a self-motivated way; when they do so, as when Andrew objects to going to Mermedonia, the aberration is immediately censored. Consistently they function as agents of heaven; all the instructions guiding them through their various adventures come from above. They engage in building gold-halls, arks, and churches, in setting up the cross, in resisting the attacks of fiends, and in protecting their souls from the world and the flesh. Most of the time their stance is negative and renunciatory in relation to this world, to the point where they do not impress us as human figures so much as bizarre patterns made of human forms. It is not difficult to imagine Saint Guthlac as a static figure, with a rigid masklike face, surrounded by the twisted bodies of serpents, beasts, and birds cunningly interlaced—or Helena, with gold halo and large protruding eyes, standing stiffly at the head of a dragon-prowed ship as she concentrates intently on her task of crossing "the sea beast's home" (237) toward Jerusalem.

All genuine human action in this poetry is seeking Paradise or heaven; each particular deed has significance only in accord with this underlying teleology, and each meaningful act has its paradigmatic model in the great creative works of God, especially Creation and Redemption. The Anglo-Saxon Christian, like Cædmon in Bede's account, or like Cynewulf in his signatures, thinks of himself as having a soul addressed by God—directly or through "ancient writings" or by means of the liturgy or through the order of the created world itself—so that a vision of higher reality claims his loyalty. He is not like the romantics, Wordsworth, for example, an originator of artistic contructs who takes his inspiration from "nature" or from his own inner being. (To comment on this historical difference does not imply a value judgment on either body of poetry.) Creativity, or any significant action, for the Anglo-Saxon Christian, involves being responsive to the Creator's revelation of himself and his works and then going on to "shape" things—damascened swords, gold circlets, timbered halls, illuminated manuscripts, jeweled crosses, poems—that commemorate the mighty acts of God. Only in this way does man in middle-earth have contact with reality or vest his life with meaning. This implies that the poet is not limited to description of the fallen world, though when desirable he does so with considerable vividness; he has divinely established models always needing to be revealed once more. This freedom from the fallen world is never presented as a freedom to indulge in wild romantic fantasies, or as a freedom from facts, but rather as a loyalty to the only really important facts.

Since it is God who summons the human soul, finally it is only through God that any real action is possible. When, in *Daniel,* Nebuchadnezzar falls to worshiping himself and his great works, the Ozymandias theme follows logically, because the rebellious, proud king has cut himself off from the body of God, the source of all real power. Adam's fall in *Genesis* is not so much doing anything as failing to remain loyal to his Lord and not enjoying enough the gifts provided for him in the paradisal dryhtsele. Falling to temptation is giving way to a cowardice of the mind and soul. It is failure to respond to divine imperatives. If at times the appropriate response means simply standing still, as it often does, if it means displaying spiritual steadiness and tenacity but not physical strength, this is to be construed as revealing true power. The grace that makes it possible for the three boys in *Daniel* to stand in the fiery furnace singing a hymn to God, or for Juliana to go on praising her Creator while she is boiled in hot lead, obviously has little to do with physical heroism of the kind described, for example, in *The Battle of Finnsburh.* To think it has would of course make utter nonsense of the poem. On the other hand, this concept of ideal humanity, or of the Christian hero as primarily an enduring sufferer so moved by the flame of love for Christ that he will meet any physical terror with spiritual weapons alone, would seem to have a great deal to do with the kind of stylistic abstraction and hieratic patterning characteristic of so much Old English poetry. The spiritual, heaven-oriented purpose of the poems necessitates that almost all physical spontaneity and freshness must be sterilized out of the hero or heroine's actions. In this, it would seem, we have a measure of the very large gap between the religious sensibilities demonstrated in this poetry and those of ourselves. Almost inevitably, as products of a postromantic world, we respond sympathetically to just those individualistic, energetic, or passionate acts of human or diabolic rebellion that the Anglo-Saxon poets decry as damnable.

If we set beside the wars fought by Andrew, Juliana, and Guthlac that of Byrhtnoth and his dryht in *The Battle of Maldon*,[21] the different concept of heroism is at once evident. The champions of Maldon are engaged in a war apparently firmly based in the actual world of men and historical events.[22] Many of the images and trappings, the "treasure giver" (278), the "boasts" (15), the "shield-walls" (277), and "spear rushes" (32), are identical to those in the romantic poems, but the narrative myth is displaced much further in the direction of plausible realism. *Maldon* is a panegyric celebrating exemplary deeds and deriding shameful ones, deeds performed by men who display recognizable human emotions of loyalty or treachery. It is interesting to notice, however, that even in a work as "mimetic" as *Maldon,* a poem which realistically describes a splendid vindication of the dryht ideal even in the midst of military defeat, the traditional imaginative sense of the three-tiered universe and the heavenly guidance of human affairs makes itself felt. As Byrhtnoth dies, he prays to "the Ruler of princes" (173), giving thanks for all the joys he has known in the world and praying that *helsceaðan* (180, hell-sent enemies) will not be allowed to harm his soul as it ascends to heaven. His worldly task of defending the homeland of his prince and people was a God-given one, he has done his best, and he now anticipates his reward. The heathen (55, 181) Vikings he has fought are very palpable enemies, but they too, like the heathen troops of the more mythical poems, are associated with hell, since *hæþene* means "devil worshiping" in an early medieval Christian context.

If the typical heroic act is to give unquestioning loyalty to

---

21. *PR* 6.7–16.1–325.

22. George Clark, however, has recently mustered strong arguments against what might be called the orthodox view, that *Maldon* accurately represents "what really happened" in a battle in August 991; see "The Battle of Maldon: A Heroic Poem," *Speculum* 43 (1968): 52–71.

the heavenly Dryhten and to obey on earth those rulers or princes who recognize his lordship, the typical demonic act in this poetry is, as we have seen in Essay One, the attempt to rival God, to set up a throne and kingdom in the northern region of heaven, to build a tower meant to scale heaven, to feast drunkenly in Babylon with the sacred vessels stolen from the temple in Jerusalem. Nebuchadnezzar and Holofernes display a kind of wild exuberance in their boasting and carousing that to a modern eye may look attractive, compared with the frozen virtue of Juliana or the managerial skill of Helena, but the tree of Nebuchadnezzar's kingdom is relentlessly cut down and Holofernes loses his head. In a poetry dedicated to furthering loyalties to heaven, any action based on self-assertion or carnal passion has to be exposed as finally antithetical to reality itself.

There are two particularly striking passages that illustrate the complete absence of real power that Satan and his tyrants normally symbolize in Old English poetry. In *Judith*, the Assyrian followers of Holofernes are so enslaved by him that they have no wills of their own. Under attack from the Bethulians, they cannot bring themselves to burst in on their prince's supposed sexual enjoyment of the heroine but instead stand around outside, unable to enter but equally unable to leave, while the enemy comes closer. A more purely mythical or abstract depiction of the same death of will and power can be seen in the tiresome whining of the fallen Lucifer in *Christ and Satan*, climaxed, in the same poem, by the ludicrous figure of the fallen archangel completely conquered by Christ and measuring with his hands the dimensions of hell.

In sharp contrast to the figure of the fallen Lucifer measuring hell we can set the Old English poetic image of a creature of God still in possession of a full measure of heaven's grace. The fabled bird, the phoenix,[23] is at once the complete opposite to the fallen exile and the ultimate metaphorical extension, in the surviving poems, of the idea and images of saintly perfection in the context of middle-earth. The funeral pyre and flames of the aged phoenix abandoning its physical body

23. *The Phoenix*, PR 3.94–113.1–677.

are, according to the poet, the sufferings and trials of the martyrs (518 ff.).

In *The Phoenix* the complex, rich poetic symbolism of the golden dryht in both its earthly and heavenly forms reaches a climax of concentration and beauty. The mode of composition, at once visionary and allegorical, comprehends a veritable ingathering of many of the symbols and myths we have seen functioning in the poems discussed in Essays One and Two. Despite its partial origins in the *De ave phoenice,* attributed to Lactantius, and in Ambrose's *Hexaemeron* (and ultimately in a myth associated with sun rites at Heliopolis in Egypt), and despite also the very widespread use of the legend in patristic texts, *The Phoenix* is deeply involved in characteristic Anglo-Saxon images, metaphors, and myths.[24]

Its overall design or archetypal shape is that of the completed quest-romance of the Bible, from Paradise lost to Paradise regained, refashioned in terms of an account of the earthly existence of the fabulous and unique bird which is the central image of the poem. Patterned—like *Genesis A* and *B, Exodus, Daniel, Christ and Satan,* and the *Guthlac* poems—according to the antithetical symbolism of the paradisal dryht and the westen, *The Phoenix* culminates (589 ff.) in an exultant vision of the emergence in heaven of the new society of the blessed. But this new, transcendental society of adoring angels round their Lord is also old; it is the eternal, unchanging dryht of heaven described at the beginning of *Genesis A* and in numerous other places in the canon. It is the order of reality attained when the flames of the bird's funeral pyre, or of the Christian martyr's torments, have cooled, so that new life, freed of all earthly imperfections, is realized. As with the aged heroic form of Beowulf, so with the phoenix wearied by one thousand years of triumphant life, the destruction by fire is an anticipation of the Judgment flames beyond which lies absolute release (cf. *Beowulf* 2820). Also as with the story of Beowulf, *The Phoenix* describes, by its pervasive use of the

24. For a summary account of the development of the phoenix legend in classical and patristic texts, see Norman F. Blake's edition, *The Phoenix* (Manchester, 1964), pp. 8 ff.

heroic diction of dryht poetry, a complete life pattern, through buoyantly exuberant youthful acts to the final quelling of heroic energy. The phoenix and Beowulf are, in relation to the saintly protagonists of the narative romances, exceptional. We have seen that physical stasis and bodily endurance are the marks of the Christian hero or heroine in this poetry. But Beowulf and the phoenix are the very embodiments of that spontaneity and freshness Guthlac and Juliana lack. I shall consider at more length the special case of Beowulf in this respect in Essay Four, making only a few anticipative comments here. The essential difference between the phoenix and the four saints of the romances is that, where they with heaven's help must build their paradise or found their church, the fabulous bird from the very beginning of the poem inhabits Paradise and is in possession of that heaven-sent power toward which the others aspire. In *The Phoenix,* because of its romance qualities and its redemptive themes, the emphasis is on rebirth and triumph, whereas *Beowulf* focuses intently on a tragic tale of human defeat within the context of middle-earth.

As a poem *The Phoenix,* in its depiction of the heavenly resolution of all earthly troubles, obviously goes far beyond the tragedy *Beowulf*. There is in existence somewhere in Latin America a comic-book version of *Beowulf* which ends with flights of angels singing the hero to his heavenly rest, a kind of dryht-of-heaven resolution of the tragedy on the earthly level; but the *Beowulf* poet knows nothing of this. Such a conclusion, however, is structurally and thematically consonant with *The Phoenix,* where faithful and heroic souls from middle-earth come as perfume-bearing phoenixes to share in the *dreama dream* (658, joy of joys) with "the best of princes" (621). Earlier he has given them, in their roles as loyal thanes, good gifts; now he sits in glory waiting to receive their songs of praise. Described by the poet as a *soðfæstra gedryht* (635, a dryht of righteous ones) or *gæsta gedryht* (615, dryht of souls) and shining like the sun with bright rings of precious jewels above their heads (602–605a), the troop of thanes sings a magnificent hymn of triumph. At this point in mythological time

all actions in the universe, even those of the earthly Paradise,
have been left behind; the Phoenix-Christ has taken all worthy
souls above the roofs of the sky which throughout history have
covered the hall middangeard.

The dominant structure of images in *The Phoenix*, then,
is centered on the radiant figure of the unique, perfect bird
which is the protagonist of the poem. Described first in a context of music, light, fresh water, and undying vegetation, the
phoenix is a creature of youth and beauty. But then, like all
exiles from heaven, however perfect, it must move away from
the "joy of the homeland" (348b–349) into a wilderness (161,
169) where, like Guthlac, it builds a lonely dwelling and prepares to undergo a purgatorial, cleansing experience culminating in rebirth. From the wilderness and death it returns to
its ritual task of sun worship, of measuring with its daily and
millennial movements the cycles of the hours and years of
history. Finally, at the end of its life of devotion, it ascends
into heaven, taking with it the eager feathered dryht of birds
which, in its isolated perfection as an *anhoga* (87, 346, solitary
one), it has always previously rejected.

This structure of images, centered on the phoenix, connects
with another, bringing into the poem an additional dimension of meaning. The allegorist tells us that the life of the
phoenix signifies the story of Adam and Eve and their progeny,
the human race. After their "gloomy banquet" (*sarlic symbel*,
406) inspired by the envy of the fiend, the first human pair
had to abandon the ideal hall and fair plain of Paradise—
willsele, willwong, wilgedryht (the hall, plain, dryht of man's
desire), *eðles wyn* (the joy of the homeland)—and wander on
"the long journey" (440) of earthly existence, during which they
fell into the clutches of evil ones and "wretched monsters" (442).
Finally they were plunged into the "valley of death" (416)
from where they have had to be rescued and taken into heaven.

There is also a third pattern of images in the poem, cunningly interconnected with those of the phoenix and of Adam's
race. This one is indicated only briefly but symbolically underlies and gives meaning to the other two. It concerns the work
of the heroic Christ, who, as the poem explains (see especially

632 ff.), took on himself the form of a child, was born, died on the cross, and was raised by the Father so that he might ascend into heaven to take part in the Judgment. All three structures of images—centered on the phoenix, Adam, and Christ respectively—at certain points in the poem are distinct and separate. Finally, however, they are identified with each other, on that level where similar images coalesce into metaphor and the myth takes its poetic expression. In the highly inclusive symbol of the phoenix, the stories of Adam and Christ, or of Adam-Christ, are intricately fused, so that, observed separately or in terms of their metaphorical resonance, they all contribute to the shape of the divine *commedia*, a circle or brilliant ring beginning and ending in an ideal dryht but including within itself a movement into the lower, darkened order of human history. In his earthly existence, Adam, like the phoenix, knows only the green plain and the wilderness, until that apocalyptic time when the power of Christ triumphs on all three levels of the cosmos.

Since *The Phoenix* is almost unimpededly mythical in its mode of imagining, and because its thematic concern is with human resurrection and saintly or Christlike perfection, most of the images function close to the boundaries of fulfilled human desires. We notice again that it is not possible, finally, to separate the modes of myth and romance, since both fall into the broad area of mythopoeic literature. The land of the phoenix is the only part of God's original Creation that exists in the postdiluvian world of human history (41b–49). Paradise is a place where nothing impedes the will of God: "þurh metodes meaht" (6, "by the power of God"), "þurh est godes" (46, "by the grace of God"), "swa him god bebead" (36, "as God commanded them"), "Is þæt þeodnes gebod" (68, "It is the Prince's will"). As such, it is remote from all those "fallen world" attributes and experiences normally associated in Old English poetry, especially in elegy and in judgment contexts, with the middangeard. The poet explicitly tells us (50 ff.) that here the state of exile, feuding, war, storms, winter, sickness, death, and hell are entirely absent. There is nothing in the earthly Paradise of that inexorable fate which pursues the

Wanderer and engulfs Hrothgar's dryht. The paradisal or idealized "victory plain" and joy-filled "hall" emerge less completely, and in more obviously threatened forms, in other poems, whenever God's champions succeed in restoring some part of the original *neorxnawong* (Paradise)—in Noah's vineyard; in Lot's green, fertile lands by the Jordan; in the halls of Salem at the beginning of *Daniel;* and, as will be seen in Essay Four, in Heorot in its unfallen aspect. The radiant light, moreover, which shines on the phoenix in its Paradise is the same one that descends from heaven to envelop the "sunbright" Juliana, to receive the devotions of the dying Guthlac, and to herald the youthful Beowulf's triumph over the wintry, chaotic waters of the sea and of the mere. The green loveliness and blossoms of the rare bird's remote dwelling place are one with the benevolent nature associated with the saints in their moments of triumph—with, for example, the flowers that spring up on the rocky slopes of Mermedonia wherever Saint Andrew's blood has been spilled.

Hope Has Wandered in Exile
Patterns of Imagery in Old English Lyrics

In this essay we turn our attention from poems involving sustained or continuous patterns of organization to shorter, more episodic lyric works. Before individual poems are considered, however, certain preliminary matters need discussion: the general question of the relation of the myths and romances, on the one hand, to the lyrics, on the other; the use of the term *elegy* to denote a branch of lyric and the relation of elegy to tragic verbal structures, as well as to a concept of an ideal order or state; the basis of narrative continuity in Old English poetry, including further discussion of the way human actions are depicted in this poetry. This last, and its connection with the ideal order assumed by elegy, will serve as a useful approach to the commentary on the mental, spiritual, and emotional conditions described in the lyrics and shorter poems which are the main concern of this essay. Here again, as in the preceding essay, the concept of myth and of displaced myth will be important.

If *lyric* is the genre of obliquity or private utterance, as is commonly held, it seems reasonable to begin a study of the design of Old English poetry with the longer narratives and their accounts of the actions of God, Christ, angels, and saints and then proceed to the more allusive, more cryptic works. We have seen that the narrative romances involve a continual reworking of the traditional mythological account of the war between heaven and hell, a war which is fought on all three levels of the universe and involves, in middle-earth, rituals of sacrifice. In the completely mythical poems the sacrifice is the Passion of Christ; in the more displaced works the rituals of sacrifice are modeled on the life, death, and triumph of Christ. Such narrative subject matter is traditional and public

in nature; in Old English lyric poetry, however, we find a
somewhat more private world of sound and image, a poetry
based on the use of word play and ambiguity appropriate to
the expression of personal emotions and thoughts. Where the
poems of action begin with the formula *We gefrugnon* (We
have heard) and clearly are addressed to a tradition-based
community, the lyrics, in the main, exploit the first-person
pronoun and work in discontinuous units of feeling and
thought. As readers, we "eavesdrop" on the woman in *The
Wife's Lament* or on the solitary exile in *The Wanderer;* in
Exodus or *Juliana* or *Andreas* we are, fictionally, part of the
same Anglo-Saxon audience once involved, by the communal
nature of the rhetoric, in the action and values of the poem.
We are meant, according to the epos conventions [1] of oral
delivery of poems to a live audience (whether the oral situation is actual or simply part of the rhetoric), to imagine that
we are addressed directly by the poet; that, for example, we
are meant to do something about Cynewulf's urging of right
behavior before the arrival of Doomsday in the *Ascension*
poem. There are elements of the epos mode of presentation
in the shorter poems—for instance, in the poet's didactic comments at the beginning and ending of *The Wanderer*—but
the major emphasis is on private, individual situations and
utterances.

If it is true, as I think it is, that all poetic imagery is
founded on metaphor or displaced metaphor (simile) and if,
moreover, the brevity of lyric art often leads to unexpected or
violent poetic paradoxes and identifications, it follows that in
studying a body of poetry as formulaic and conventional as
that in the Old English poetic records the reading of a lyric
must be based on close attention to the same kind of metaphorical identifications that take place in the longer poems,
where the descriptive possibilities are greater and where any
given motif can receive more amplification. Even a casual
perusal of Old English poetry would reveal that the lyrics and
the longer narrative works do use many of the same formulas

1. For discussion of this term, see Northrop Frye, *Anatomy of Criticism:
Four Essays* (Princeton, 1957), pp. 248–50, 251–62, 269–72, 293–303.

and themes—exile, wandering, seafaring, bondage, rescue, and so on—but in the shorter compositions the utterance is often so oblique in its reference as to present truly formidable problems of interpretation, a fact demonstrated, for example, by the number of studies of *The Wanderer* and *The Seafarer*.

Still, even taking into account the special qualities of lyric art, one can proceed some mental distance in reading a poem like *The Wanderer* by learning the symbolic language of Old English narrative poetry, by recognizing the traditional mythology that appears to shape and inform almost the whole corpus of Old English poetry, and by bringing to each lyric a knowledge of the relevant parts of that symbolism and mythology. It is a main contention of this essay that the patterns of public ritual described in the longer poems—building churches, rescuing enslaved peoples, and sacrificing one's physical being for spiritual ends—provide the underlying structure of the private dreams and aspirations expressed, sometimes by techniques of indirection, in the lyrics. The mythical designs described in Essay One and elaborated in Essay Two frequently appear to be assumed by the lyricists, who then go on to define highly personal, elusive, and meditative verbal patterns that have their own internal density of meaning but constantly need reference to the larger construct if they are to be understood. In that group of lyrics sometimes called elegies, for example, we have the *penseroso* works of Old English poetry, meditative verse that serves as a complement to the poetry of heroic or saintly action.

In its simplest definition, *elegy* is a generic term, having come to mean the kind of lyric which is a song of mourning, a short poem of lamentation or regret for someone dead. But a reading of two such different elegies as Milton's *Lycidas* and Gray's *Elegy Written in a Country Churchyard* shows that themes other than lamentation over the death of an individual are taken into the elegiac genre. In *Lycidas* the lament over a dead poet is expanded until it becomes a dirge for the whole fallen world of man and nature. Gray's *Elegy* is a lament for a dead community, for the passing of a way of life. In both poems the death of an individual is a small but important part of a much wider tragic pattern involving the whole world of man's experience, and the death lamented is simply the most obvious symbol of human defeat within the order of nature.

In Old English poetry there are several laments over the deaths of individual persons. There are many laments over the nature of human existence in the ruined dryhtsele of middle-earth. When the terms *elegy* and *elegiac* are used, then, in this essay, they are frequently meant in an extended sense. To restrict them to their germinal idea of lamentation over the death of one man would be to make them useless for describing several of the lyrics conventionally designated elegies, to say nothing of the elegiac themes in other poems. The essential element always is a melancholy sense of the passing away of something desirable, whether that something be a life, a civilization, a human relationship, a beloved object or activity, or perhaps a state of spiritual or emotional harmony. Elegy involves a frustration of human desire, followed by a sense of unhappiness or misery, which, if the mood is allowed to develop, will probably take the form of lamentation or sympathetic utterance in relation to the object of desire.

It can be seen readily enough that such a thematic concern is likely to be associated with tragic verbal structures built round themes of death, disintegration, loss, waste, or any of tragedy's many possibilities. *Tragedy* is a structural term, however, and *elegy* appears to be a thematic as well as generic one, involving both subject matter and mood. Structural elements are usually more easily recognizable in a literary fiction, and they are certainly more easily described, than sense and mood are. But an attempt to do the latter can proceed a long way by resort to the former; a knowledge of the tragic structures in Old English poetry is, in fact, basic to any discussion of the related elegiac development.

In the closing scenes of *Beowulf* the gradual isolation of the hero from the world and from the society in which he has lived out his "loan-days" is accompanied by a bleak sense of the passing of time, by a burdensome awareness of the end of effective human action and the need for meditation, and finally, after the wounding, by resignation in the face of the tragedy of human existence in a world of bloodshed and destruction. The old warrior-king, gazing as he dies on the "works of giants" (2717), the ruins of human aspiration and ambition, can be taken as a typical elegiac figure; his personal tragedy is part of the tragedy of the race, and the order lamented in his passing has wide significance both in *Beowulf* and in other Old English poems, notably in the elegiac lyrics. To recognize this is to face the question of what that order of life is that is threatened by the death of an Old English poetic hero. What forms does it take in the poetry, and why is their destruction cause for lamenting? What is the ideal shape of human life in Old English poetry, to which the poets give their loyalties and their abilities in shaping words? In Essays One and Two a main purpose has been to suggest answers to these questions, in terms of the Old English dryht, an essentially simple concept denoting the bonds of loyalty between lord and thane but one capable of becoming a complex, many-faceted symbol embracing the dryht of heaven, the dryht of hell, the dryht of the earthly Paradise, and the ruined or tyrannous dryhts of middle-earth. It will be necessary to keep these ideas in mind during discussion of the lyrics.

Also relevant to both the longer poems and the lyrics is the way in which Old English poetry, in its use of images and symbols, as well as of underlying concepts, seeks in very obvious ways the typical and recurring. It has been noted how the triumphs of God and his champions are normally associated with radiant light and with the emergence of the green plain (or of related vegetation imagery) and also how defeats or near defeats are associated with a darkened wintry wasteland. Juliana, in her hour of triumph, becomes "heaven's candle." Andrew, at the nadir of his physical torment, is presented in a night-shrouded world where gray frost-warriors lay fetters on the land and homes of the Mermedonians. The Old English phoenix, allegorically symbolizing man as both Adam and Christ, is described in a rich mythological profusion of images of sunshine, fresh water, undying vegetation, music, and precious gems. The phoenix, like all men, however, even Christ, must pass through a westen on its way back to its green plain and paradisal streams and also, like restored Adam, the saints, and Christ himself, is finally taken out of the natural cycles of middle-earth.

In the Old English *Menologium*,[2] the month of March is associated with frost and fierce hailstorms (35) but also, since it contains the vernal equinox, with God's Creation (44b–47) and with the angel's Annunciation to Mary that she is to bear the best of kings (48–54a). The *Menologium*, in its account of the journeys of the times and seasons of the year, an account given in terms both of changing weather and of the acts of the Dryhten and his thanes, is only the most obvious example of an almost ubiquitous Old English poetic motif whereby the cycles of nature, night and day, summer and winter, are represented as symbolizing spiritual truths which completely transcend the natural order. May is not only the month in which a beautiful spring maiden, clothed in vegetation, comes journeying into the strongholds of men (75b–79) but also that time of the year in which Helena found the cross (83–87a) and Gregory the Great despatched Augustine to Britain (95b–106a). The point is this: the Old English poetic uses of images of the cycles of nature, in the wastelands and green plains of middle-earth, is a major symbolic device for giving a sense of movement and order to the poetry, even as it points to the pervasive supernaturalism of this art of words.

To speak of *movement* in Old English poems, however, can be misleading, if by the term we understand naturalistic or dynamic description of physical bodies in motion. There are sea voyages, battles (earthly and cosmic), and banquets, but there is very little sense of actual people or physical shapes moving from one place to another. There is no literary equivalent of three-dimensional perspective in painting, nor would we look for it in this period of history. The imaginative world that emerges in the major Anglo-Saxon poetic codices is caught in a peculiar stasis, so that where we might expect movement, change, and development, the poet gives instead successive and

2. *PR* 6.49–55.1–231.

continuous states of being: the condition of heroism or of cowardice, the state of *dream* (theological or simply social) or that of wretched exile, the condition of blessedness or that of damnation. Even the descriptions of the times and seasons, the daily and annual cycles, do not point to naturalistic principles of movement and development so much as to successive states of being. The *Beowulf* poet's comparison, in the context of Grendel's mere, of the vanishing of the sword blade, accompanied by radiant light, with the melting of ice in the springtime sun symbolizes the favor of God returning to the land of the Scyldings. It is clearly not a naturalistic account either of the destruction of a blade or of the return of spring to a wintry world.

Similarly, in *The Seasons for Fasting*,[3] an exhortation to ritual observances, fasting, and piety on the model of ancient Israel under Moses, we do not find a temporal or chronological ordering of human actions; instead, the poem presents an overall symbolic and thematic contrast between God-fearing Israel in ancient times and the contemporary degenerate state of the Church as observed by the poet. The four Ember seasons (the first week of Lent, the week after Whitsunday, the week before the autumnal equinox, and the week before Christmas) are not climatic, meteorological, or natural times of the year. They have a status independent of what we think of as nature: they are simply special occasions on which followers of Christ attempt to approach closer to the dwelling of angels, where, the poet tells us, their Prince has gone after his Resurrection (31–38).

There is, of course, a kind of narrative movement and chronology in many Old English poems whereby one event succeeds another, but there is never anything even approaching a story for a story's sake. The concern is relentlessly with clear thematic distinctions and with the character or action types involved. As we have seen in Essays One and Two, movements and changes in the human sphere are normally represented as precipitated by heaven or hell. That this is an adequate explanation for any given condition or experience is

3. *PR* 6.98–104.1–230.

simply an underlying assumption. Often we have the sense that man as we know him is not yet born. Even in a passage where a degree of verisimilitude is present, as, for example, in the scene when Unferth baits Beowulf, we are apprized of the thyle's role as a mar-peace (*un-ferth*) and fratricide so that his malign connotations will be perfectly clear. We have already been fully informed that it is the progeny of the archetypal fratricide Cain who are destroying Heorot. Unferth, then, picks a fight with the would-be rescuer of Heorot because it is his function, as a fratricide, to feud and kill, not to welcome deliverance and peace. Verbal warfare, giving the hero a sword that proves worthless, and killing one's brothers are not differentiated; their status in defining Unferth is of the same order. His silence later, after Beowulf's successes, means simply that he has failed, at least temporarily.

For us, though, Unferth is a problem. The Old English poets' defining of men and actions by means of attributes and of the direct influences of heaven and hell prohibits explanation or understanding in a modern sense. We, from perspectives of behavioral psychology, with at least some degree of confidence in plausible empirical explanations, find it difficult to accept as given a poetry that normally uses phenomena only as a means of pointing to a reality that is noumenal. The *Guthlac* poems and *Juliana* are to an extent special examples, but their otherworldliness is typical enough. Their assumption that physical existence is a burden or a torment to be borne and then gotten rid of as soon as God permits is a very long ideological distance from most modern readers. They proceed according to the principle that earthly life itself is a temporary or *læne* disturbance in a universe whose reality is in heaven. Mythologically, the whole human race from the time of the Fall is in a condition of dismemberment and division, of Babylonian confusion, necessitating the resurrection of the body of man so that the original unity of humanity with divinity may be restored. The lyrics as well as most other Old English poems work within this context.

In the mythical poems and romances discussed in the first two essays, we saw functioning poetically the metaphor of the created world as the mighty dryhtsele of God, a magnificent edifice in which the Deity doles out to men the gifts that symbolize his love for his creatures. This metaphor of the ideal earthly dryht combines with that of the green plain, to give the two main Old English symbols for the paradisal or ideal state of existence on the earthly level. But the physical world of the cycles of nature—within which, after Adam's treachery, sacred history unfolds and earthly kings dispense their gifts— exists in a double aspect, with the result that the dryht of middle-earth may be represented in a particular poem either as the ideal golden one or as a society of fratricidal acts paralyzed by pride and enslaved to a wolf-hearted tyrant, like Nebuchadnezzar. But the golden dryht and the society of Cain or Babylon are only terrestrial images of the dryhts of heaven and hell, those two divergent societies involved in the war in heaven that we see described at the beginning of *Genesis A* and mentioned in dozens of other places throughout the canon. Out of these antithetical dryhts arise most of the possibilities of narrative as such in Old English poetry, inasmuch as man's middle position in the cosmos involves him in two possible kinds of action, either ascent to the eternal, unchanging dryht of heaven or descent "down under the headlands" into the joyless hall of Satan. Constant interaction between the macrocosm and the microcosm determines that each observable action will be set in a theological context and, in terms of literary criticism, in a mythological one.

The mythical poems and the romances make clear that real human action can take two forms. The individual may become a being apart from human society, shaping a small paradisal dwelling for his soul while waiting for death and ascension into heaven, or else he may become an apostolic thane repeating among men the works of Christ, by establishing a sacred space (the gold-halls of Abraham or the church founded by Helena) somewhere in middle-earth. In both acts the ultimate goal is the same, the reception, after the death of the body, of earth's only substantial treasure, the perfected human soul, into the golden dryht of heaven. At that moment in earthly existence when the individual thane of the heavenly

Dryhten becomes the totally obedient servant of his Lord's purposes, he exists at what Eliot has called "the still point of the turning world"; he is freed from the Babylonian confusion of the ruined dryht-hall of earthly existence, even though his physical body may for a time have to remain in the ruin of the paradisal hall.

Most Old English poetry constantly invites its reader or audience to focus not on the physical surfaces of the harps and swords of the earthly dryht but on the moral and spiritual truths revealed through them. The brief description of the cunningly fashioned fortress of Salem at the beginning of *Daniel,* for example, is a poetic device at the very start of the poem for detaching a certain portion of undefined space, to make it manageable for the human mind and to vest it with spiritual meaning. The curious sword hilt brought back from Grendel's mere not only is a striking physical object but also serves a major thematic purpose in the poem, by making clear the apocalyptic or mythical significance of Beowulf's destruction of the monsters. We are continually reminded that we are not only to look at the images of the text but to ruminate on or look through them. Perhaps one of the most vivid illustrations of the kind of spiritual illumination sought occurs in the unfairly despised poem *The Order of the World.*[4] The apparently peremptory, almost "preachy" tone encountered here, which has alienated some modern readers—"Wilt þu, fus hæle" (1, "Are you willing, eager man"); "Leorna þas lare" (23, "Study this teaching"); "Gehyr nu þis" (37, "Now hear this") —comes from a thematic concern that the reader will so rouse his mental powers, by contemplation of the splendid, complex artifact of God's Creation joined harmoniously in all its parts, that he will attain to true visionary wisdom. At the same time, the poem stresses the limitations of the earthly order and of the powers of human understanding. This emphasis on the finitude of natural creatures is skillfully handled, in terms of light symbolism and of the intimate relation between the golden dryht of Creation and the society of heaven.

The Order of the World has been indicted as uninspired

4. *PR* 3.163–66.1–102.

and structurally weak, because half of the description of Creation takes the form of a glorification of light.[5] Why this should be cited as a structural weakness is difficult to understand, either in terms of the immediate poetic context or in terms of the wider uses of the Creation myth throughout the canon. Since the theme of the poem concerns the gaining of wisdom and the illumination of the mind of man by God's revelation of himself through created things, the beautiful description of the solar cycle seems entirely apposite. The mysterious submarine journey of the sun, incomprehensible to human faculties, becomes the symbol of the boundaries established for man's mind by God. It is by thinking on the wonders of Creation that human beings attain to the wisdom necessary for that renunciation of sin that leads to heaven, heaven symbolizing the end of mystery and the completion of man's vision of an ideal reality. There is none of the diffused melancholy here that in some poems accompanies the disappearance of light or the mention of man's crimes against heaven. The focus is almost completely on the order symbolized by the "gold-bright sun" (73), an order that does not decline but is held fast, in the poem's language, by mighty locks placed round it by God (86–89). Unlike the impermanent land of the phoenix and unlike Heorot, whose iron locks can be torn away by Grendel, this Creation does not suffer tragic destruction. Heaven and earth are in primal harmony, and neither Doomsday flames nor outer darkness intrude. Clearly the poet is not describing the world of actual human experience, the world of the ruined dryht brooded over by the elegist, but rather the ideal world whose lasting form is in heaven and to which all human endeavor ideally turns. His knowledge of such a world derives not so much from actual life in a historical society as from traditional Church teaching, with its revelations of the deeds of God. It is this kind of knowledge and vision which, when it is obscured or remains only in dreams, gives rise to Old English elegy. But always in the background in poem after poem, whether elegiac or not, is the longing for complete absorption into heaven, for the

5. C. W. Kennedy, *The Earliest English Poetry* (London, 1943), p. 323.

restoration of a primal unity; and always there is the desire
for a world of pure metaphor where the *hæleþ* (warriors) are
angels, banqueting is not fleeting, and the lord is the Dryhten,
God himself.

The dryht, as a complex of images, has traveled a long
distance in imaginative space from a poem like *The Battle
of Finnsburh* [6] to *The Order of the World*. From the loyalties
enacted by a band of *geoguð* (young warriors) in a purely
earthly hall under attack in *Finnsburh,* the bonds of the dryht
idea have reached out to signify two levels of being: the place
of the presence of God and the angels, that is, the empyrean
of the old Ptolemaic cosmos; and secondly, the level of ideal
or paradisal existence in middle-earth. This latter, as we saw
in Essay One, is the reality brought into being when the
Scyppend (Creator) began to fashion the empty, useless *westen*
in *Genesis A* into a gift-hall for men. But *The Order of the
World* shows only half the picture, the upper two of the four
levels of imagery found in Old English texts. Here there is no
mention of Babylonian confusion, ruined fortresses, and vanished joys, of society fallen into a wasteland world of winter
and darkness, or of that level of imagery which shows the
parodied or perverted dryht of hell. But as we approach other
Old English lyrics with their ambiguities and cryptic utterances it is necessary to keep in mind the interrelations between
all four of these levels of possible poetic meaning and action.

The Wanderer [7] is a poem about the world beneath the
heavens, where divine grace (1–2) is not visibly operating and
where everything is seen to be under the sentence of Judgment
(85–87). The exile who is the subject of the poem,[8] however

6. *PR* 6.3–4.1–48.

7. *PR* 3.134–37.1–115.

8. It will be evident from what follows that I accept the now fairly
general view that the *eardstapa* and the *snottor on mode* of the poem are
the same man. John C. Pope, however, has recently revived the older view,
that there are two speakers in addition to the poet himself, thus making
dogmatism in the matter unwise. See his "Dramatic Voices in *The
Wanderer* and *The Seafarer,*" in *Franciplegius: Medieval and Linguistic
Studies in Honor of Francis Peabody Magoun, Jr.,* ed. J. B. Bessinger, Jr.,
and Robert P. Creed (New York, 1965), pp. 164–93. I agree with Pope,

intensely personal his lament, is treated not simply as an individual but as a representative as well of man's life in the physical world of fallen nature, that same world anticipated by Adam in *Genesis B* when he first began to realize the implications of his treachery to his Dryhten and when he saw that he must now become a wanderer in a wasteland and a seafarer through stormy seas. The typical or exemplary function of the Wanderer is evident, in his namelessness and in the fact that he is simply "the solitary one" (1) waiting for the advent of grace, like the wretched inhabitants in the ruined dryht in *Christ I*— "hu se earma sceal are gebidan" (70, "how the wretched one must wait for grace")—and forced with heavy heart to make his way over the dark waves.

His identity with the fallen physical world is intricately worked out in the body of the poem, especially in relation to three aspects of nature. His daily experience, unlike that of Andrew or Guthlac or Juliana, includes no mention of radiant sunlight, only of "morning care" (8–9) and of the shadow of night casting gloom over the world of men. His yearly cycle is incomplete, the only seasonal imagery being that of winter and its storms. The water symbolism associated with him is that of the icy sea, of hail and snow, the antithesis of the flowing streams of Paradise described in *Genesis A* and *The Phoenix* and of the waters of Baptism in *Andreas*. Night, winter, and chaotic waters are the symbols of the Wanderer's unredeemed or spiritually lost condition.

Adam outside of the dryhtsele of Paradise, then, is the

---

however, that the question of one or two speakers does not greatly alter the total meaning of the poem as a sequence of ideas and emotions. See John C. Pope, ed., *Seven Old English Poems* (Indianapolis, 1966), 79–80. In presenting my interpretation of *The Wanderer,* within the context of this book, I have decided against entering into a lengthy discussion with the many other interpreters of the poem. Of all the studies I have read there is one, however, that of P. L. Henry, which seems, both in its overall thesis and in its handling of details, to be most congenial to my argument, although Henry sees the Wanderer as achieving God's mercy in the poem and I do not: see "The Wanderer," chap. 8 in his very rich interpretative study, *The Early English and Celtic Lyric* (London, 1966), pp. 161–75.

archetype of the eardstapa (wanderer), the same poetic model which lies behind the numerous other exiles wandering through the fallen world in Old English poetry: Abraham seeking a permanent dwelling place where he may live in the Dryhten's favor; Moses leading the Israelite troop through the wilderness and the Red Sea; Noah seafaring at God's command. Like Adam, who no longer can enjoy the gifts dispensed to him in Paradise, the Wanderer is separated from the joys of the dryht. His experiences illustrate the workings of inexorable *wyrd* (what is to be), once the grace of heaven is withdrawn or absent.

The theme of potential salvation, through the purposeful seeking of God's mercy, is kept alive in the poem by the introduction (1–5) and by the conclusion (111–115), but the body of *The Wanderer* presents a stark vision of life as almost unrelieved tragedy and misery. The absence of any release is intimately involved in the fact that the exile is in bondage to his own desire to regain the past, to return to a world that no longer exists. Despite the fact, however, that he is described throughout as imprisoned in a fatally determined order of existence, his experiences do lead him through a kind of intellectual progress to the point where he sees his individual miseries and the disappearance of the dryht to which he once belonged as part of the wider, universal tragedy of all life in middle-earth (58 ff.).

The extensive repetition of sound patterns in the poem, especially of initial words and expressions (*Oft . . . oft; Forðon . . . forðon; ne to . . . ne to; Hwær cwom . . . hwær cwom; Eala . . . Eala*), is perhaps the most obvious indication of the pondering, deliberative mental process that makes this intellectual advance possible. In the poetry of feeling and meditation which is involved here, there is an almost palpable quality to some of the lines, a sense of the rhythm being prior to the choice of words—"Oft him anhaga are gebideð"; "earmne anhogan oft gebindað." There is also a semihypnotic verbal incantation in which the patterns of sound are meant to absorb the listener, even as they establish a sense of melancholy solemnity. If we are to appreciate in *The Wanderer* the intensity of its bleak vision of life in the world of the vanished dryht and if we are to perceive the force of the meditation on the meaning of wisdom in the latter part of the poem (58 ff.), it is important to recognize the complex of images by which the exile's experiences are described, and also the basic metaphors informing these images.

One might suppose that a poem with a "wanderer" as its central symbol would have to do with wide open spaces and journeying through many lands, but this is not what we find. In spite of the solitary exile's four references to his journeys throughout the years, he is on the whole a static figure of confinement and introspection, a man almost frozen in body and soul who sits deep in thought. His lament, like the necessity of his exile itself, is compulsive, not voluntary. He is in a state of fear in which he dares not utter confidences to anyone and, above all, feels that he must cultivate reticence. He says that he must bind fast or hoard within the "enclosure" or "treasure chamber" of his mind his unhappy thoughts (13–14), thus implicitly suggesting an analogy with the cessation of joy in the world of the hall where the end of treasure giving means the withdrawal of the lord's favor. The sharing of counsels, like the sharing of treasure, is an integral part of the life of the dryht.

It should also be noted that the description here of a lamenting exile's heart presents the emotional antithesis of the mood of the hero engaged in action. Beowulf, who rejoices at his "night work" of monster killing (827), Guthlac doing spiritual battle against legions of demons, and Helena with her dryht eagerly setting out for Jerusalem, all are active participants in extending a divinely sanctioned order of reality. Beowulf, in the fullness of his youthful powers, tells the lamenting Hrothgar that it is better to avenge a friend than to mourn greatly (1384b–1385), thus providing a clear contrast between the elegiac and the heroic figures. The Wanderer, unlike Beowulf and the other champions, is not the recipient of heaven's grace; his metaphorical affinities are with those who are part of the bondage of the dryht of hell, whether their captivity be endured in middle-earth, as with the demons in

Guthlac A and *B,* or down beneath the headlands. Like Juliana or Helena or Guthlac, the figure of the exile here is static and rigidly stylized even when speaking of his actions. Unlike the saints, however, he is not in a spiritual condition of freedom from the treasures and human loyalties of the world.

To recognize the mythical connection with the dryht of hell is not to suggest that the Wanderer is depicted as actually damned—for no human soul, however devoid of grace, can theologically be damned while life remains during which the receiving of salvation is still possible—but simply to indicate that his paradoxical experience as an unredeemed, *wintercearig* (24, weary with winter) man, burning with desire for human society and kinship relationships once his but now gone, is closer to the spiritual condition of the fallen Lucifer than to that of those figures who are the recipients of grace. The mythical meaning of his bondage and wandering lies in the poetic descriptions of Lucifer or Satan as the fallen, captive archangel, bound in his own pride-based sins and, at the same time, wandering apart from the Body of God from which he has cut himself off. He is like Guthlac's thane, as has often been noted in modern times, in that his loyalties are all earth bound.

The Wanderer, like all men in the postlapsarian world, is an exile from Paradise, not yet received into the dryht of Christ and therefore overwhelmed with terror and hopelessness before the threat of nonbeing symbolized by the "rime-cold sea" (4) and winter storms. Other than the fact that he is now "lordless," earth's darkness having years ago covered his generous prince (22–23), and the fact that "many slaughters" (7) have taken away the hall-men he once knew, we are not told in the first part of the poem why he is doomed to search in vain for a mead-hall and a treasure giver who will show him love and counsel. Unless, however, we reject the relevance to the body of the poem of the clearly theological statements at the beginning and the conclusion, there is no difficulty in recognizing that the Wanderer is a study of a man, whether through individual sin or simply through the working of an inexorable and malevolent *wyrd,* apart from God's grace. It follows, then, in line with what I would call the dominant symbolic conventions of Old English poetry, that the imagery associated with him will derive from a vanished paradisal dryht and from the dryht of hell itself. He remembers the comrades of his youth, the receiving of treasure, and the joyful embracing of his lord, but this "paradise" is now irrevocably gone and he, once again like the fallen Lucifer, is a prisoner of memory. As with the captive archangel at the end of *Christ and Satan*, the vast desolation of his surroundings is the objective counterpart of his own sense of nonbeing, of his knowledge that he is now cut off from the body of the lord whose presence established reality and meaning in his life. So also, his spiritual bondage is like that of hell's captives, and he accordingly has a paradoxical sense of himself as being forced to wander far and wide but of existing, at the same time, in fetters. His body is *ferðloca freorig* (33, a chilled place of confinement for the soul and the wintry world in which he exits is one in which all treasure, joy, and love are either hidden or permanently gone. In other words, the poem has its major informing metaphor in the identification of the Wanderer, body and soul, with the settings—the wintry sea and the rocky, wind-swept slopes beside the ruined hall—in which he is placed.

Within the frame provided by the introduction and the conclusion, two major themes are developed, the tragedy of the individual Wanderer's existence and the more general theme of the transitoriness and doomed character of all earthly existence. These two concerns are centered on the figures of the exile and the wise man respectively, the latter being the man whom the Wanderer comes to realize must emerge from the kind of experience he has undergone. The initial indulgence in nostalgic dreaming must give way to depiction of the waking consciousness or the rational mind to provide a unified state of vision in which all the emotional and rational powers are involved. The wise man must perceive, says this *penseroso* figure, how it will be "when all worldly wealth stands wasted, as even now, here and there throughout this middle-dwelling, walls stand beaten by wind, covered with frost, the habitations falling in ruins" (74–77).

From line 58 on, the poem expands the account of an indi-

vidual tragedy to include the whole of human existence: the
Wanderer's spiritual wasteland becomes unmistakably the
wider vision of a fallen world, the poetic antithesis to the
vision of Creation described in *The Order of the World*. Even
as his individual happiness has been shattered, "so each day
this middle-earth declines and falls" (62b–63), and the image
of the grave into which his lord has been placed (23) is now
symbolically extended to encompass the whole of fallen nature,
to the point where the vision of ruined fortresses and dwellings is, in effect, that of a universal graveyard filled with
crumbling monuments to past glory. Rulers lie dead, mighty
warriors in their pride have fallen by the wall, and the gray
wolf has done his work (78–80a). J. E. Cross has seen the
references here to the wolf and the bird as part of the traditional Christian theme of "ways of death," represented, for
example, by Cyril of Jerusalem's description of vultures and
ravens flying away over all the world.[9]

The *eardstapa* (wanderer) who becomes the *snottor on mode*
(wise man) explicitly identifies the cause of desolation with
the activity of the Creator himself: "Thus the Creator of men
laid waste this earthly dwelling until, deprived of the tumult
of its inhabitants, the ancient work of giants stood empty"
(85–87). We recall that the adjective in the formula *idlu
stodon* (stood useless or empty) is used to describe the dark
waste prior to Creation in *Genesis A* (106) and that a firmly
established Old English poetic image for God's earthly Creation is that of the world as a dryht-hall. Here again the same
dryht is seen plunged into desolation and ruin, following the
end of the life of its once-proud inhabitants. The *enta geweorc*
(87, works of giants), or ruins of man's ambition, it will be
remembered, is a theological motif found in the Judgment
contexts of the destruction of the tower of Babel, the kingdom
of Nebuchadnezzar, and the devil worship of the Mermedonians. (Only in the last of these is the formula *enta geweorc*
itself used; *Andreas* 1495.) It seems clear that the wise man has

9. J. E. Cross, "On the *Wanderer* Lines 80–84: A Study of a Figure and
a Theme," *Vetenskaps-Societetens Årsbok* (Lund, 1958–59), pp. 77–110,
especially p. 88.

arrived at the traditional Doomsday vision. Having pondered
deeply "this dark life" (89), he comes to realize that in spite
of all human aspiration and temporary joy, the "decree of fate
changes everything in the world beneath the heavens" (107).
The horse, the warrior, the treasure giver, the gold-hall, and
the bright cup have all disappeared as if they had never been,
and in their place "stands a wall, wondrously high, glistening
with serpent shapes" (97–98).

If it seems unconvincing to read *The Wanderer* as a poetic
amplification, somewhat "displaced," of Adam's lament in
Genesis, it is worth remembering that all Old English poetic
references to Adam in one way or another exploit the idea of
his thaneship in relation to his Lord. In *The Descent into
Hell,* Adam, as the leader of the "assembly of heroes" (47),
welcomes Christ as a guest to the hall of hell, saying that now
he himself can take courage at the end of his long exile, knowing that if he trusts in the grace of his Lord the "hostile fetters" (65) will be removed from him. The fall of Adam is conventionally described as a bitter banquet, the fatal apple given
Eve by the serpent metaphorically being a poisonous drink.
The result of this feasting is the exile of Adam from the bright
hall of Paradise and the attendant ruin of that hall. If, as I
am suggesting, this set of conventional metaphors is working
in *The Wanderer,* then the climax of the poem—the vision of
the former place of the race of heroes, now characterized by
the ruined wall glistening with serpent shapes and beaten by
storms sent "to the torment of men" (105)—is fully and powerfully executed, on the basis of the ancient myth of Paradise
lost. From the perspective of the ruined earthly dryht, with its
overtones of the dryht of hell, the Wanderer looks back to a
former idealized and golden world. The poet's comment, that
it is well for any wretched man to seek comfort and mercy
from the Father in heaven, "where all security stands" (115),
provides the larger context of the eternal dryht of heaven, of
hope and salvation.

Like the Wanderer, the narrator in *The Seafarer* [10] is an
exile cut off from human companionship, who often has made

10. *PR* 3.143–47.1–124.

his difficult way through wintry seas, even as he thought back to the joys left behind. For years, he recalls, he has been acutely aware of the lonely rigors of his perilous life of seafaring. The poem is a symbolic depiction of spiritual pilgrimage, using the vivid traditional imagery of physical seafaring. Like the Wanderer, the Seafarer is troubled by unsatisfied longings, seeking a fulfillment that as yet has not been granted him. Toward the end of his meditation on life and death he arrives, as does the speaker in the other poem, at a vision of that decline and destruction of all worldly glory permitted by God, who long ago "established the solid foundations, the regions of the earth and the sky above" (104–105).

But the Seafarer is fundamentally quite different from the Wanderer, whose meditation is almost entirely nostalgic and retrospective in its statement of frustrated human desire and whose wandering is an exile apparently externally imposed by a hostile fate. The journeys of the Seafarer are voluntary, even though they bring him great physical misery; his exile is self-imposed, in line with his conviction that the rigors of seafaring are preferable to the peaceful delights and prosperity which could be his, at least temporarily, on land. The Wanderer is lost. He is in bondage to the malign circumstances of his life and compelled alternately to wander and to lament, with no assurance that he will ever break out of the closed circle of his passionate memories of time past: "Often I had . . . to make known my care" (8–9); "a weary spirit cannot withstand fate" (15); "He who long has to do without the wise counsels of his friendly lord knows" (37–38); "Care is renewed for him who must send his weary spirit once again over the binding of the waves" (55b–57). He looks back on his former homeland as a place of warmth and joy, as an ideal existence to which he would eagerly return.

In contrast, the Seafarer's mind "is wandering far and wide with the ocean, across the homeland of the whale" (58–60); his spirit is urged on irresistibly by the screaming "lone flier" (62), and the desire of his soul always urges him to seek the dwelling of strangers. There is close metaphorical identification of his turbulent soul with the restlessness of the waves—"min

modsefa mid mereflode" (59, "my spirit with the sea flood")—
and of his solitary spirit—*anfloga* (lone flier)—with the desolate
cries of sea birds.[11] His emotions are depicted by the oxymoron
of cold body and burning heart (8b–11a), but the burning involves desolation in terms of human relationships in favor of
identity with nature in its bleaker aspects. The images of a
resurgent nature—groves breaking into blossom, the strongholds becoming fair, the plain quickening with springtime
vegetation (48–49)—are the conventional symbols associated
with Old English paradisal and redemptive themes and are
intimations of the desired state which is not yet his. His seafaring, he says, like that of any man, is filled with anxiety,
since there is no knowledge of its final results (39–43), but he
does not look back longingly on what he has abandoned
(44 ff.). His attitude to the world of harp music, ring dispensing, and joy with a woman is fiercely renunciatory and ascetic:
"þis deade lif, / læne on londe" (65–66a, "this dead, fleeting
life on land"). He has no thought for any earthly delight, for
his mind knows only the rolling of the waves; "the joys of the
Lord are keener" (64b–65a) for him than the fleeting pleasures
of the world. He has no faith that earthly riches or the life of
the prosperous man on land have any lasting worth and so
resolves to strive against the hostility of fiends, against the
devil, in the faith that afterward he will have honor among
angels and be exalted by men (66b ff.). His rejection of the
world, the flesh, and the devil is absolute, to the point, apparently, where he despises even the honor shown a dead
kinsman, on the ground that no earthly treasure will alleviate
the wrath of God if the soul is filled with sin (97–102).

In a thematic sense *The Seafarer* is a sequel to *The Wanderer*. The man who looks back in despair on a vanished dryht

11. The reading of *anfloga* as meaning the Seafarer's soul, like many
other things in this much-discussed poem, is controversial. *Anfloga* has
also been taken as the cuckoo, as *draco,* as a "disease-bringing, malign
influence," or as a metaphor describing the Seafarer's imagination as a
lonely sea bird. For a recent, extended argument in favor of the
anfloga as the Seafarer's restless soul, see Henry, *The Early English and
Celtic Lyric,* pp. 137–49, 154. Henry's discussion includes a summary of
previous comment.

is bound by necessity, but the one who voluntarily becomes an exile for Christ and resolves to do battle with the devil looks forward to grace (107b) and freedom. The Wanderer is introspective, melancholy, and, since there is no indication that he will act on the poet's counsel to seek God's mercy, doomed. The Seafarer is actively heroic, in the way that Guthlac is, and has accepted the spiritual view of ultimate reality that comes into clear focus only in the introduction and conclusion of *The Wanderer*. In this latter poem, the relations of the earthly dryht are both treated sympathetically (by the exile) and revealed (by the poet) as fated to be destroyed by God. In *The Seafarer* the same ties are held in contempt, as deterrents in the quest for the only authentic dryht. In each poem the vision of middle-earth is the same, all earthly glory and beauty being treated as insubstantial and moving inevitably toward ruin, but in *The Seafarer* it is the exile himself who passes judgment; the Wanderer is an integral part of the order doomed by the Creator. In terms of the controlling Christian myth, the Seafarer has progressed further on the road to grace by his denial of the very world idealized by the Wanderer.

There is a subtle but important difference in the emotional attitude of each of the two speakers, in relation to their quite similar views of the decline and fall of the world of the earthly dryht. The Wanderer's "Alas, bright cup! Alas, byrnied warrior!" (94) is permeated by a nostalgia and idealism unspoiled by irony, but the Seafarer's words—"The days have passed away, all the proud trappings of earth's kingdom" (80b–81)—are imbued with the harsher note of judgment. The elegiac figure takes a position of lamentation in relation to the doomed structure of the world, but the more homiletic Seafarer turns aside potential elegy by saying that the object of desire is unworthy. It is this renunciatory attitude consistently maintained throughout *The Seafarer* that makes it impossible to call the poem an elegy.

In *Resignation*,[12] another homeless exile describes himself as driven forth "without friends" (91) and "deprived of the

12. PR 3.215–18.1–118.

joys of society" (90). Because he has sinned and committed evil deeds, he has incurred the wrath of God (78b ff., 91). Cut off from both man and God, for years he has been severely punished in the sight of the world, has suffered "a heavy martyrdom" (81–82) of poverty, hardship, homelessness, and fear. Dependence on the alms of men has only increased his misery, for with the alms given he has had to endure bitter reproach (93–95a). Like the heart of the Wanderer, his is described in formulas of gloom and near despair: "always his heart is sad, his spirit sick in the morning" (95b–96a). His plaint is that "thus solitary and cut off from social joys—the wrath of God is upon him—a friendless exile can no longer live" (89b–91).

Resignation is an elegiac prayer, similar in its mode of expression to the penitential psalms. The rhetoric of prayer seems to demand, especially in the first, nondescriptive part of this poem, the stringing together of many short phrases and formulas invoking God to single out for redemptive care and acceptance the penitent who speaks: "Possess me" (1); "Help me" (2); "Mark me" (10); "Forgive me" (19); "Grant me" (22); "Establish my mind on thee" (37); "Raise my spirit" (39). The poem is essentially lyric, in that it is clearly a private utterance directed toward God, the Deity being designated by ten different epithets in the first fourteen lines. The penitent exile begins his lament by placing his whole being, his soul, body, words, deeds, limbs, and all his many thoughts, before his Lord (5b–9). Above all, his prayer is for guidance: how can his soul best observe God's will and thus build up for itself benefits?

As the diffuseness of the rhetoric gradually allows the reader to get a picture of the man's whole life, it is established that the penitent is looking back on a miserable and friendless existence brought on himself by his sins. At the time of making his plaint he is about to depart on a journey toward God and away from this world (41 ff., 70 ff., 96b ff.). For him earthly life is the conventional "fleeting time" (31) before man enters into the permanence of heaven. His problem in setting out on the journey is that he has no gold with which to buy a boat and no friend to help him on his voyage. "The forest may abide in its destiny, putting forth branches," he reflects, but because of disgrace he "cannot in his heart love any man in the land" (105–108a). The contrast between the man out of charity with his fellows, and therefore unable to thrive spiritually, and the tree which does flourish as it should seems to be a variant of that kind of mythological imagery we have observed in other contexts, in which natural, vital images of vegetation symbolize the redemptive power of God. Earlier in the poem the penitent has referred to himself as the "limb" of God's body and has prayed that the devil will never be able to lead this "limb . . . on a hateful journey" (53). The idea of a tree unable to grow and that of a limb cut off from the divine Body which is its source is an apt, conventional metaphor for the spiritual sterility of the man who is an exile both from human society and from heaven.

Where the Wanderer has been deprived of the joys of the earthly dryht by the relentless workings of wyrd and where the Seafarer voluntarily has chosen the path of exile, this third man has, by his own report, brought all his miseries on himself; he suggests no other cause for his hardships. Friendship and possessions are fleeting for him, as for the other two exiles, but the fault is in himself. The poem resulting from this central concept of individual guilt is essentially private in its tragedy, whereas in *The Wanderer* and *The Seafarer* the themes of exile and of the transience of the world are more universalized, more removed from the exclusively private reference, by their amplifications of reflection on an individual's fate into a vision of the whole fallen world. The particular figure of suffering is central in all three, but in the less carefully structured *Resignation* the speaker remains concerned only for his own salvation. The force of God's wrath is represented as directed only toward the exile himself, there being no suggestion that the world of the earthly dryht is being judged or is even doomed. The fact that the tragedy is conceived in purely personal terms seems to be the reason that, as an elegiac lament, *Resignation* seems somehow trivial when compared with *The Wanderer* and *The Seafarer*. The gnomic

conclusion, concerned with stoicism and the means of enduring in this world rather than with how to live for the
next, does little to break the closed circle of feeling within
which the would-be pilgrim stays: "Yet it is best, when a man
cannot change his fate, that he endure it well" (117–118).

The Riming Poem [13] appears also to be an elegiac lyric—
it is one of the most obscure pieces in the canon—uttered by
a prince toward the end of a glorious life in the context of a
happy worldly dryht (1–42). For many years he has engaged in
the delights of feasting and has ridden long-legged and richly
ornamented horses as they galloped over the plains. He has
entertained many guests, has gone seafaring, and has been the
proud owner of a splendid troop and hall, of great estates, and
of a princely throne. Wherever he placed his foot he controlled the produce of the earth, because it was his. Year after
year friendships endured and the harp string resounded, as
servants made their way about the bright hall. He gave wise
counsel and wealth from his throne, and loyalty flourished.
As a mighty prince he was nobly adorned, and his pleasures
were those of the earthly dryht wrought to perfection ("wæs
min dream dryhtlic," 39a).[14] In all his activities he fulfilled
the high calling of protector of the land and folk.

But this splendid existence in a Heorot-like world has now
come to an end, and the golden dryht has become the vanished
dryht, lamented by the man who was once its most illustrious
figure. Like the Wanderer, he looks back from a condition of
misery in the present to a time of former happiness. Then the
vision alters (43 ff.), into a description of a fatally determined
world changing continually in its mad pursuit of hatred and
thus bringing shame to a vanishing race. The fundamental
change in the prince's condition or state of being is symbolized, quite unnaturalistically, by a complete change in the

13. PR 3.166–69.1–87.
14. To translate this clause as "my joy (or my happiness) was noble
(or lordly, or excellent)" would delimit the rich connotations of the phrase
in the context. What is involved in nothing less than a full life of
happiness and apparent fulfillment in the world of an earthly dryht
or kingdom, with all pleasures and activities of that world enjoyed from
a position of great privilege and honor.

character of the world in which he lives.[15] One by one the
heroes age and die, all the wealth and might of the world
grow old, and bravery ceases to exist. The conventional formulas for man's fate in the fallen world appear: the relentless
passing of time and its inexorable grip on human life, the
darkness of night, death's seizing of each man from his native
land, the corpse devoured by worms. This melancholy vision
inspires the elegist to enjoin his listeners to turn away from
sins and hasten to the true God.

Though metrically quite different, *The Riming Poem,* in its
broad outline and in many of its details, is similar to *The
Wanderer.* But the perspective of the one who laments is not
that of a thane in exile; it is that of the lord of a vanished
dryht, thus making possible a poem which, in this sense, is
complementary to the other. In *The Riming Poem,* moreover,
it is the unhappy man himself who turns his aspirations
toward the joys of heaven, not, as in *The Wanderer,* the poet.
The general vision of a declining world is present, but the
theme of personal tragedy dominates, as it does in *Resignation,* and the imaginative range is narrower than in *The
Wanderer* and *The Seafarer.*

The Ruin [16] is the least personal and perhaps also the least
oblique of all the well-known Old English shorter poems.
Although we must take into account the fact that the poem as
we have it is fragmentary, still it should be noted that *The
Ruin* records nothing of personal loss, as do *The Wanderer,
Deor, The Riming Poem, The Wife's Lament,* and *Wulf and
Eadwacer,* and nothing of private feeling and spiritual aspiration of the sort we find in *The Seafarer.* In its freedom from
looseness of description and sentiment and in its presentation
of precise images of "hardness" and clarity, the fragmentary
Ruin is very close to what we in the twentieth century know

15. J. E. Cross has seen the cause of the change as *avaritia* or *cupiditas*
and links it to the Christian tradition of paralleling the progress of man
and of the world. See his "Aspects of Microcosm and Macrocosm in Old
English Literature," *Studies in Old English Literature in Honor of
Arthur G. Brodeur* ed. S. B. Greenfield (Eugene, Ore., 1963), pp. 11–15.

16. *PR* 3.227–29.1–49.

as an "imagist" poem. From the very specific introductory image of the *wealstan* (1 wall stone), the poem develops with objectivity and clarity its contrast between the present ruin and the past splendor of a great fortress.

If we recall what Wordsworth does with a similar image in *Elegiac Stanzas* (beginning "I was thy neighbour once, thou rugged Pile!"), a poem in which the artist's own changing consciousness provides the mythos, we can easily see the markedly direct quality of the Anglo-Saxon poet's observation. To Wordsworth's central image, an ancient castle in calm and then in storm, he attaches two widely divergent emotional states of his own, his former illusory and romantic dream of Elysian quiet and then a mood of deep distress over human suffering, which while writing the poem he feels is closer to reality. The theme of Wordsworth's elegy is the rude awakening of a poet's sympathies by the experience of a deep personal loss. It is easy to say that the theme of *The Ruin* is the transience of human glory, but the objectivity of the poem itself avoids any overt expression of either feeling or didacticism. At most the thematic content is implicit. There is no first-person lyrical voice and, aside from the expression of admiration or fascination in the first half-line—"Wrætlic is þes wealstan" ("Wondrous" or "curious is this wall stone")—and the flat, prosaic comment—"Þæt wæs hyðelic" (41, "That was handy")—on the subject of the hot baths, there is no indication in the poem of what, from the point of view of the speaker, we are to make of the structure of images put before us.

In terms of genre, it is a poem on a dead community, a meditation on the ruins of a society that existed "a hundred generations ago" (8–9). The complete absence of any lament, despite the centrality of images of mutability, means that only to a limited degree is *The Ruin* an elegy; it does present a vision of the passing of a desirable world, but the poet's sympathetic response to what has passed away is at most suggested. Structurally the composition depends on the contrast of the crumbling, frost-covered "works of giants" (2) before the artist's eye in the present and the mead-halls filled with joyful and tumultuous men, conjured up from the past. The note of heroism and idealism is obvious, in the imagining of those "bold in spirit" (19) who once lived "light of heart and bright with gold," shining in their armor and gazing on rich treasures (33–34). No suggestion of irony undercuts the sense of excellence, and no attribution of guilt on anyone's part is stated or implied to explain the fall of the once-superb fortress. There seems to be no suggestion that the ruins symbolize the worldly fate of those who banqueted without God's blessing. The causes of destruction are various, all of them impersonal: fate (*wyrde*, 1, *wyrd seo swiþe*, 24); frost (*hrim*, 4); age (*ældo undereotone*, 6); storms (*under stormum*, 11); days of pestilence (*cwoman woldagas*, 25); and death itself (*swylt*, 26). There is nothing here, although there may well have been in the complete version, of the tone of judgment that appears so frequently in Old English poetry to minimize the works and splendors of human achievement and thus to dispel, wholly or in part, the mood of elegy.

The *byrig* (fortress) of the poem—these mead-halls and towers filled with gold, silver, and precious stones—is located in the midst of a plain (*wong*) which crumbles when the *Hryre* (3, fall) comes and when wyrd the mighty begins to turn "bright dwellings" to "waste places." This fortress is described, though not interpreted, by traditional formulas of the archetypal dryht of Paradise mentioned in other Old English poems: "enta geweorc" (2, "works of giants"), "dreama full" (23, "full of joys"), "on þas beorhtan burg bradan rices" (37, "in this bright city of a broad kingdom"). Discussion as to whether the ruin described is historical (Hadrian's Wall, Bath, or some other Roman city with hot baths) has tended to obscure this fact, but to recognize this conventionality is not in any way to reduce the imagistic particularity of the description or the possibility that an actual historical ruin may have provided materials for the artist. Such recognition simply points out that the poem's apparent tendency toward idealization seems naturally to lead into an established Old English language of mythological symbols. In terms of the dominant mythology of the period, the city described here would be located somewhere in time between the Fall and either the Advent of grace, which restores ruined cities and crumbling walls through the power of Christ the *wealstan,* or the Last Judgment.

The description of the way in which the wall foundations were originally bound together—"weallwalan wirum wundrum togædre" (20, "the foundation of the wall wondrously together with wires")—suggests the same cunning "shaping" or fashioning of objects, buildings, or the world itself described in other poetic contexts whenever real human work or the work of God is involved. Once again we remember the goldhalls built by the patriarchs in *Genesis,* the ramparts of the fortress of Salem in *Daniel,* and, with a wider metaphorical force, the hall of middle-earth in Cædmon's *Hymn.* The image of the ruined *enta geweorc* which introduces the poem is, we recall, the climactic formula in the Wanderer's vision of the fallen world under the sentence of doom. The aged warrior-king Beowulf, as he dies from the venom of the *eorðdraca* (earth-dragon), knowing that he now has used up his share of earth's joys, also gazes on *enta geweorc* (2717). So does the protagonist of *Andreas,* at that point in his experiences when God is preparing to release him from his miseries at the hands of the Mermedonians by devastating their fallen kingdom (1492–1495a). In *The Ruin,* in keeping with its visionary clarity and freedom from moralizing, there is no articulation of a Doomsday theme and no sure indication that the theme of the fall of a city is to be thought of as an image of the fallen world of Christian myth, although the images in the main are those normally found in the myth of the ruined or vanished dryht. What a complete text might have shown is a matter for conjecture, but we cannot base a complete and confident interpretation on speculations about lines that do not exist.[17]

The Old English poem which provides the most concen-

17. Hugh T. Keenan recently has argued that the ruin described in the poem is Babylon and that the literary antecedents are Book 15 of the *De civitate Dei* and the Book of Revelation. See "*The Ruin* as Babylon," *Tennessee Studies in Literature,* 11 (Knoxville, Tenn., 1966), pp. 109–17.

trated vision of death as the final isolation of a man from all that he holds dear on earth is entitled simply *The Grave*.[18] In contrast to the lyrical utterances of the Wanderer, the Seafarer, and the penitent in *Resignation*—but rather like the objectivity of *The Ruin*—this memorable poem is not a personal expression of feeling in the face of human defeat. It takes the form of an apostrophe directed to someone designated simply as *ðu*, possibly implying Everyman, and has the basis of its rhetoric in an imitation of direct address rather than in the lyric indirection of an overheard meditation. In reading *The Grave* one is neither invited nor required to imagine a specific context for the central images of grave and corpse. It is a markedly asocial poem with nothing of the trappings of the world of the dryht as seen in the other poems considered so far in this essay. The reason is not difficult to see. Although it is possible that *ðu* once referred to an actual historical person, there is no evidence for this; the universality of the theme and of its application would, in any case, tear the poem away from so restricted a context. The absence of dryht imagery and of overt mythological references, as well as the chronological lateness of *The Grave* in relation to other Old English poems, perhaps should remove it from the scope of this book. I have included it here, however, because of its inherent power as a poem and because it serves admirably to illustrate a kind of end point or final statement of the ruin of the body of man and the cessation of all human action, the absolute frustration of man's desires in this world, by the overriding fact of that death brought into the Creation, as the Christian mythology puts it, at the time of the Fall.

    The Grave is not an elegy, despite its concentration on the central elegiac fact of death. It does not engage in the conventional idealization of the one who has died, nor does it,

---

18. The text is not included in the collective edition, *The Anglo-Saxon Poetic Records*, but is available in an article by Arnold Shröer, "The Grave," *Anglia* 5 (1882): 289–90. A translation into modern English can be found in Kennedy, *The Earliest English Poetry*, p. 331. The poem comes very late in the Old English period and includes linguistic terms clearly indicating the transition to Middle English.

in a mood of lamenting or pensive melancholy, nostalgically re-create a former happy state now disrupted by death. It does not move, as do many elegies, beyond the vision of death and human defeat to a release from lamentation through stoical resignation or hope in an afterlife. Restricted in range, grimly realistic in tone, and refusing to idealize, *The Grave* creates an irony completely hostile to the elegiac mood. It is a poem of warning, a grim reminder of the inevitability of death, and is composed of an almost gloating depiction of the confinement of the grave and the imminent putrefaction of the human body to be placed in it. Macabre and monitory, like the dance-of-death poems of later times, *The Grave* puts to work the stylistic devices of Old English poetry (verbal repetition, antitheses, metaphors, kennings, and alliteration) in a vivid account of the triumph of the worm.

Like all ironic writing, *The Grave* depends in large part for its particular effect on what it leaves unsaid. The ideal or desirable aspects of life force themselves on the reader's attention only because of the narrowness of compass in the images chosen: "This dwelling was built before you were born" (1), the fact of the grave superseding the significance of birth itself; "Nor is your house erected on high" (7), implying a contrast between the low house of the corpse and the high-walled residence of the living man; "There you are locked fast and Death has the key" (14), exploiting the implied mental picture of a home where people come and go freely. When, a few lines later, the actual decay of the body becomes the subject, once again the method is to imply something desirable by speaking of its absence:

Thus soon you will rot and be loathsome to see . . .
Soon your head will be deprived of its hair,
All the fairness of your locks will be ruined,
And soft fingers never will fondle them again.

The related subjects of death, the grave, and the disintegration of all earthly achievement appear frequently throughout Old English poetry, and it is not unusual to find them in elegiac contexts, but in themselves these matters are neither

tragic, elegiac, homiletic, gnomic, nor ironic. Rather they are
indifferent units that may be used by a poet according to his
particular purposes. Cynewulf, in his signatures, and the poets
of *The Wanderer, The Seafarer, Resignation,* and *The Riming
Poem* are interested in the theme of death in contexts that
emphasize the transitory nature of all mortal life. The poet
of *The Ruin* stops short of any thematic use of his images and
simply lets them exist in their own poetic world of time present
and time past. The poet of *The Grave* moves in another direction. He does not present the imagery of mutability with de-
tachment, nor does he seek to inspire feelings of regret; rather
he bends his efforts to the evocation of apprehensions of gloom
and terror, in the manner of an austere homilist.

When we turn from *The Wanderer, The Seafarer, Resignation, The Riming Poem, The Ruin,* and *The Grave*—lyrics
having in common themes of human defeat and death and the
mutability of all earthly things—to the four poems *Wulf and
Eadwacer, The Wife's Lament, The Husband's Message,* and
Deor, we might appear at first to be abandoning our mythological theme, since these latter four do not work openly
within a context of biblical myths and symbols. But there is,
as I shall attempt to demonstrate, an important connection
here, to do with the view that the Old English poetic records
are best approached as an environment of images.

As we have already seen, the conflict between private longings and an externally hostile or fallen world which destroys
or removes the objects of desire takes a variety of forms in
a large number of Old English poems, most notably in those
lyrics we have just discussed. In *Wulf and Eadwacer, The
Wife's Lament,* and *The Husband's Message,* this general
thematic concern is specifically focused on separated lovers,
and in *Deor* two of the seven exemplars of misery in the poem,
Beadohild and the "Geatish lover" (or "Geat," if it is a proper
name), are represented as suffering the ravages of a sexual relation that brings no happiness.

If one accepts the view of *Wulf and Eadwacer* [19] normally
taken, it is read as a dramatic monologue expressing the feel-

19. *PR* 3.179–80. 1–19.

ings of frustration and isolation of a woman in captivity to a tyrannous husband and apart from her outlawed lover.[20] Whether this is the narrative situation or not, we do not know. About all that is indisputably clear is that *Wulf and Eadwacer* concerns someone in a condition she finds lamentable and that her emotions are given elegiac expression. The treatment of the theme of separation (4, "Wulf is on one island, I on another"), is handled in cryptic fashion, to the point where the lyric is an enigmatic and ambiguous puzzle. Even so, it may well be that no additional knowledge of the identities, fictional or otherwise, of the principal figures in the poem would add to an appreciation of the restrained art of this very private lyric.

The poem contains no suggestion of self-pity on the part of the speaker, as, perhaps, the Wanderer's lament does, with its more extended account of personal miseries. Various elements combine to create a mood of frustrated longing: the fact that each of the lovers is on an island removed from the other by a fenland; the presence of what I would call "Cain-like" or, as the poem says, of "bloodthirsty" (6) men on the island with Wulf; the metaphor of the woman's desires and hopes as a wanderer in exile (9) while her physical body sits weeping in the rain (10); the embraces, both pleasurable and painful, of her "battle-ready" captor (11–12, Wulf or Eadwacer?); the metaphor of intense emotional misery as sickness or starvation (13–15); and the despised child (16, fathered by Wulf or by Eadwacer?). The final two lines complete a conventional pattern; first, there has been elegiac lament, and now resignation follows. Here, however, the paradoxical gnome which concludes the lyric takes on a peculiar pathos of its own because of the particular situation described: "They can easily separate that which was never joined together, the song of us two to-

20. For an excellent account of the varying interpretations of this lyric and also for a very incisive analysis of what makes it an effective poem for many readers, regardless of what interpretation they put on it, see Alain Renoir, "*Wulf and Eadwacer:* A Noninterpretation," *Franciplegius,* ed. J. B. Bessinger, Jr., and Robert F. Creed (New York, 1965), pp. 147–63.

gether." *Wulf and Eadwacer* is the *cri de coeur* of a woman denied the possibility of singing a happy love song. The devices of interrogation, refrain, direct address, and gnomic assertion combine in nineteen lines to form a lyric outstanding for its understated but intensely conveyed loneliness and melancholy. The basic conflict is one between a private love and a world, both of men and nature, hostile to that love.

The same essential conflict is present in *The Wife's Lament*,[21] another dramatic monologue, by a woman who says that she has never endured such miseries as she does now at the time of uttering her "song of deep sadness" (1). Exiled from the man she loves and plotted against by his kinsmen who wish to separate them in *woruldrice* (13, the kingdom of the world), fearful for her very life and dwelling in an old "earth-hall" (29), her lot is similar to that of the woman in *Wulf and Eadwacer*. Her misery began when her "lord" (6) left his people and went seafaring. The reason for his turning away from home and loved ones is not stated, but, following her husband's departure, the woman has become the conventional *wineleas wrǽcca* (10, friendless exile), a social outcast and an exile of love, living in a lonely dwelling in the forest. The former devotion of her husband, for some undefined reason, has now cooled and "is as if it had never been" (24–25a), so that she has to endure his hatred as well as that of his kinsmen.

As in all elegy, so in *The Wife's Lament*, there is a sense of the loss of something desirable, in this case the former happy relationship between the woman and the man, a union in which they used to pledge each other that nothing but death would divide them (21–23a). As in many elegies, the human melancholy that gives the poem its emotional focus is reflected in images of a ruined or bleak nature. In *Wulf and Eadwacer* the lamenting woman sits in the rain on an island, separated by a wasteland from her lover. In *The Wife's Lament* the one who makes her plaint sits beneath an oak tree (28), in a wilderness setting of "dim valleys," "high hills," and "sharp" or "bitter enclosed fortifications overgrown by

21. *PR* 3.210–11.1–53.

briars" (30–31). She imagines her "friend" (47) sitting under a rocky slope, chilled by storms and surrounded by water. The utter solitude of the woman in *The Wife's Lament* is emphasized by her thoughts of other people loving and happy in their beds while she, each morning at dawn, makes her way to her "earth-cave" to spend the long summer's day lamenting her exile and miseries, knowing that she cannot ever allay the *modceare* (grief) and longing that have overtaken her in this life (33b–41). At this point of the woman's lament she sounds a little like the Seafarer, who also sees himself as fated throughout his earthly life to bear a heart heavy with care. The source of restlessness is, of course, different; it is not a divinely prompted discontent that sends the woman into solitude but social persecution and a love turned to hatred.

The depiction of the woman's loss and complaint is succeeded by generalized gnomic comment with an objectifying function in the poem. The gnome shows the woman mentally placing her own misery in perspective and also indicates the catharsis effected by the elegy: "It is misery for the one who must endure longing for a loved one" (52b–53). By uttering her lament, the woman, like the Seafarer and the Wanderer, is led to a realization of something of the universal nature of human misery: each individual exile, including the exile of love, is only one of many in the solitary places of middle-earth.

The Wife's Lament is spoken, according to the lyric persona adopted by the poet, by a woman from whom happiness in love has gone. *The Husband's Message*,[22] whether the circumstances of the poem's composition or its contents have anything to do with *The Wife's Lament* or not, is addressed to a woman for whom happiness in love is about to become possible. The theme of estrangement present in both poems moves in opposite directions, toward a despair with no relief in the one and toward a fair dwelling with the loved one in the other. The first woman's suffering is caused partly by the fact that her former lover has broken his vows to her; the second is receiving a declaration of love and a concrete proposal by which she may rejoin her husband. The time reference of

22. *PR* 3.225–27.1–53.

The Wife's Lament is limited to the present and the past, to
the exile and the vanished object of desire, whereas the time
reference of *The Husband's Message* includes time past,
present, and future, with the emphasis on the last of these. In
the past, both couples have been caught up in social hostili-
ties—we are told that the second man has been driven away
by a feud (49). In *Wulf and Eadwacer* and *The Wife's Lament*
the sea is an isolating factor, but in *The Husband's Message* it
is to become the way leading toward a secret reunion: "Go
down to the sea, the home of the gull" (26). The fact that *The
Husband's Message* looks toward future happiness as one of
its main emphases is the chief determining factor in making it
a nonelegiac lyric.[23] The elements of frustration and misery
attending the loves described in *Wulf and Eadwacer* and *The
Wife's Lament* are in the process of being dealt with in this
poem; the essential elegiac characteristics of lament and melancholy are absent. The result is a lyric of hope and consolation, not of gloom or complaint.

There is a mystery in the center of *The Husband's Message,*
cloaked in runes and meant apparently to be readable only by
the wife. R. W. V. Elliott has argued that each of the runes is
to be given its name, since as they stand they spell no known
word. He suggests, moreover, that read in this way the letters
are the husband's message, embracing the main themes of the
poem, and read something like this: "Follow the sun's path
across the sea to find joy with the man who is waiting for
you." [24] If one has in mind the definition of a lyric as something private which is overheard, then it would seem that in
an additional special sense this poem is the essence of lyric.
In its concealment and obliqueness it is also close to the rid-
dling convention, in which inanimate objects speak, enig-
matically, and where the real point is never stated openly or

23. For a recent, somewhat different view see R. F. Leslie, ed., *Three
Old English Elegies* (Manchester, 1961), p. 21.
24. R. W. V. Elliott, "The Runes in the *Husband's Message,*" *Journal
of English and Germanic Philology* 50 (1966): 1–8. Leslie, *Three Old
English Elegies,* pp. 15–18, summarizes the history of the interpretation of
these runes and discusses Elliott's reading.

described fully but left as something unexplained to be puzzled over. Also contributing to the mystery is the sense of threatening forces surrounding the secret message, the same forces, presumably, that have driven the man away over the sea in the first place. The husband's cautioning of his wife to let no man hinder her leaving and the concealment of the message from all except the one to whom it is directed give an air of private intrigue to this account of true love. The lovers' rapport is with each other and with certain aspects of nature, the latter being symbolized by the sea as an avenue of hope, by the cuckoo in the grove (23), by the "fair land" (38) to which the prince's daughter is being called, and by the speaking stave of wood that has come bringing a welcome message to the "treasure-laden" (14) woman.

Deor[25] is not a lament and is less lyrical or personal than all the poems commented on so far in this essay except *The Ruin* and *The Grave*. The exiled scop who speaks mentions briefly seven individuals or groups of people who, at some point in their particular lives, find themselves in tragic or barely tolerable circumstances. The poem is presented as the product of the mind of a dispossessed scop who correlates other human afflictions with his own. The materials he refers to are, in the main, legendary,[26] that is, traditional and communal possessions of the world of the Germanic dryht, and the rhetorical position from which he speaks or sings of them is that of the dryht community's craftsman of words. Where the Seafarer or the Wanderer or the principal figures in most of the other lyrics we have been examining sing "songs of themselves," using principally the first-person pronoun and adapting traditional patterns of myth or structures of images to highly personal feelings and thoughts, Deor works primarily with the epos convention and within the public domain: "Many of us have heard"; "that was known to many"; "We have heard." It is not until the last eight lines of the poem that the personal, lyric reference enters, and even then it does so with a re-

25. *PR* 3.178–79.1–42.

26. See especially the notes in Kemp Malone, ed., *Deor,* 3d ed. (London, 1961).

strained, stoical objectivity. There can be little question that
the admiration extended to this poem in modern times is at
least in part due to the reserve and impersonality with which
it treats subject matter which in the hands of a more senti-
mental artist could easily have turned maudlin.

The seven representatives of human experience to whom the
"wise Dryhten" (32) has given "a sorrowful portion" (34) are
as follows: a famous warrior, exiled and mutilated by his
captor (1–7); an abused woman, the victim of rape and an
unwanted pregnancy (8–13); two lovers, frustrated and in-
somniac (14–17); an exiled king (18–20); the unhappy subjects
of a tyrant (21–27); an unnamed, typical figure, the *sorgcearig*
(sorrowful, oppressed) man (28–34); and finally, a dispossessed
scop, who is the speaker of the poem (35–42). Each section is
skillfully put to work in the fashioning of a verbal fabric
symbolizing human misery in several typical aspects.

Weland, the Germanic world's mythical counterpart to
Vulcan and Tubal-Cain, is presented in traditional formulas;
he experienced "wintry cold exile" (4), he knew what it was
to have sorrow and longing as his comrades (3), and he existed
for a time in a condition of bondage (4b–6). He was, then,
the bound and nearly frozen wintry man encountered so often
in Old English poetry, when the overall thematic concern is
to depict characteristics of the fallen world in which human
desires inevitably are frustrated. There may, as at least two
interpreters have suggested,[27] be a specific reference, as in the
Volundarkviða,[28] to Nithhad's hamstringing of Weland, in the
mention of the *seonobende* (6, bonds made of sinews) put on
him by his captor, but the imagery of exile, bondage, and
mutilation is also an integral part of the conventional tragic
suffering of victimized figures in Old English poetry.

27. See *Ibid.*, pp. 5–6; and L. Whitbread, "The Binding of Weland,"
Medium Ævum 25 (1956): 13–19. In the latter, the scene of the mutilating
of Weland on the Franks Casket is used as a basis for interpreting
swoncre seonobende (6a, supple sinew-bonds) as a reference to the actual
cutting of Weland's sinews, which from then on were "bonds" making
impossible his escape.

28. See Lee M. Hollander, trans., *The Poetic Edda*, 2d ed. rev. (Austin,
1962), p. 163.

Beadohild, raped and impregnated by the much-abused Weland when the latter finally takes his revenge, is a figure roughly analogous to the woman who, in *Wulf and Eadwacer,* is forced to suffer the unwelcome embraces of an enemy and give birth to a child fathered by someone she does not love. The "Geatish lover" or "Geat," if that is the person described here, along with someone called Mæthhild, both of them hopelessly and sleeplessly in love with each other, are figures unknown to us except in this poem, so that what seems to be an allusion of the scop—"We þæt Mæðhilde monge gefrugnon" ("Many of us have heard that for Mæthhild")—can evoke no confidently informed response from us, although Malone [29] has seen a connection with a Scandinavian ballad that has survived in a Norwegian and in an Icelandic version. Nonetheless their typical or exemplary function in the poem seems clear enough. Both they and Beadohild, in the previous section, are only three of a fairly large group of Old English poetic figures depicted as the victims or near victims of sexual passion or of a human love interfered with by some external force. There are not only the estranged couples of *The Wife's Lament, The Husband's Message,* and *Wulf and Eadwacer* but also Juliana and Judith, both threatened with sexual violation. In *Genesis,* Sarah, "of elfin beauty" (1827), is temporarily claimed as partner by the Pharaoh and by Abimelech, and in the same poem Hagar, as an exile from the love of her lord and plotted against by her lord's wife Sarah, wanders "gloomy in spirit" (2270) in the wilderness, terrified of wolves and starvation and worrying about the fate of her son Ishmael, until a "thane of glory" (2268) appears to offer her consolation. In *Christ I,* Saint Joseph is "gloomy in spirit" (173) and deeply distressed at what he takes to be the disgrace to himself and to his betrothed Mary because of Mary's premarital pregnancy. Finally, we remember the figures of the immediately postlapsarian Adam and Eve in *Genesis,* sitting separate and alone in the forest (like the wife in *The Wife's Lament*), lamenting each morning their lost happiness.

It is perhaps in this last description of the broken love union

29. Malone, *Deor,* pp. 8–9.

of man and woman that we find the paradigm or model which implicitly—but not necessarily consciously on the part of the particular poets—includes the other poetic manifestations of it. In the case of Adam and Eve it is devils, not "kinsmen," that have taken counsel together and then acted successfully to separate them from their Lord and from each other, so that they become exiles lamenting in wilderness places. The overall imaginative context of the love lyrics is indicated in the phrase *in woruldrice* (in the kingdom of the world),[30] in the imagery of desolate places and dismal weather, and in the emphasis on feuding as the social environment for the suffering of the lovers. It is very much the world that Eve's lord, Adam, antici- pates when in *Genesis A* he realizes he is now an exile who must go on a long sea journey to merit the return of heaven's favor. The primal unity between earth and heaven, between man and nature, and between man and woman has been dis- rupted. The feud that began between Lucifer and God, was then extended to Adam and God, and finally to all the mem- bers of the race of Cain throughout human history, provides the basic mythical outline within which the lyrics are located. The patters of imagery in the love lyrics, depicting private emotions and relationships, are displaced from the mythical abstraction of the myth of Eden in the direction of a greater realism, in a manner analogous to that of the more realistic handling of the battles fought in *The Battle of Maldon, The Battle of Brunanburh,* and *The Fight at Finnsburh* compared to those fought by the saints of the romances. But the con- crete patterns, the physical images, are the same.

In the fourth section of *Deor,* we hear of a ruler called Theodric who was known by many, according to the poet, to have "owned" or "ruled" for thirty years the stronghold of the Mærings, apparently (although the reference is very cryptic) while in exile from his proper kingdom.[31] The following sec- tion is about a kingdom under the sway of a "savage" tyrant who holds his warriors "bound in sorrow" and wishing for the end of his reign. Like Nebuchadnezzar and Holofernes,

30. *The Wife's Lament,* 13b.
31. For discussion see Malone, *Deor,* pp. 9–13.

Eormenric is "wolfish-minded" (22), metaphorically a beast of prey feasting on his carrion subjects, not a wise, charitable ruler.

In the sixth part of *Deor*, we hear of a "sorrowful man" who sits deep in melancholy, thinking that his share of sufferings is endless. Like the Wanderer, he is an exile from all joys or happiness and hence begins to ponder the inequity of men's fates. He concludes that the manifestly unequal distribution of worldly success and sorrow in this life is in accord with the will of the "wise Lord." This unnamed *penseroso* figure, with his insight into the meaning of the gifts-of-men theme—quite different from the same theme in *Christ II* where it leads to reflection on the necessity of preparing the soul for Doomsday —provides the singer Deor with a means of transition to the subject of his own career, with its alteration from joy and prosperity to adversity. The poem's song of general human woe now becomes briefly a "song of myself"—"þæt ic bi me sylfum secgan wille (35, "I wish to say this about myself")— as Deor recalls the favor previously shown him by his protector and lord, a favor dispensed now to a rival instead. But the personal reference includes no bid for pity, not even a suggestion of lament over the reversal of fortune.

The evident primary theme of *Deor* is the misfortunes of men, in the context of an overall divine or providential wisdom. The poet has selected seven tragedies in little and presented them in a context of stoical resignation, mixed with hope for a better future. The clear implication is that time is to be thought of as the great healer. *Deor* is one of the least romantic of all Old English shorter poems. It sets aside heroic or idealistic themes in favor of that kind of irony that derives from the poetic attempt to reveal the all-too-realistic aspects of man's existence. The one reference to the transcendental power of God is made in terms of the mutability and apparent injustices of life in this world, not of the more desirable heavenly order. But the absence of a complementary vision of heavenly fulfillment is not the only basis for the poem's ironic, astringent quality. Even on the level of middle-earth, where the imaginative focus is set, the objects of desire are almost totally obscured, attention being given instead to conditions of misery and frustration. With one exception (Deor's own story), each of the tragedies mentioned includes no open reference to what would be a more desirable state for the individual or group involved, other than by implication in the refrain.

It is this realistic or nonromantic quality in *Deor* that distinguishes it sharply from such an elegiac poem as *The Wanderer,* where a powerful vision of the world of tragedy and frustration is presented more diffusely than in *Deor.* In *The Wanderer* the golden dryht is also there, both in the solitary one's dream and in the vision of eternity supplied by the poet. As a meditative lyric, moreover, *The Wanderer* is more didactic than *Deor* in its injunction to take up the quest for divine grace and, in the body of the poem, in its emphasis on the necessity for the attainment of the kind of wisdom that comes only through experience of the fallen world. *Deor,* in spite of its reference to a wise God, is fatalistic, its irony deriving from an emphasis on the immediate spectacle of human suffering on earth rather than on any theoretical way of avoiding or going beyond human problems in this world by means of wish-fulfillment dreams or heavenly quests. A theological concept does emerge in the sixth part, to inform the scop's reflection—the idea of divine control of the fates of men—but at no point is there mention of an eternal resolution or release from earthly miseries, as one finds in *The Wanderer* and, much more elaborately, in the asceticism of *The Seafarer.* As a scop dispossessed or worldly goods and honored position, Deor does not adopt a perspective outside of time and space; his utterance is therefore not apocalyptic in any way. He himself is in a position of catastrophe within a tragic world, and he waits stoically for a change on earth.

I have said that *Deor* is nonromantic, concerned almost exclusively with one possible attitude in relation to human tragedy, but this does not imply that the poem is pessimistic. On the contrary, taken as a whole, *Deor* is an optimistic statement about human life. The repetitive sound and sense of the refrain, along with the apparently stanzaic organization, serve to resolve the catastrophes one by one, and the whole verbal pattern is cathartic in relation to the scop's own predicament. In terms of developing logic, the final use of the refrain, verbally identical with the others, is very different in significance. Presumably *þæs* in each of the other sections refers to the particular tragedy just indicated, *þisses* to Deor's as yet undisclosed suffering.[32] But at the end of the poem what has passed away is not a melancholy exile or frustrated love but Deor's own highly desirable position as honored and wealthy scop. Logically, then, *þisses* in its last occurrence must refer to Deor's present condition of loss and demotion. The refrain in the first five uses of it turns on a *þæs* (the particular catastrophe in the past, just described by Deor)—*þisses* (Deor's own catastrophe in the present, not yet revealed) antithesis. In the final occurrence, however, the meaning is different: *þæs* now refers to a period of happiness and success, Deor's own, in the past and just now described for the first time, and *þisses* to Deor's present unhappy position. The references to time past and time present are identical in all six uses, but the meaning is subtly reversed in the last line of the poem by virtue of its different context.

It can be seen, then, that there is a skillfully developed logic inherent in the structure. Each tale alluded to is in one sense completed by the refrain ("That passed away"), but at the same time the refrain points obliquely ahead, to something yet to be learned by the reader ("So can this"). The theological problem of suffering in a wise God's world, that is, the traditional problem of theodicy, is led up to in the first five sections, brought into the open in lines 28–34 and (at least poetically) resolved, in terms of confidence in God's wisdom and of the necessity for stoical resignation. What emotional stress there is in the poem—undoubtedly several lines have this as an important content—is handled or "contained" throughout, in both the detached perspective of the scop (even

32. Malone has suggested, rather oddly, it seems to me, that *þisses* in each case has an indefinite reference, to the reader or the hearer in search of consolation (see his *Deor*, p. 17). While possible, this view has the disadvantage of assuming that each hearer or reader has some catastrophe he must come to terms with.

in relation to his own misfortune) and in the aesthetic objectivity provided by the refrain.

In *Deor, Wulf and Eadwacer, The Wife's Lament,* and *The Husband's Message,* there is almost no sense of a heavenly order as a basis for hope when earthly miseries become too oppressive. In *Deor* we have the reference to the gifts-of-men theme, but the Lord's apportioning of grace or of misery concerns primarily life "in this world" (31) and does nothing to diminish the overall stoicism of the theme of consolation. In *The Husband's Message* the wish is expressed that Almighty God will make it possible for the man and woman to engage in the dispensing of treasure and studded armlets to warriors, thus opening up the motif of the golden dryht and the prospect of human happiness and fulfillment, but here too the reference appears to be entirely to this world. In the other two poems there is no mention at all of God or heaven.

This underemphasis or absence of theological meaning indicates that these four compositions are unlike *The Wanderer, The Seafarer, Resignation,* and *The Riming Poem;* the causes of suffering and lamentation, or of stoicism, have nothing directly or explicitly to do with the contrast between the fleeting nature of joy in the dryht-hall of this world and the permanence of joy in the fortresses of heaven. Tragedy and misery are caused entirely by the disintegration of human relationships, private and social, and there is no suggestion that matters will be resolved in heaven. Consolation takes the form of resignation and gnomic wisdom, of learning how to endure in this world. In this sense the imaginative range (though not the poetic value) of these texts is more limited than that of the openly religious or mythological lyrics, suggesting a closed-in quality in the descriptions of individual tragedies that has its own undeniable effectiveness. It may be significant that it is in *The Husband's Message,* the one lyric in the group in which God is most clearly associated with potential human happiness, that tragic elements are least important. In addition to the husband's own heroic achievements, making him the possessor of all the joys of an earl on earth, the wife is to become another of those gracious, liberal, and gold-adorned ladies cited as ideal in Old English poetry.

The immediate impact of all the poems examined in this essay derives from a vision of the world and human life in their tragic aspects. The elegiac passages depict either a rocky, barren wasteland filled with ruins and located between stormy seas, a landscape of rocks blasted by wind and rain, snow and hail, or a lonely seascape, equally driven by the forces of winter and storms. Through this imaginative space solitary exiles, from a dryht-hall or from a love union, make their way. These conventional settings, with a human outcast at the center, are the major Old English images of the fallen world. As poetic conventions they would be ineffective, in terms of elegy, stoic resignation, or heavenly hope, if the poets did not combine with them a contrasting vision: the ideas of fall and ruin assume the complementary idea of former, more desirable modes of being. Similarly, the idea of the possible fulfillment of human desire—of reentry into a dryht or reunion with a loved one—postulates a better future. If it is true that the most vulnerable human faculty is the memory, we can see how appropriate it is that the images of fleeting shapes attack this part of the human mind and heart, reminding the exile how "in days long ago" the wine-hall, the earthly Paradise, and the vows of true lovers endured in their original harmony.

In Old English poetry the paradisal state occurs at one of three points in imaginative time: at the beginning of the myth of man's experience; at that point somewhere later in his experience when he seems temporarily to recover his earlier happiness or to have his desires fulfilled; and thirdly, after death, if his life has been heroic or wise. In Essays One and Two we considered at length the third of these points in time—when the flux of history is left behind in favor of eternity—and showed how entrance into the golden dryht of heaven at the end of mythical time is, metaphorically, also the return to the guest-hall of Eden, described at the beginning of the total narrative. In the lyrics this same myth of eternal return works itself out in more immediately personal contexts. If the protagonist of the lyric looks only to the past or to the ruined present, his situation remains at best a stoical compromise with a repugnant reality, at worst a mental and emotional bondage to a lost world. If, as in *The Husband's Message* and *Deor,* the speaker holds out some promise of a better experience in the future in this world, a measure of triumph over adversity is seen as possible. If, however, like the Seafarer, he aspires beyond the order of time and space, there opens up the possibility of the triumph of the human soul and of eternal joy in the society of heavenly beings.

Heorot and the Guest-Hall of Eden
Symbolic Metaphor and the Design
of *Beowulf*

Beowulf [1] is a poem about hell's possession of middle-earth. Within its overall tragic structure, the joys of the golden dryht and the actions of good kings and heroes are presented as capable of a splendid but precarious realization; the dominant vision, however, is of the defeat of man in the kingdoms of this world by the powers of darkness. Essay Two described a group of narrative poems constructed around heroic, saintlike protagonists caught up in actions that are inspired, and also largely controlled, by heaven. In these poems the war of the champion against his enemies or tormentors is recognizable as another episode in the Christian mythology of the battle between Christ and Satan. The large involvement of heavenly influences in the fictional action assures a "romantic" conclusion to the narrative, so that, on one level of interpretation, *Andreas, Juliana, Elene, Guthlac A,* and *Guthlac B* can best be understood as ritual enactments of an otherworldly Church community's desire to escape the insubstantial joys and miseries of life on earth. In several of the lyrics examined in the third essay there is expressed, in abbreviated form, a more realistic or tragic vision of human existence, with a corresponding emphasis on defeat and the frustration of desires for love, possessions, and communal pleasures. At the same time the tragic vision is represented in several of the lyrics as only part of a larger myth which tells of the potential triumph of heaven over all the miseries of the earthly kingdom.

Part of this essay has been published, in somewhat different form, in *Mediaeval Scandinavia* 2 (1969): 78–91.

1. The edition used throughout is F. Klaeber, *Beowulf and the Fight at Finnsburg*, 3d ed. (Boston, 1936, with supplements in 1941 and 1950).

The *Beowulf* poet takes a tale of heroic action, in its naïveté not unlike those of Essay Two, and subjects it to the kind of brooding, deliberative treatment illustrated in the elegiac lyrics. The result is a romance set inside a tragedy—perhaps we could call it a "tragic romance" or even an "elegiac tragedy"—serving the same Christian view of the fleeting nature of all man's earthly joys that we see throughout the canon. But *Beowulf,* because of its sustained fusion of the elements of romance and tragedy, is different. Where the other poems either leave these two narrative structures, romance and tragedy, separate or with their interconnections only briefly traced (the emphasis normally being on the transcendental reality of heaven), *Beowulf* submits the world of the golden dryht of middle-earth to the prolonged reflections of a mind and sensibility apparently deeply attracted to that world but acutely aware of its doomed nature.

We have seen how works like *Genesis A* and *B, Exodus, Judith,* and *Daniel* are symbolic depictions of two kinds of society, each with a natural and a supernatural aspect: on the one hand, we have the idealized dryht of Noah, Abraham, Moses, Judith, or the Israelite remnant, working in harmony with heaven's purposes; on the other, we have the society of Cain, Babel, Egypt, Assyria, or Babylon, characterized by bloodshed and tyranny and, above all, by a hell-inspired enmity to the society of God's chosen champions. Individual heroes (this holds true for the hagiographic romances as well) are simply exemplars of the kind of society or order of human life that is trying to emerge, however briefly, in middle-earth. Their reality, their acts, and the pattern of their lives are set down in the life of Adam-Christ or biblical man, and their thematic importance in the poems in which they appear exists only in terms of their exemplary function. There is almost nothing in Old English narrative poetry of what might be called interior mental event which would individualize the human figures presented. What we learn of the emotional or rational processes of Moses or Andrew or Helena, we learn by means of the poets' comments on them or by their own stylized speeches to the community or people in whose fate they are involved. Even in the lyrics, where one might expect to find a more individualized depiction of thought and emotion, the particular human figure central to the poetic meditation is scarcely less typical or conventional. The Wanderer is a "wanderer"; Deor is a dispossessed scop. *The Wanderer* is about the world of the vanished dryht; *Deor* is about the possibility of stoicism, even optimism, in a world of misery and suffering.

Similarly, *Beowulf* is not about an individual as such but about a man of archetypal proportions, whose significance, in the broadest and deepest sense, is social. The poem is an imaginative vision of two kinds of human society, one symbolized by the gold-hall and banqueting and characterized by generosity, loyalty, and love, the other by monsters of darkness and bloodshed who prey on the ordered, light-filled world man desires and clings to. Despite the lyric overtones to the poet's presentation of his theme (that brooding, melancholy reflectiveness that every reader recognizes), *Beowulf* is not about a complex, individual character whose interior mental processes lead plausibly to certain actions and relations with other people. Beowulf does not have an ego, despite his boasting, and certainly has no discernible id; he is publicly conceived, all superego and controlled by the divine favor he bears. We do not know why, psychologically, Unferth behaves so oddly or what Hrothulf is thinking at any point. We learn a little more about what goes on in the mind of Hrothgar or Wealhtheow or the aged Beowulf (late in the poem) but only in terms of their functions in relation to God and to the kindred and dryht in whose social fabric their lives have meaning. They are all functionaries playing out their roles as long as wyrd permits, not images of real people but exemplars of human types. If this assessment of the way life is presented in *Beowulf,* and more generally throughout the Old English poetic records, is correct, it is important that the structure and meaning of the poem be considered primarily in terms of the myth of human society presented in it. The poet's interest in different kinds of societies and their implications, for all three levels of the three-tiered universe, is deeply involved in the

way he arranges and paces his materials. It is to these matters
we must turn our attention if we are to understand the poem's
vision of human life.

It is generally recognized, by Klaeber, for instance,[2] that
Beowulf is not, in any very consistent way, lineal in its organization. What is more, it gives little evidence of a concern on
the part of the poet for plausible or realistic ordering of events
according to a causal sequence. Rather, one event is associated
with another—past, present, or future—because of symbolic
or thematic appropriateness. The narrative is discontinuous;
it does not in any representational way point out for each
phenomenon mentioned its determining agents or antecedents.
In fact many things happen in *Beowulf,* and in other Old
English poems, that do not have causes in any phenomenal
sense. Heaven and hell, as I shall try to demonstrate, are too
much involved. In more purely critical terms, to use Tolkien's
expression, *Beowulf* is a product of "the mythical mode of
imagination." [3] This means that it works in implicitness of
connections, in simultaneity of association, in narrative discontinuity. The images all point to the main ideas and the
ideas are not time bound, not determined by orderly chronology. This kind of imagining makes unavoidable the use of
metaphor, which means that the modern interpreter of *Beowulf* must be sensitive to poetic identities cunningly suggested
in the associative imagery but not spelled out for the logical,
skeptical mind. It means also, however, that he must not force
identifications in ways uncongenial to the connections built
up by the language of *Beowulf* itself or in a manner unsup-
ported by the conventional metaphors observable in other
Old English poems.

In my examination of the mythical design or structure of
Old English narrative romances I tried to show how the constant remembering back to an ancient time, designated as

2. Klaeber, *Beowulf,* pp. lvii–lviii.

3. See J. R. R. Tolkien's influential article, *"Beowulf:* The Monsters
and the Critics," *Proceedings of the British Academy* 22 (1936): 245–96;
reprinted in Lewis E. Nicholson, ed., *An Anthology of Beowulf Criticism*
(Notre Dame, Ind., 1963), pp. 51–103.

ær or *in geardagum,* that is, to a primordial beginning, often associated with the myth of Creation, balances a complementary tendency to look forward to an apocalyptic Doomsday when human or earthly history will be annulled. We saw also that the heavenly fulfillment of man's quest is his starting point transformed, the celestial dryht being the perfect, eternal model of the guest-hall of the earthly Paradise. Such a pattern is of course precisely in harmony with the traditional Christian idea (whether Anglo-Saxon or not) that the work of Christ both abolishes and renews history. It establishes a term for history but periodically renews the Church and the individual soul in the liturgical cycle of the Christian year. Renewal takes place through the sacramental repetition of the archetypal acts of Christ and the saints, since these, by virtue of their divine source or cause, do not bear the burden of time and are therefore capable of freeing a Guthlac or a Juliana or the dreamer in *The Dream of the Rood* from that bondage to sin and death which is the chief determinant of man's fate in the *læne* world. The poets' insistent harking back to the old or the traditional is witness to the belief that the old is the new; the ancient Creation is the newly redeemed order emerging from the depths of the Red Sea or from the waters of Baptism.

But *Beowulf* is unique among Old English longer poems in several important respects, the most obvious being the large amount of its story materials that derive from a Scandinavian milieu rather than from a biblical or Mediterranean or even English one. Despite a measure of agreement nowadays about its having something of a Christian character, it is not as clearly and unmistakably shaped and informed by Christian myth and symbol as are most of the poems examined in the first three essays of this book. The apparent obliqueness of its Christianity poses a whole set of questions that continue to puzzle most thoughtful readers. Is Beowulf, in any demonstrable sense, an imitation of Christ, as some have surmised? What really is the meaning in the poem of the references to Cain and the Deluge? Are they simply mythological embroidery, or do they have a deeper purpose? Why has the poet associated the building of Heorot with God's Creation of the world? If

Beowulf is to be thought of as a redeemer figure based implicitly on Christ, why does the poem give so much attention to his physical death and to the social desolation surrounding it, with scarcely a hint of anything in the bleak closing scenes to suggest resurrection or redemption? How can a poem so resolutely engaged, even while recounting heroic triumphs, in the depicting of death, disintegration, treachery, loss, and the waste of human effort be construed as Christian, especially since so many of the human acts described, not only the hero's, are represented as bound by time in a way that we have seen to be foreign to the Christian belief in the possibility of escape from time, even during earthly existence? These questions, and others like them, do not admit of simple or easy answers, but I should like at least to make certain suggestions, working with the patterns already described as constituting the Old English poetic mythology and also with the definition of myth as symbolic metaphor.

Standing back mentally from the whole text and thinking of it in terms of its abstract design, one can see that *Beowulf* is about two earthly kingdoms, Denmark and Geatland, that go down to defeat, despite the deeds of the man whose heroic acts are deeply involved in their corporate lives. The story of the house of the Scyldings is sketched in its entirety, from the mysterious emergence from the sea of the eponymous ancestor, Scyld Scefing, to the final conflagration in which Heorot is destroyed. The main focus is on the reign of Hrothgar, during which Grendel takes possession of the royal gold-hall and along with his monstrous mother has to be destroyed by the hero who has come across the sea from Geatland. The story of Beowulf's own people, the Geats, does not emerge so completely. Although we hear several times of Hygelac's reign and its disastrous conclusion in the land of the Franks, and although we can piece together, from various references, Beowulf's own life among the Geats, from "dummling" youth to venerable king, the story of this kingdom does not emerge into the foreground of the poem with the clarity and definition characteristic of the scenes in Denmark. The reasons for the difference of treatment are deeply embedded in the structure of the poem, in the fact that Heorot, for all the gloomy foreboding about its ultimate fate, is the scene of the youthful hero's major achievement and recognition as a champion against the forces of darkness. Hrothgar's kingdom is the setting for the romance and the marvels that are central to a tale of how God works, through his chosen hero, to rescue a doomed people. Geatland, whose gold-hall is never visualized in the poem, is, on the whole, the setting for tales of death, confusion, and social chaos. Aside from that part of the narrative in which Beowulf tells Hygelac the story of his Danish adventures—the imaginative focus there is almost exclusively on Denmark—the kingdom of the Geats appears as one wracked by wars and feuds, except during Beowulf's reign, when he manages to hold an insecure peace against threatening forces. In brief, Geatland is the main symbolic setting for the poem in its tragic aspect.

Moving a little closer to the text but still thinking of it in terms of its overall design, one can recognize four major myths or symbolic episodes, each of which is concentrated at appropriate points in the narrative but also extends its effect, with varying emphases, throughout the whole poem. In the emergence of the Scylding dynasty, climaxed by the construction of Heorot, we have a *cosmogonic myth* explicitly connected by the poet with the Christian biblical account of the origins of the created world. This in turn is followed by *the myth of the Fall and the beginnings of fratricide and crime,* as the Grendel kin of the race of Cain begin to lay waste Hrothgar's hall. Next comes the account of the advent of the hero and *the myth of the heroic redeemer,* and finally as the poem moves into its decisively tragic phase, we have *the myth of the hero's death and the return to chaos.*

Beowulf begins with a description of a lordless people and ends with another lordless people; the overall tonality is elegiac, and one of the major symbols of the poem's beginning, as of its conclusion, is the funeral of a great king. It is as if the poet had composed his work in the manner of a symbolist poem: starting with the effect he wanted, he then backtracked to the point from which we must begin to get that effect. From the dirgelike lament and ritualistic movements of Scyld's followers in the midst of the dynastic vision that introduces the

poem, the Anglo-Saxon artist fills out and intensifies his
pattern. At the same time, however, the aesthetic and thematic
balance between the funerals of Scyld and Beowulf provides
a very important contrast: Scyld's funeral is followed by an
augmenting of the powers of his dynasty, but Beowulf's, so we
are led to believe, is to be succeeded by social and political
disintegration for the Geats.

   The creation of Heorot is anticipated from the first line of
the poem. The exordium introduces immediately the heroic
world of the "Spear-Danes," those great warriors who "did
deeds of glory" in days long ago (1–3); this is followed by a
description of the mysterious appearance in Denmark of the
foundling child who was to rise to a position of eminence as
the mighty king of the people. During his life Scyld terrifies
and subdues the enemies of the Danes and, even in his death,
is splendid, surrounded by symbols of royal power and wealth.
Like his father, Scyld's son Beow (Beowulf I) also is exemplary,
described as a gift of God to the Danes, a comfort to them in
adversity. He gives treasure generously and performs noble
deeds; his eager comrades return willing service in time of
war. He in turn is succeeded by the "high Healfdane" (57),
another ideal dispenser of rings and the father of Hrothgar.
The motifs involved in this description of the Scyldings are
those of the golden dryht, the continual interchange of treasures, services, and protection being the very lifeblood of such
a society. This interchange takes place vertically in the imaginative space of the poem, as well as horizontally, since it is
God, the "Prince of life" (16) and "Ruler of glory" (17), who
sends splendid lords one by one to show generosity and protection to the Scyldings.
   Hrothgar, one of the three sons of the patriarchal Healfdane,
is given success and honor in war, so that his retainers follow
him eagerly and his troop prospers. At the zenith of his
glory (64 ff.), Hrothgar decides to have built a might mead-
hall, such as the sons of men have never heard of before, as a
place for feasting and the giving of gifts. With the help of
many peoples throughout middle-earth, "the greatest of halls"
(78) towers up "high and horn-gabled" (82). Hrothgar does

not forget his promises but puts the marvelous building into use as a place of communal joy where heroes drink mead while listening to the sound of the harp and to the voice of a scop singing about God's great original gift to men, the whole created world.

The imagery of the primordial Creation we have seen before: the *wlitebeorhtne wang* (93, plain radiantly beautiful) surrounded by water, the sun and the moon as lights for land dwellers, the branches and leaves ornamenting the regions of the earth, and all living creatures. In this account of the building and initiation of Heorot, the sense of ritual repetition by man of the work of heaven is, to me, unmistakable. The implication seems to be that the construction of the gold-hall, whose light is to shine over many lands, is a hierophantic act, a manifestation of the sacred in the world of men, metaphorically identifiable with the Creation of the world itself.[4] For the Old English thane the gift-throne is the center of the world; apart from it, he "wanders" in a life devoid of focus and meaning. The hall, the throne, and the good king can all be seen as images of the divine power that gives protection and significance to human life. Heorot is a sacred enclosure, thought of

4. In the use here of the terms *hierophantic act* and *manifestation of the sacred in the world of men* and in certain others that follow—*center of the world, sacred enclosure,* and so on—I show directly an influence which is further in the background but important in other parts of this book, that of the writings of Mircea Eliade, most especially his *Cosmos and History: The Myth of the Eternal Return,* trans. Willard R. Trask (New York, 1954, 1959), published originally as *Le Mythe de l'éternel retour: archétypes et répétition* (Paris, 1949); and his *The Sacred and the Profane: The Nature of Religion,* trans. Willard R. Trask (New York, 1959, 1961). So far as I have been able to determine, Eliade never discusses specifically religious forms of early England, but his observations on traditional religious or "sacred" societies can throw a good deal of light on the cultural patterns evident in Old English poetry. I note with interest that Edward B. Irving, Jr., also shows an Eliade influence in his discussion of Heorot; see *A Reading of Beowulf* (New Haven, 1968), pp. 89–90. Irving's book has preceded mine considerably in its publication. Readers of both will notice several similarities between his interpretations —of Scyld, of the "creation" of Heorot, of Grendel—and mine. At the same time we see a rather different overall meaning in the text of *Beowulf.* The two views were worked out and written quite independently of each other, although we have recently discussed them together.

as towering upward, to ensure communication with the heavenly gift-throne and the Prince of life. It is one of several examples in Old English poems of halls built by God's champions, like those of the patriarchal princes in *Genesis*, for example, whose archetype is the celestial dryht that endures *in æternum*. Heorot, like the others, is paradisal in symbolic import. Hrothgar, whose name appears to mean "glory spear" or "spear of triumph" or possibly "spear of joy," is, like the heavenly Dryhten, a lord of victories. As with God's Creation in *Genesis* so here, Hrothgar's mighty creation comes after triumph over the chaos of internecine war. Again as in heaven in numerous Old English poems (for example, *The Dream of the Rood*, 139–141), the condition of *dream* (joy) is symbolized by banqueting in the hall. Like Adam and Eve in the guesthall of Eden, the Danes, so the poet tells us, immediately after the Song of Creation, "lived in joy, blessed" ("Swa ða drihtguman dreamum lifdon / eadiglice . . . , 99–100a). Still innocent of the *feond on helle* (fiend, or enemy in hell) who lurks without, they slept after the banquet given by their lord, not knowing "sorrow, the misery of men" ("Fand þa ðær inne æþelinga gedriht / swefan æfter symble: sorge ne cyðon, / wonsceaft wera").

The name Heorot can be explained not only in terms of naturalistic imagery to do with stag antlers on the gables of the hall,[5] or even as a symbol of royalty like that on the Sutton Hoo standard,[6] but also in terms of scriptural association.[7]

5. Klaeber, *Beowulf*, p. 129, note on line 78. It is usually accepted by *Beowulf* scholars that if there ever was an actual geographical counterpart for Heorot, it was probably near the ancient Hleiðr (modern Lejre, on the northern coast of Zealand), the royal seat of the ancient Danish kings.

6. The possible significance for *Beowulf*, line 78, of the bronze stag above the Sutton Hoo royal standard has been discussed a good deal in recent years; see especially R. L. S. Bruce-Mitford, "The Sutton Hoo Ship-Burial," in R. H. Hodgkin, *A History of the Anglo-Saxons*, 3d. ed. (London, 1952), 2: 696–734.

7. C. L. Wrenn makes this suggestion, but does not develop it, in "Sutton Hoo and *Beowulf*," in R. W. Chambers, *Beowulf: An Introduction to the Study of the Poem* (Cambridge, 1959), p. 518.

If we recall the psalmist's use (Ps. 42) of the analogy of the hart or stag thirsting for healing streams and the human soul in its desire for God, and if we remember that we are told later in *Beowulf* by the king of Heorot that the "hart strong in his antlers" will give up his life rather than enter the hellish mere (1368–1372), the possibility emerges that Hrothgar's mighty hall is imagined primarily as the earthly dwelling place of the human soul, both communal and individual. Where the mere, the poem's antithetical image for Heorot, is loathsome and terrible and infested with monsters, Heorot is described as "the most famous of buildings under heaven" (309–310a), "the bright dwelling of brave men." As a communal symbol of an ideal earthly dryht, the newly created hall is in paradisal harmony with heaven. The question of whether Hrothgar's hall in the midst of the conventional "plain" (225) has an individual reference as well as a communal one may be partially answered by remembering a use of the ideal-hall motif in *Guthlac A* (742). There, when the saint has triumphed in war over his enemies, his barrow, the dwelling of his newly perfected soul, is a *sele niwe* (new hall, dwelling) standing in the protection of God in the midst of a "victory plain," a very succinct correlation of the two major metaphors for Paradise in the Old English poetic mythology.

But Heorot is a fated image, existing in a double aspect. Even at the moment of its first towering upward, the poet speaks of the "fierce heat and hostile flame" that wait for it and of the "sword-hate" between son-in-law and father-in-law that will spring up because of bitter enmity (82b–85). So also, the description of the Danes living in a state of blessedness is interrupted by the first mention of Grendel and the race of Cain (99 ff.). Heorot and the world of the golden dryht exist as a splendid ideal, as *wlitige* (beautiful, fair), throughout the poem, but as earthly images they are also doomed, in the mind of a Christian poet, to become *unclæne* or polluted and thus to fall into the necessity of being "cleansed."

In the poet's use of *the myth of the Fall and the origin of fratricide,* he often specifically connects the Grendel kin with hell, which should make it easy to recognize the metaphorical structure barely concealed beneath the relatively slight surface realism of the poem. On one level of meaning, *Beowulf* can best be understood as a reworking of the same war between heaven and hell that emerges in its undisplaced mythical form in *Christ and Satan* and other poems. As in the Christian mythology, where demonic powers are assumed to have taken possession of the world shortly after the Creation, so in *Beowulf* a monster comes out of the mere and possesses the poem's *imago mundi,* Heorot. This necessitates a war between a heaven-sent champion and the monster, a war in which the champion's victory is a "cleansing" and a preliminary defeat of the feond on the earthly level, as in Christ's victory on the rood. But, again as in the Christian story, the deliverer's victory in the world must be extended and consolidated by a further triumphant battle in the very depths from which the demonic attacks have come. Whether the hell referred to in *Beowulf* is from Teutonic myth or from Christian myth or, more plausibly, from a mixture of both does not alter the fact that the images of bondage, darkness, endless pain, joyless exile, fire, ice, wind, storm, and enmity against mankind, images associated with the monsters and their haunts, are the same ones found over and over again in the Old English poetic accounts of man apart from God. Nor does the fact that Grendel and his mother seem in some ways to be trolls from a different legendary background diminish the connotations they draw from Christian symbolism; it means only that they have this additional extension, as compared with a less poetically complex demon like the one tormenting Cynewulf's Juliana.

In several passages Grendel is described as directly connected with hell, even though he is not altogether a medieval devil.[8] As a being metaphorically identified with Cain and therefore also with fallen Adam, he is perverted or fallen man, a parody of the human form as it was created by the *Scyppend* (Creator); like other fallen men he treads exile paths (1351b–1352). The related ideas of sin, rebellion against God, and

8. See Tolkien, *"Beowulf:* The Monsters and the Critics," pp. 276 ff.

enmity to God's creature, man, are explicit in various expressions used to describe the monster:—"laðgeteona synnum beswenced" (974–975, "the malicious enemy afflicted with sins"); "fyrena hyrde" (750, "keeper of wicked deeds"); "Godes yrre bær" (711, "bore God's wrath"); "manscaða" (712, 737, "wicked enemy"—at line 1339 Grendel's mother is also described by this term, and so is the fire-dragon at line 2514); "synscaða (801, "sinful enemy, one who wickedly does harm"); "Godes andsaca (1682, "God's adversary"). As an image of a "hall-thane" (142), who lives "in a hostile hall" (1513) or "death dwelling" (1275) gleaming with a demonic light that parodies the radiance of Heorot, Grendel is the companion of other monsters exiled from both the Dryhten and the golden or ideal society of Heorot. Described as *hæþen* (852, 986, heathen), he is the symbolic antithesis of a Christian hero. His heathen nature unavoidably links him with the devil worship of the Danes, a practice to which they are driven by this heathen warrior. The poet explains that the Danes in their efforts to defend Heorot sought help from "the slayer of souls"; they "trusted in the hope of the heathen," "remembered hell in their hearts" (175 ff.). It is worth recalling, in this connection, that normally in Old English poetry heathen peoples—the Egyptians in *Exodus,* the Babylonians in *Daniel,* the Mermedonians in *Andreas,* and the Assyrians in *Judith,* to name only four—are presented as "devil worshipers." There is no suggestion, however, in *Beowulf* (though it has often been assumed by readers in modern times, on the basis of assumptions about the historicity of the poem's Scyldings) that the Danes, prior to Grendel's incursions, are heathens or devil worshipers—the Danes of pagan Denmark in the sixth century—or anything other than God-fearing recipients of heaven's favor. The other references to heathenism in *Beowulf* are to the fated hoard in Part 2 (2216, 2276).

When Grendel is held fast in Beowulf's grip, he utters a song of defeat and, as "prisoner of hell" (788), bewails his wound. At the time of his death his soul goes to hell, as the surging waves of the mere receive him: "þær him hell onfeng" (852b, "there hell received him"). A little later, Beowulf indi-

cates that Grendel will have to endure God's Judgment: "there
he must wait for the mighty Judgment, for what the glorious
God decrees for him" (977b–979). It is important to notice,
however, that it is not only at the time of his death that
Grendel's hellish characteristics are evident. Even though
feond may mean simply "enemy," as Tolkien has pointed out,
the whole formula feond on helle, describing Grendel long
before he dies (101)—combined with helrunan (163, those
skilled in the mysteries of hell) and with helle hæfton (788,
prisoner of hell), also used before he has died—seems to indicate clearly enough that Grendel is the unblessed member of
the hellish society both before and after his death. It is true
that he is called by terms applied to ordinary men (wer, rinc,
guma, maga), but he and his mother are also called deofla
(1680) and he flees to the "company of devils" (756a) in the
darkness when the hero strikes terror into him. Early in the
account of his ravages of Heorot he is called "an accursed
spirit" (133); in Hrothgar's homily about the slayer coming
with winged bow to kill the unwary king, the devil is also
referred to by this same formula (1747).

Perhaps most important of all Grendel's demonic connotations is his association with Cain.[9] Early in the poem when
Grendel is first named and connected with the archetypal
fratricide, the reader is confronted with a pattern highly suggestive in its possibilities for adaptation to tales of bloodthirsty
feuding in Germanic society. The poet of Maxims I tells [10]

9. See the following four articles: Oliver F. Emerson, "Legends of
Cain, Especially in Old and Middle English," PMLA 14 (1906): 831–929;
S. J. Crawford, "Grendel's Descent from Cain," MLR 23 (1928): 207–208;
S. J. Crawford, "Grendel's Descent from Cain (lines 107–114, etc.)," MLR
24 (1929): 63; Marie Padgett Hamilton, "The Religious Principle in
Beowulf," PMLA 61 (1946): 309–31. Also see Stephen C. Bandy, "Caines
Cynn: A Study of Beowulf and the Legends of Cain," (Ph.D. diss.,
Princeton University, 1967); abstract published in Dissertation Abstracts
28 (1967): 1780A. Most recently there is a more complete study, including
examination of legal codes and patristic texts, by David Williams, "Cain
and Beowulf," (Ph.D. diss., University of Toronto, 1970).

10. PR 3.163.192–204.

how, after the earth swallowed Abel's blood, Cain's criminal hatred did not die out in the world but spread, with ever-increasing malice, until it was known to all peoples. Men throughout the earth became busy with the "strife of weapons" and devised the hostile sword, so that shields, spears, swords, and helmets have ever since had to be ready for conflict. By his murderous action, the gnomic poet seems to be saying, Cain set the pattern in which all men are caught. This traditional view of Cain and Abel, elaborated at length in Book 15 of Augustine's *De civitate Dei*—in terms of the unending conflict throughout history of the society of carnal man, or Cain, and the society of the elect, or Abel—is also given a poetic use in *Genesis A,* apparently in an attempt to show the special significance for the poet's own period in history of fratricide and conflict among mankind. All strife and human misery are depicted metaphorically as the branches of the demonic tree which sprang up from Abel's spilled blood. The crime of Cain is linked with the guilt of Eve, and both are associated with wyrd, indicating that it is only in the fallen world that "cruelly destructive fate" holds sway. Cain's exile, depicted in the same formula as Adam's exile earlier, leads inevitably to an intensified enmity between Cain's descendants and God, this warfare culminating finally in the Deluge. Noah, the chosen of God, is warned after the Flood that anyone who takes the life of another destroys his own soul's happiness. But with the sin of Ham the old enmities break out again and the conflict continues, in the form of the building of Babylon by Nimrod.

The curse of God on Cain and his race is permanent: they are eternally damned, beyond the possibility of grace either on earth or in heaven. This tradition of the Cain figure who can expect no favor from heaven throws light on a much discussed crux in *Beowulf:* "no he þone gifstol gretan moste / maþðum for Metode, ne his myne wisse" (168–169, "he could not approach the gift-throne, the treasure, in the presence of God, nor did he know his love"). It is well known by readers of *Beowulf* that there is ambiguity surrounding almost every

word here, even if attempts are made to delimit possible
meanings.[11] Is it Grendel or Cain who is not allowed to approach the throne? [12] And whose throne is referred to, God's or
Hrothgar's? Perhaps an approach involving recognition of
levels of metaphorical meaning and of mythological identities
will help.

It has been noted that Grendel is "of the race of Cain" (107).
He is, in fact, a Germanic manifestation of Cain preying on
the fraternal society of Heorot and, like his biblical archetype,
forever barred from the throne of grace. The gift-throne in
Hrothgar's hall is a seat of ring dispensing, a symbol of royal
favor on earth that reflects the grace shown toward men by
the heavenly Gift-dispenser. Even as God's throne in heaven
is the source of all power and grace, so on earth the throne of a
good king ruling at God's command is a source of grace and
well-being. We have already noted that the beginning of
banqueting in Heorot is accompanied by the scop's Song of
Creation, suggesting that the building of Heorot is analogous
on the human level to God's acts of Creation on a higher level.
God's guest-hall is first marred by Adam who is sent into exile,
then by Cain who is also exiled; Hrothgar's splendid hall is
threatened by Grendel from the moment that the harp first
is heard. Cain is forever joyless and barred from the throne
of grace; Grendel also is joyless and can never be part of the
ritual life around Hrothgar's throne. We do not have to de-
cide, then, whether *he* in line 168 is Grendel *or* Cain. In terms
of the imaginative connotations established by the poem, the
figure of Grendel, who functions literally in the narrative, is
also metaphorically Cain, "God's adversary," and can approach
neither Hrothgar's heaven-sanctioned gift-throne nor God's

11. See Klaeber's discussion of various readings in his edition; also
Emerson, "Legends of Cain," pp. 882–84; and Hamilton, "Religious Principle," pp. 116–17. C. L. Wrenn has suggested a reordering of the text, to
make *he* clearly refer to Cain; see his *Beowulf, with the Finnesburg
Fragment*, rev. and enl. ed. (London, 1958), pp. 188–89.

12. It has even been argued that *he* refers to Hrothgar; see Arthur G.
Brodeur, *The Art of Beowulf* (Berkeley, 1969), pp. 200–205.

own throne of grace in heaven. All literal treasure in Heorot, like all spiritual treasure from heaven, is denied him.

The feuding or Cain motif, with its related idea of two kinds of men or human societies—those loyal to the Dryhten and those who rebel against him—lasts throughout the poem, becoming almost omnipresent in Part 2, even though the explicit naming of Cain and Abel has by then faded out. It is almost as if the deliberate reconstruction of biblical myth in Part 1 is succeeded in Part 2 by the reality itself. No longer is it necessary to establish biblical antecedents, now that the ravages of warring kinsmen are so unmistakably the same in both biblical and Germanic story. A survey of the main uses of the two-societies or two-dryhts motif will illustrate something of the way in which the poet gives mythical resonance and unity to his complex verbal pattern.

Emerging from a cleansed mere to return to a cleansed hall, Beowulf carries "the twisted hilt with its snake adornments" (1698), the remains of the ancient sword miraculously provided for him by God when Grendel's mother had almost defeated him. This is one of the high points in the heroic action of the poem. As Hrothgar scrutinizes "the ancient relic, upon which is inscribed the origin of primeval strife," he recalls "the rushing deep" and the brood of giants alien to God, who suffered terribly when destroyed (1687 ff.). This is not mythological ornamentation but imagery illustrating a central structural fact about *Beowulf*. The sword with its serpent ornamentation and its runic inscription, about the original sinful Creation destroyed in the Deluge, indicates the mythical identity of God's deliverance of this later creation, Heorot, through his champion Beowulf, with the rescue of the good Noah and his family. The Grendel kin and the other monstrous inhabitants of the mere are, as Marie Hamilton has shown,[13] the society of reprobates who, in Genesis and throughout human history, persecute the just. Also, there were the Egyptians who "fought against God" in *Exodus,* who worshiped devils and were destroyed by "an ancient sword" of judgment in the midst of

13. Hamilton, "Religious Principle."

the chaotic, bloodstained "mere," the Red Sea. The traditional typological associations of the Deluge, the Red Sea crossing, the descent into hell, and the immersion of the individual in the waters of Baptism were recognized in Essay One. In Beowulf's descent into the hellish mere to destroy those monsters that plunge men into sin and devil worship, and thus to cleanse the blood-filled, turbid waters, we have a fusion, both unmistakable and imaginatively very rich, of traditional symbolism for the restoration of a ruined Creation to its Lord.

In the account of Heremod's life the Cain-Abel configuration appears again, this time the attention being focused on a joyless prince whose destructive actions are diametrically opposed to the *dream* and fraternity of dryht ideals. Heremod's stinginess about giving gifts to the Danes (1719b–1721a) is similar to Cain's clinging to the produce of his fields. Like Cain, Heremod in his rage has killed his close companions and then turned from human joys to live alone, a savage spirit welling up in him. The description of Heremod is almost identical in places with that of the malice-filled social outcast Grendel: "joyless he lived, so that he suffered the reward of his hostility, the long evil to the people" (1720b–1722a). Heremod's notoriety shows that he too is under the curse of Cain, a man directly antithetical to Beowulf who is to be a lasting comfort to his people and a help to the race of heroes (1717b–1719a).

The theme of illiberality and covetousness associated with Cain carries over into Hrothgar's picture of the proud, well-favored king to whom God has dispensed wisdom, lands, and rank and whose spirit he has allowed to wander in delight until overbearing pride grows too great. At this point "the guardian, the protector of the soul, sleeps" (1741b–1742a), and this Nebuchadnezzar-like king, who never gives circlets, meets his doom from the piercing arrow of death. Following the figure of the arrogant ruler in Hrothgar's thematically important discourse, comes one more like Abel, who doles out treasure generously. It is to this example that the patriarchal king directs Beowulf's attention for emulation. He seems to be saying that it is possible for the spirit of Cain and the spirit of Abel to coexist in one man, making necessary an initial choice and continual alertness against the avaricious, murderous Cain elements in human nature: "Bebeorh þe ðone bealonið, Beowulf leofa, / secg betsta,   ond þe þæt selre geceos, / ece rædas; oferhyda ne gym, / mære cempa!" (1758–1761a, "Guard yourself, dear Beowulf, best of men, against this baleful wickedness, and choose for yourself that better part, eternal benefits; avoid pride, great hero").

The young prince, Hrothgar says, must not become arrogant because he finds himself full of strength, for there are still many ways in which he may be destroyed—sword, fire, flood, knife, arrow—or, failing these violent means, there is always the prospect of old age waiting to dim the brightness of the hero's eye. It is partially this last, apparently, along with a relaxation in vigilance, that has plunged the venerable Hrothgar into decline. For fifty years, he tells Beowulf (1769 ff.), he upheld his role as guardian of the people, protecting the Ring-Danes from many tribes, until he came to believe that he had no foe beneath the expanse of heaven. But then the other half of the Abel-Cain cycle came around, and with the rise of Grendel the "ancient foe" (1776) brought sorrow after joy. Now, however, following Beowulf's triumph, the old king makes thanksgiving to the Creator that he has been enabled to gaze on the bloodstained head, *ofer eald gewin* (1781a, after the old struggle). The use of this formula, recalling once again the primordial nature of the conflict between God and the race of Cain (not just the twelve years of Grendel's attacks), precedes Hrothgar's command for *symbelwyn* (1782, banquet joy) to be resumed in Heorot. The conclusion, to me, is unavoidable, that the poet consciously and deliberately has exploited his sense of the timeless quality and the immediate relevance of the ancient biblical myth. Once again, he is saying, heroic action and the return of God's favor have restored that paradisal banqueting terminated years earlier by the emergence of the savage *deaðscua* (death shadow).

Before Beowulf's descent into the mere we are told, in the description of Grendel's mother (1258 ff.), that "many fated spirits" sprang up after Cain and, "marked by murder,"

went to live in the wilderness. Grendel was one of these but
was struck down by a hero who "trusted himself to the
Lord for grace" (1271b–1272); now, we are clearly meant to
understand, Grendel's mother is another in the series. She, as
the poet's foreboding about the ultimate fate of Heorot implies and as Beowulf himself says to Hygelac (2006–2009), is
not by any means the last murderous enemy of the hall.

In the Grendel kin, all human murderers in *Beowulf* find
their metaphorical signficance. Heremod, as already noted,
is a figure in whom the Cain spirit plays havoc. Unferth, who
also has slain his brothers (587 ff., 1167 ff.), scoffs at Beowulf
and is shown as jealous of the hero's success (501 ff.), recalling
Cain's feeling about the favor accorded Abel by God. Despite
those critics who would excuse Unferth of any wrongdoing,
there is something very sinister, I think, in this figure of
"mar-peace" or Discordia within the confines of Heorot, a
sinister element that plays its part in establishing the doomed
atmosphere. His seat in the court at the feet of the king appears to be one of distinction. The deference shown him,
however, comes only from within Heorot, not from Beowulf
or the poet. We are told, through Beowulf's speeches, that
Unferth's crime of fratricide has gained for him punishment
in hell, despite the fact that it seems to have been overlooked
in Heorot. If the Cain metaphor is as significant in *Beowulf*
as the centrality of the Grendel kin in Part 1 would seem to
indicate, then the presence within Heorot of a sanctioned
fratricide, who at first opposes the hero's mission of rescue
and then gives him a sword that will not work, is surely
another of several clear indications of the fated nature of
Hrothgar's "fraternal" hall. The ingrate Hrothulf, closely
associated by the poet with Unferth and destined, despite the
favor shown him by the king and queen, to plunge the hall
into bloodshed, is another indication that the brotherhood
established in Heorot, within the context of Hrothgar's
patriarchal *dryhtscipe* (lordship,) and symbolized by the
passing of a gold cup, is only a temporary joy doomed to
pass away.

The venerable patriarch Hrothgar and his gracious, gold-adorned queen Wealhtheow are, on one level of the poem's abstract meaning, a primal or mythical family from whom younger men try to seize power, assisted in their rebellion by a figure of discord within the original dryht. The society of Cain is founded on a primal crime; the society of Abel is founded on primal loyalty to God. When Unferth, on the human level, and Grendel, on the level of the supernatural, bring the Cain impetus into the confines of Heorot, the formerly unfallen society enters into a conspiracy with the devil and engages in devil worship, a common participation in religious sacrilege, which is also the sin of Lucifer and his followers. Lucifer's primal crime in the war in heaven is, like Hrothulf's anticipated treachery, the work of one especially favored by the Lord of the dryht, the act of a traitor who goes on to betray the mutual loyalties of thane and Lord; he denies the concept of lordship itself, refuses to worship anyone other than himself, and thus disrupts the primal body of heaven. This in turn leads to the ruin of the dryhtsele of Paradise and, inevitably, to the crime of fratricide.

The war in heaven is described in *Genesis* as metaphorically a dismemberment of the body of God. The war in Heorot is the same but on the human level. Beowulf, like the hero of *Andreas,* does battle against cannibals, eaters of the body of man. The goal of Christian mythology is the resurrection and restoration of each bloodstained, embattled, and mutilated human body, so that humanity may be taken into the mystical body of Christ. The body of Christ which is mutilated in a poem like *The Dream of the Rood* is, as we have seen, the body of the world. The dryht called into being by that signal warcraft brings into old English poetry a new meaning for "banqueting," the same meaning that Beowulf, with the strength of thirty men provided him by heaven's favor, must impose on Heorot where the cannibalistic Grendel, who seizes thirty men at a visit, has destroyed the primal creation and *dream.* A little later in the poem, the image of the dead Æschere's head lying on the sea cliff by the bloodstained mere (1420–1423) is the apt symbol for a created social body now rent in pieces by the demonic spirit of Cain.

The agony of the Danes as they gloomily look at this latest sign of the deadly feud that has engulfed them is based on the realization that their world is literally being dismembered by powers beyond their own capacity for retaliation. They are what is left of a diminished totality. They now know the results of violent division of the originally unified society once the self-destruction of devil worship, symbolized by the cannibalistic monsters, has taken over a formerly good creation.

When Hrothgar first builds his mighty hall, he as king is free to dispense all gifts given him by God except public land and the lives of men (73). It is this right of property that distinguishes the free men from the slaves, and it is a divinely established right. It is precisely here, then, that the demonic thrust of the race of Cain is directed, to destroy the world of the gold-hall. The monsters have no respect for property or for the lives of men. Grendel ravages the hall and feeds on the bodies of warriors and so is barred from the gift-throne of man and God. The freedom and joy of Heorot before Grendel's incursions are liberty and human fulfillment based on the responsibility to use the gifts of God—treasure, loaned weapons, natural faculties, various skills—in service to the l(L)ord who gave them. It is recognition of the ultimate lordship of God that makes slavery impossible in any earthly dryht. Once this is forgotten, hell's destruction is unleashed and bondage to Grendel follows. In the poetry of the world of the dryht, on both the heavenly and earthly levels, when the source of gifts is despised or betrayed (the war in heaven; *Beowulf,* Part 2; *The Battle of Maldon*), the most heinous of crimes follows. The brotherhood of the dryht is possible only on the basis of the patriarchal principle of lordship. Old English poetry is, to a high degree, the story of the clash of Abel and Cain, of the true son or thane who remains faithful to the father or lord and of the faithless son or thane who murders rather than render obedient service. One's sense of the imaginative centrality of *Beowulf* in the total canon is based on a realization of the sustained way in which it, as a poem, comprehends and explains in symbolic terms this central concern of the Anglo-Saxon poetic version of the Christian mythology. Heorot is an attempt at *concordia* (harmony) into which Unferth and Grendel penetrate. Beowulf silences Unferth temporarily and kills Grendel, but the discordant elements eventually triumph.

The Finn episode (1063–1159), focused on the unhappy queen Hildeburh, includes one of three ceremonial funerals spaced at the beginning, middle section, and end of the poem. With its concentration on a marriage and a funeral pyre, the Finnsburg tale shows a kind of "funeral baked meats"—"marriage tables" theme in reverse. The episode has a supporting connection with the Cain-Abel motif. The queen, in serving as a "peace weaver," finds herself as ineffective as Wealhtheow and Freawaru do among the Danes and the Heathobards respectively. Her husband Finn kills his brother-in-law Hnæf. Her son is killed by Hnæf's band. An uneasy truce spoiled by brooding thoughts of revenge, a tense winter of sharing a wine-hall, and the feud breaks out again with disastrous consequences. A band of Danes slaughter the Frisian king and carry their kinswoman back to her homeland. Vengeance, slaughter of kinsmen, plunder, and futility make this cruel tale a fitting statement in miniature of the same Abel-Cain cycle in which Heorot is bound.

The human actions of murder and feuding derived from Cain gradually take over completely in Part 2. The bright dwellings of the Geats are laid waste by the fiery dragon (2312 ff.), and Beowulf's own wine-hall is destroyed (2324 ff.). Symbol follows symbol as the poet recounts a massive destruction that extends into past, present, and future. Cain figures, men disloyal to the fraternal order of the dryht, wander on the earth in the coldness of the lordless state, outlaws hateful to man and God. Not all killers are legally culpable, and the degree to which the spirit of Cain possesses individuals varies. In the main, the world of *Beowulf*, Part 2, is inexorably and fatally caught in guilty bloodshed. For sheltering the exiles Eanmund and Eadgils, King Heardred is murdered by Onela (2373 ff.). Hæthcyn accidentally kills his brother Herebeald; Hrethel, the father, dies of grief (2435 ff.). Following the death of Hrethel, the vigorous, warlike sons of Ongentheow come to Geatland to kill Hæthcyn (2472 ff.). In revenge, Eofor kills the Swedish king Orgentheow (2484 ff.). In the midst of these feuds Hygelac is served well by Beowulf, but Beowulf is not a murderer of kinsmen, however much he is obliged to become part of this tangle of feuds. Just before his death, while revolving many memories, he rejoices that when his life passes from his body the Ruler of men will have no need to punish him for the slaughter of kinsmen (2741–2743a). It is almost as if he were remembering God's curse on Cain or the divine prohibition against murder laid on Noah. The death of this last protector is to be followed by further conflict between the Swedes and the Geats, by a common feud across the waters, apparently with total annihilation of the Geats coming at the end of the long, bloody trail that leads from Abel's corpse to *Hronesnæs*, "the Headland of the Whale," or "Whale's Ness," or "Leviathan's (?) Ness." [14]

All fraternity, *Beowulf* seems to say, is potentially fratricidal, and brothers in the fallen world are brothers to dragons. The warring, schismatic, confused tribal world, then, in which Beowulf dies is symbolized by a dragon. In such a world the tree from Abel's blood flourishes, as the poet of *Genesis A* (987 ff.) puts it, and a curse rests on all men: hence the endless *fæhðe* (feuding, enmity, hostility) of Old English poetry and the relentless dual themes of vengeance and the guilt of fratricide. It was narcissistic self-love accompanied by

---

14. Kenneth Sisam, in *The Structure of Beowulf* (Oxford, 1965), pp. 154 ff., has stated that outside *Beowulf* (in the poem, he says, "considerations of manpower" probably do not have much relevance to the "marvellous adventures" described) there is little evidence for the very early history of the Geats and none at all that they were annihilated by the Swedes. For a much fuller though controversial treatment of the Geats in documentary sources see Jane Akomb Leake, *The Geats of Beowulf* (Madison, 1968). Sisam quite rightly, in my view, stresses that the poet is concerned not with actual history but with a poetic fiction devoted, at this point in the poem, to describing the mood generated by the death of a great king.

a conspiracy of thanes that disrupted the primal society of heaven and led to the creation of hell. It is disloyalty followed by vengeance that destroys the harmony of the *neorxnawong* (Paradise). It is fratricide which characterizes human history. Grendel cannot approach Hrothgar's gift-throne, nor Cain God's, and the dragon destroys Beowulf's hall because the fratricidal enemy of society seeks to destroy the ritual harmony embodied in the gift-dispenser on his throne. When war takes over, men become *wælwulfas* (carrion wolves), subhuman, and rend the body of man.

It is, finally, only death that can mark Beowulf off completely from the relentless vendettas of life in the northern lands, a life that has become an intricate, bloodstained pattern of accidental, vicious, or legally required murders. Beowulf's life has risen like a parabola from an inauspicious youth to the role of mighty hero and king, but now that life sinks again, penetrated by the fire and venom of the serpent. What remains, once the rituals of lamenting have ended, is a large memorial barrow towering high above the waters of the northern Leviathan or sea beast, a barrow that is to serve other seafarers in the perilous floods of existence in middleearth as a reminder of one truly exemplary life.

The social chaos or Babylonian confusion of all the feuds revolving in the background of Part 2 throws into greater prominence the collapse of the dryht of which Beowulf is the center. The ten cowards emerging from the trees, bearing toward their dead lord the weapons loaned them earlier (2845b ff.), epitomize the end, except for Wiglaf, of the faithful Abel element among Beowulf's thanes. To his men the lord has given prosperity and safety, but, like Lucifer and Cain, they have withheld faithful service. The one loyal warrior utters a scathing denunciation of his fellows' treachery, prophesying for them and their families an inglorious life of exile and disgrace (2864 ff.). The cowards are now members of the outlawed race of Cain; their treachery has made them integral parts of the monsters that prey on ordered human society. The Grendel kin are now more alive than ever, in spite of the illustrious way the hero has used up his "loan-days." The poem concludes its reworking of the Abel-Cain motif with one resurgent Abel, Wiglaf, rising to carry on the struggle, while ten more figures of nihilism go forth.

By persistent foreboding, the poet prepares for the ultimate laying waste of both the Danes and the Geats: "fate is exceedingly near" throughout the poem, not just at the hour of the hero's death (2420b). The ideals made explicit in Heorot and in the person of the hero are lamented as doomed even before they are revealed in their full splendor, so that the resultant tonal unity of *Beowulf* is profoundly elegiac, deriving from the poet's deep sense of the tragic nature of his story. In the midst of the most triumphant lightfilled pictures, the demonic is present. It is really only a matter of time, of another triumph of fate, before the emblem of the gracious Wealhtheow passing the communal cup of fellowship is replaced by that of the fugitive thrall ransacking the dragon's hoard to steal a cup with which he hopes to buy himself a place in another dryht (2278–2286). The warmth of human companionship in the golden dryht of middle-earth is continually set against the Cain exile in his cold, joyless state and his Lucifer-like envy of the society of thanes bound together by golden circlets. Man in a world of endless murders thinks back to Eden, and Cain, like Satan in the dryht of hell, has regrets.

There can be no tragedy in literature without a sense of glory or happiness or fulfilled ambition potentially within human grasp, a glory shown finally not to be obtainable, or, if it is obtained temporarily, not capable of being preserved. As the *Beowulf* poet brings his hero to work on behalf of Heorot in its ideal aspect, he demonstrates his realization of this fact of tragedy. His particular poetic version of *the myth of the heroic redeemer* has an overall tragic shape, as it combines with the myth of Fall and fratricide, but the tragic effect is possible only because Heorot in its ideal form remains as an image of what once was and what still might be, however precariously, if pride, envy, avarice, and murder could be controlled. It is to the restoration and realization of this potential Paradise—what I have been calling the golden dryht of middle-earth—that Beowulf bends his efforts in Part 1 of the poem.

When he comes to Heorot the Danes are living in a state of Babylonian confusion or lower nature, a world of bloodshed, terror, and devil worship. Every night for twelve years the hall has been possessed by a monster of destruction. Like the desolate waste in *Genesis* before God begins his acts of Creation, Heorot is *idel and unnyt* (413, cf. *Genesis* 106, empty and useless). Time and fate have worn the once-splendid hall. Hrothgar sits *eald ond anhar* (357, old and very gray), a typical elegiac figure wrapped in melancholy thoughts about the tragedy that has overtaken his world but powerless to take heroic action to free it from its bondage. It is clear that Heorot has fallen to its present level from an earlier condition of *dream,* a state at once more desirable and more human than that of the demonic possession symbolized by Grendel's ravages. In its earliest manifestation, Heorot is an image of the kind of life established by the Scyppend as natural to man: it involves a high order of heroism, the achievement of social and political peace, and harmony with heaven. Its immediate social symbols are rings, banqueting, and harp music; its cosmological symbols are the sun and the moon shining on the plains of the world, plains ornamented with branches, leaves, and all living creatures. When, however, the Danes fall into the clutches of the *feond on helle,* they lose most of their original world. Still, the poet makes clear throughout Part 1 that all those things that are good for man —heroic actions, remembrance of former happy times, music, beer drinking, pledges of generosity and loyalty, brotherhood, and mindfulness of God's creative acts—can temporarily restore the Danes to their earlier Paradise, with the help of God and Beowulf. Hrothgar, as ruler, is meant to embody the ordered world and to demonstrate the generosity and protection of heaven. For a time he has done so splendidly, but as an earthly king and almost through no fault of his own, he is highly vulnerable to the demonic influence that emanates from the mere and from the hell in the frightened hearts of his subjects (179–180) as they ponder their disastrous situation.

Beowulf's advent into the ruined dryhtsele, as Hrothgar immediately perceives, is through the grace of God (381 ff.). As Hrothgar also knows, it is only God who "can easily restrain the mad destroyer from his deeds" (478b–479). It is as if the divine favor forfeited when Heorot fell, twelve years before, is now about to be restored. Hrothgar is an aged Adam waiting for grace and deliverance, and Wealhtheow, trying to provide for her sons a life free of crime and bloodshed, is a latter-day Germanic Eve trying to repair the ravages begun at the fateful banquet long ago in the archetypal guest-hall of Eden. In line with his elegiac rather than homiletic theme, however, the poet is careful not to censure Hrothgar and Wealhtheow but to emphasize the fateful nature of the conflict in which they are caught and to show them ready and eager to receive God's new and necessary gift to them, in the form of the hero's deeds. The underplaying of a theme of guilt in the handling of Hrothgar and Wealhtheow is analogous to the treatment of the Fall of man in *Genesis B*, discussed in Essay One. Beowulf, as the deliverer of the ruined dryht of the Scylding Adam is, by symbolic association, the second Adam who now comes to do battle on behalf of those who have fallen into the clutches of the fiend.

In the account of the hero's journey from Geatland, his arrival in Denmark, and his subsequent actions in restoring Hrothgar's kingdom, we see once again how in Old English poetry the myth of heroic deliverance or redemption exploits the myth of Creation for much of its imaginative significance. Beowulf, like the champions of the mythical and romantic poems discussed in Essays One and Two, engages in ritual reenactments of the cosmogonic myth, in his splendid sea voyage, in his restoring of Heorot to its former glory, in his conquest of the chaotic waters of the mere, and in his gift giving to both the Danish and Geatish societies. With each generous act something of the original dryht of middle-earth again is revealed.

With the account of the hero's departure from Geatland,

we see a dryht other than that of Hrothgar, this one centered round "the strongest of mankind . . . noble, and powerful" (196–198a) and including fourteen of the boldest young thanes. The omens are favorable, wise men of the Geats do not let their affection for Beowulf impede his plan, the hero is a *lagucræftig mon* (209, man skilled in the sea), and his followers are eager to set sail, their war gear shining with bright ornaments. The "foamy-necked ship, most like a bird" (218) makes its way, impelled by the wind, until it arrives at the gleaming cliffs and high hills of Denmark, where the crew, their coats of mail rattling, go up on the *wang* (plain) and give thanks to God for easy sea paths (224b–228). The whole introductory description of the hero's dryht is spirited and buoyant. The imagery—bursting with life, expectation, and a sense of spaciousness—contrasts sharply with the mood of melancholy and the sense of claustrophobia in the preceding description of the hall possessed by the *deorc deapscua* (160, dark death shadow). The ship is a ship of life, with a clear destination and manned by fifteen willing champions —*weras on wilsið* (men on a desired journey)—in the fullness of their powers, in vivid contrast with that earlier ship of death surrounded by mourning thanes reluctantly dispatching the dead Scyld Scefing to his unknown destination.

Not since the poet has described the Song of Creation a hundred lines earlier has there been this sense of exuberant and purposive action. It is as if the heavy sense of time as duration—*fela missera, singale sæce* (many half-years, continual conflict)—into which Heorot has been plunged, is now in the process of being abolished in favor of an earlier sacred time when divine favor for Denmark was directly evident. It is also as if the experience of time only as duration brings the peril of forgetting what is fundamental, that existence itself is given by God, with the result that the Danes who now do not know the true God have fallen into devil worship. One is reminded, too, by the account of this sea voyage, of the importance in Old English poetry of the boat as a symbol of the way heroic man takes part in reenacting the divine acts of Creation and redemption. Noah with his ark makes possible the emergence from watery chaos of a new creation, Andrew takes life and redemption to the Merme-donians in a boat in which he himself is increasingly en-veloped by divine wisdom, and Helena makes her way over the "sea beast's home" to discover the miraculous, life-giving cross of Christ. The exile in *Resignation*, feeling bound by his sense of guilt and deprived of heaven's grace, longs for a boat to take him out of his miseries. The Seafarer takes to his ship to escape the false allurements of life on land. And the *god cyning* Scyld Scefing comes out of the sea to bring heaven-sent prosperity to the Danes.

Hrothgar's coast guard, burning with curiosity at the au-dacity of the Geats' unexpected and open landing in a foreign land and greatly impressed by the uniquely striking figure—*ænlic ansyn* (unique or glorious form)—of the hero, demands to know the newcomers' identity (229 ff.). They are Hygelac's warriors, Beowulf tells him, and have come on "a mighty errand" to the prince of the Danes. The Geats' first glimpse of Heorot is vividly described (306b ff.), in terms of the hall's ideal aspects; it is "timbered, splendid, and gold-adorned," "the most famous of buildings under heaven," and in it "the mighty one" dwells. Its light shines over many lands, and it is approached along a road shining with stones. After due ritualistic courtesies and the impressive announce-ment "Beowulf is min nama" (343, "Beowulf is my name"), the hero, *heard under helme* (404, brave beneath his helmet) and shining in his byrnie, takes his place near the hearth in the hall and salutes Hrothgar. He tells why he has come— "Me wearð Grendles þing . . . cuð" (409, "the Grendel affair was . . . made known to me")—gives his credentials, in terms of a boasting speech about his earlier heroic exploits, and indicates his belief that with his handgrip he can cleanse Heorot of the monster who brings death and terror and refuses to fight with weapons. If not, he will bow to fate and die willingly. Even at this point in the action the hero has exercised restorative influence. A great weight is lifted from the mind of the old king, and the primal, golden dryht re-appears briefly:

>   Scop hwilum sang
>   hador on Heorote.   Þær wæs hæleða dream,
>   duguð unlytel   Dena ond Wedera.   [496b–498]

> [From time to time a scop sang
> Clear-voiced in Heorot. Then there was joy for the
>   heroes,
> No little glory, for the Danes and the Weders.]

Beowulf repeats his resolution to conquer or die and triumphs over Unferth in a battle of words. Again, as in olden times— "Þa wæs eft swa ær" (642a, "Then it was again as once it had been")—brave speeches resound within the hall, and Hrothgar confidently turns over to the hero the custody of the building. Beowulf and his thanes remain in Heorot, the hero trusting firmly in his "proud strength, the favor of God" (670). He strips off his armor and gives his sword to a servant. Then come gloomy reflections among the Geats, talk of murder and death and of God, and finally Grendel arrives.

Marked by God's wrath (711) and "deprived of joys" (721), Grendel is defeated by heaven's champion in a ferocious wrestling match, after which, mortally wounded and singing a song of defeat, he goes, the "prisoner of hell" (788), to seek the company of devils (808). Rejoicing in his night's work (827), the hero places the hand, arm, and shoulder of this rebel against God beneath the vaulted roof of the "cleansed" (825) hall. The next day the "mar-peace" Unferth lapses into silence, the battered Heorot is redecorated by many willing hands, gold tapestries are hung, banqueting is resumed, and again a cup is passed, giving a markedly sacramental sense of unity in one socially cohesive body. The whole sequence has interesting connections with the account of the expulsion of Lucifer at the end of the war in heaven in *Genesis*. There is the same theme of rebellion through envy against God's dryht, the same idea of God's *yrre* (wrath)—(*Genesis* 34; *Beowulf* 711)—the same wrestling motif (God seizes his foes with hostile hands, crushes them in his bosom, and drives them forth on the "long journey" to hell), and the same sense of a primal pattern of joy and banqueting in the process of being restored to its original condition by the expulsion of demonic influence. The dismemberment of Grendel and his ensuing lament, as he is driven out of Heorot, are closely parallel to the fallen Lucifer's sense (in *Christ and Satan*) of himself and his fellow rebels as stained and wounded parts of the divine body, rather than, as formerly, "limbs about the dear One." After the battle with Grendel, the lord of Heorot, believing that the eternal God must have been "gracious" to Beowulf's mother in her child-bearing, takes this "best of men" as his adopted son and prophesies for him glory "forever and ever" (942b ff.).

There are of course differences of detail, many of them, between the conflict with the foes of God and man in *Beowulf* and the conflict between the dryhts of heaven and hell in the poems of the Junius MS, but the same structural pattern is working, whether consciously on the *Beowulf* poet's part or simply through the shaping power of the traditional word-hoard. The parallels between the Christian mythology, here and elsewhere in *Beowulf*, are, to me, so striking as to suggest a highly conscious process of shaping verbal materials.

With the defeat of Grendel, the Cain spirit is only temporarily quelled. Grendel's mother (1251 ff.), in strict adherence to the destructive principles of blood-feuding, rises out of the mere to wreak grisly vengeance on Heorot, taking back to the underwater hall with her the head of Æschere and the hand of Grendel. Plunged again into profound gloom, Hrothgar describes (1345 ff.) to Beowulf what is known of the mere, that source of apparently unending hostility to his world of Heorot. At this point in the poem the myth of heroic deliverance, so far confined to the cleansing of middle-earth, is expanded to include the hellish source of evil itself, and the hero realizes that he must go "beneath the head-lands" (1360) to eradicate the still-active demonic powers. Grendel's mere, although only a few miles from Heorot (1361–1362), is the opposite pole from Heorot in the poem's imaginative space. Like the splendid hall, it is primarily an image of this world, a complex symbol of all those things in nature and in human society that human desire most rejects set against the ideal aspirations embodied in the gold-hall. But also like Heorot, indeed like most images of Old English poetry, the wider significance or supernatural reference of the mere exists on the level of myth or symbolic metaphor. Unlike Heorot, however, which at certain points is the paradisal guest-hall and at others the ruined hall of the fallen world, the mere as a poetic image has no double-ness or ambivalence in its meaning. In its entirety it is demonic.

The overall tragic vision in *Beowulf*—of a "fleeting" world caught in time as duration, in which human longings to return to the paradisal guest-hall are constantly frustrated —is clear. Similarly, the connections of the monster-infested world in *Beowulf* with the conventional Old English poetic vision of the ruined or fallen world are numerous. The mere is the poem's most complete concentration of fallen-world motifs as they merge, ostensibly on the level of middle-earth, with the imagery of hell. In several ways the underwater *reced* (building) or *niðsele* (hostile hall), inhabited by the *healðegn* (hall-thane) Grendel and his mother, is a grotesque parody of Heorot in its ideal aspect. Its location beneath the headlands and turbid waters, rather than in the midst of the "plain," its demonic light antithetical to the radiance of the gold-hall, its hoarded treasure (1557, 1613), its cannibalistic banqueting, its weird kinship loyalties, its total absence of *dream,* and its inveterate hostility to the harp music and loyalties of the fraternal dryht—in all these things it is a perversion of Heorot. The precise extent to which its character as a demonic dryht envelops Heorot—the making dark of the hall, the prevention of gift dispensing, banqueting, and music, and the symbolically implicit undermining of Hrothgar's *sibbegedriht* (387, 729, peaceful troop, band of kinsmen) by the spirit of Cain through the persons of Unferth and Hrothulf—is the measure of the fall or ruin of Hrothgar's world. The climactic detail of the mere's conquest of Heorot is the devil worship, the honoring by the Danes of those same demonic powers that are destroying them (175 ff.).

In terms of nature imagery, the mere, in a detailed way, is
a perversion of the ideal order of Creation.[15] Located out in

15. W. S. Mackie, in "The Demons' Home in *Beowulf*," *JEGP* 37 (1937):
455–61, has stressed the imprecision of the *Beowulf* poet's description of
the mere: "The poet of *Beowulf* cares little about verisimilitude and does
not greatly trouble to be consistent; his purpose is not to make the supernatural appear natural, but to invest his narrative with an eerie atmosphere of strangeness and horror." W. W. Lawrence countered this view by
stressing the clarity with which the waterfall setting emerges, although he
felt that the parallels in the *Grettissaga* represent a much better preservation of the story; see *"Beowulf" and Epic Tradition* (Cambridge, Mass.,
1928), chap. 6; also "Grendel's Lair: A Reply to W. S. Mackie," *JEGP* 38
(1939): 477–80. It is not easy, I think, perhaps not possible at all, despite
Lawrence's claim, to visualize the mere described by the poet. The problem as I see it is one of bringing the modes of perception of a different
period of culture to bear on an earlier one. It should be remembered
in discussions of what might loosely be called nature imagery in Old
English poetry that in this period there is no "nature" in the nineteenth-
century sense of phenomena as opposed to noumena. Noumena, whether
demonic or divine, constantly penetrate the earthly order for the Anglo-
Saxon, so that "nature" is thought of as exemplary, as the book of God
capable of teaching truths about the mind of God. Mircea Eliade has
reminded us, in his description of archaic or traditional societies, that
"For religious man, nature is never only *natural;* it is always fraught with
a religious value"; see his *The Sacred and the Profane*, p. 116. It is
perhaps worth remembering also that art generally in Anglo-Saxon times
is two-dimensional not three-dimensional. This has its implications for
Old English poetry. There is no fixed visual point of view for the
listener or reader, no arbitrary selection by the poet of a single static
position to create a pictorial space with vanishing point. E. H. Gombrich
has shown how the representation in art of what we call "natural appearances" is quite abnormal, a convention which has to be learned by
both artist and viewer. It is abnormal and quite unperceptible as such
to nonliterate peoples. See his *Art and Illusion: A Study in the Psychology
of Pictorial Representation* (New York, 1960). Old English poetry has
suffered much at the hands of critics conditioned by "three-dimensional
representational fiction" of later periods. In dealing with poems like
Beowulf, Andreas, and *Exodus*, we are up against art from a mythical, or
at the very least, romantic mode of perception. In it there is no
mechanistic sense of causal relations. Events do not follow one another
causally. Characters do not exist in any developed psychological way.
Scenes do not emerge with three-dimensional pictorial clarity. Rather,
one event, one character, or one scene is associated with another because
of symbolic and thematic appropriateness. Mackie is right when he says

the fens or moors beyond the plain surrounding the hall, it is a mist-shrouded wilderness (103–104, 162, 450, 710, 764, 820, 1265, 1348, 1405). We are told in *Christ and Satan* and in *Guthlac A* and *B* that some demons live in remote places of middle-earth and from there launch their attacks on men; this is precisely what the Grendel kin do. Encircling rocks, frost-covered trees, and the twisted roots of a "joyless wood" show the mere's wasteland setting to be the direct antithesis of the sunny, blossoming groves of the earthly Paradise described in detail in *The Phoenix* and more briefly in other poems. The motif of chaotic, treacherous water, beside which the "hart strong in its horns" (1369) will die rather than plunge in, connects with the Physiologus idea of the *deaðsele* (death-hall) of damnation being located at the bottom of the treacherous whale's domain, that hall of the dryht of hell to which Eleusius' dryht is plunged in *Juliana*.

At two critical points in the poem—the swimming contest with Breca and the battle in the mere—the hero's actions are a demonstration of his "mere-strength" (533); the barrow ultimately erected to his memory is meant to be visible far and wide to "seafarers." Beowulf's main credential establishing him as capable of cleansing Heorot and the mere is that he has already proven himself superior to sea beasts, giants, and the stormy sea. The "whales" (540), "nickers" (422, 575), "sea fishes" (549), "hostile deadly foes" (554), and "mighty sea beast" (558) that he has already conquered, along with five giants, anticipate the "evil broods" (111) and "demons" (163) of the mere who plunge the Danes into devil worship. When the troop from Heorot first sees the baleful waters (1416b ff.), the poet focuses attention on many of "the race of serpents," the "strange sea dragons," "nickers," "serpents," and "wild beasts" moving about in the water or lying on the nesses. Some of these, he tells us, are those who in the mornings make their way over the sea. The iconographic function of these unblessed creatures can hardly be mistaken.

---

that the *Beowulf* poet cares little about verisimilitude. It would have been very odd if any artist in that period had been greatly concerned about this particular mode of perception.

In the expressions *sædraca* (sea dragon), *wyrmcynnes fela* (many of the race of serpents), and *sædeor* (sea beast), the dragon or serpent, typical of land monsters (the biblical Behemoth), merges with traditional destroying sea beasts, like the great whale Fastitocalon in the Old English Physiologus (the biblical Leviathan), in an intricate fusion of the horrors of both the wasteland and the stormy sea. The other traditional beast of prey, the wolf, also is mentioned, in the reference to the "wolf-slopes" (1358) surrounding the mere and in the odd compound *brimwylf* (1506, 1599, she-wolf of the sea), applied to Grendel's mother.

Closely connected with Beowulf's quelling of the mere is the poet's identification of his hero's acts with certain parts of the cycle of the seasons and the daily cycle of the sun. The contest with Breca occurs in "the coldest of storms" (546) when winds from the north do fierce battle against the two human interlopers (547b–548a). The youthful hero's triumph is a victory over both wintry seas and darkness and is heralded by the reappearance of "God's bright beacon" from the east (569b–572a). Wind, frost, and rain are all prominent in the mere setting over which "the heavens weep" (1376a). The most vivid seasonal image is that of the miraculous "war-blade," recorder of the primordial conflict between God and the race of Cain, as it melts "very like to ice, when the Father who rules the times and seasons loosens the bonds of frost, unwinds the flood-ropes" (1605b–1611a). The damascened blade disappears completely in the blood of Grendel, leaving only the didactic hilt as graphic witness to the connection of God's work, through Beowulf, with heaven's periodic sustaining and redeeming work on behalf of the faithful Noahs of human history. Each important physical object, like each human act, becomes real in *Beowulf* only insofar as it imitates or repeats an archetype. It is as if, in this kind of tradition-centered poem, everything that lacks an exemplary model is meaningless and devoid of reality.

One of the most obvious image motifs of the hell-on-earth theme is that of night and darkness, with connotations both of the endless night of damnation and the primordial chaos preceding Creation. Over and over again, the Grendel kin, and later the dragon, are associated with the powers of darkness. It is always after night descends that Grendel, the *deorc deaðscua* (dark death shadow) who holds the moors "in the endless night" (161), comes to Hrothgar's hall as "the greatest of night miseries" (193). In Geatland, Beowulf has heard that it is "after the light of evening is hidden under heaven's vault" (413–414) that Heorot stands *idel and unnyt* (413a). Beowulf's battle with "the one who goes in shadows" (702b–703a) appropriately is "night work" (827b). The mere with its *fyr on flode* (1366, fire on the flood) is its most terrible at night.

The motif of destroying fire, with inevitable connotations of judgment in a poem where biblical typology helps reshape Scandinavian materials, does not come to the foreground of the narrative until Part 2, but it is present earlier: in the anticipative references to the ultimate fate of Heorot (82b–83a, 781b–782a), in the poet's gnomic comment about the soul of the wicked man being "pushed into the embrace of fire" (185), in the "horrid light" shining from Grendel's eyes (726b–727), in the flame on the mere at night, and in the baleful light shining in the depths at the time of Beowulf's arrival there (1516b–1517). The fire motif, however, is clearly secondary in Part 1 to the motifs of darkness and perilous waters. Not until the hero's life has been lived fully does the fiery serpent appear, to destroy both the *banhus* (bone-house, body) in which his soul lives and the hall at the center of his earthly kingdom.

Beowulf's katabasis or descent into the mere (1492 ff.) is at once the hero's archetypal journey into a lower world and, in Christian symbolism, the analogue to Christ's descent into hell. Despite obvious differences of detail, the narrative here derives major significance from the Old English form of the myth of the Harrowing of hell. In the Exeter Book *Descent into Hell,* Christ is described, in terms not unlike those applied to Beowulf, as a figure of warlike splendor and heroic ferocity who comes to hell determined to plunder its strength. Grendel could not be harmed with ordinary phys-

ical weapons but required for his defeat the God-given might
of thirty men embodied in Beowulf. At the edge of the mere,
Beowulf dons his armor and descends to the hostile hall for
a nearly fatal battle in which he has to fling aside the famous
Hrunting, the gift of Unferth (which has never previously
failed any man in time of war), and depend instead on his
mighty handgrip; finally, when even this is not enough, he
has to resort to the marvelous sword provided by God. Only
when all purely human means deriving from the fallen
dryht world of feuds and wars have been exhausted does the
triumph of God's *cempa* (champion, warrior) become possible. In *The Descent into Hell* the poet makes elaborate
use of warlike imagery only to point out its final irrelevance
in describing a battle whose significance is entirely spiritual.
In both poems the light of heaven shines brightly at the
moment of victory.

The connections between the two harrowings go further
than this. Christ as Creator, having by the time of his Passion carried out his miraculous work in Bethlehem, Jerusalem, and the Jordan, is urged to include hell's hall itself
in his work of deliverance. From middle-earth the Lord of
Creation goes into the depths to cleanse them, while the
dryht of the Old Testament faithful wait to be reunited with
their Dryhten. But *Beowulf* is not quite so abstract as *The
Descent into Hell.* The Geatish hero is not the Lord of
Creation, although the *soð Metod* (true God) works through
him to melt the sword and to shine heaven's light into the
mere.

In the discussion of *Exodus* as a poem about spiritual rebirth through baptismal cleansing in Essay One, there was
a close analogue for the ancient sword of judgment used
by Beowulf to smite the demonic powers at the bottom of
the mere. There were also the traditional typological associations of the Deluge, the Red Sea waters, the Harrowing of
hell, and the waters of Baptism. All these connotations appear to converge in Beowulf's climactic acts in the depths of
the hellish waters. Like Christ, the Sun of Righteousness, he
scatters the darkness and ice of paganism or devil worship
and brings back to the peaceful condition of its origin the

Danish kingdom that had been covered with obscurity by the dark shadow of sin and death. The vernal associations of his victory are apt, in that God, according to traditional typology, is believed to have raised up the fallen world by Christ's Resurrection at that very season in which he first created it out of nothing. Beowulf's immersion and emersion, then, would appear to be, mythologically, both a descent into hell or vicarious burial (the Danes and the Geats both conclude that he is dead) and a resurrection into a world newly restored by his acts of rescue. Beowulf's troop, like the thane Adam in *The Descent into Hell*, wait as patient retainers for the coming again of their lord, but they, like Christ's despairing disciples after their Dryhten's death, wait on earth, not in hell itself. After the Harrowing, Christ's faithful retinue journey with him to heaven; Beowulf's troop go with him back to Heorot, there to experience with the Scyldings the rejoicing (*dream*) of a world that temporarily has lost fear and sadness because Beowulf has cleansed it of the demonic. Christ's return to his Father in the Ascension, as described by Cynewulf, marks the final settlement of the "greatest of feuds," and he is rewarded with the "greatest of banquets." He himself then begins the lavish dispensing of treasure (salvation) to the sons of men on earth. In *Beowulf*, as in *Exodus*, a dryht in bondage to hell is led by a God-chosen "seafaring" man through its regenerative cleansing experience, at the end of which treasures are joyfully shared and the song of those released from hell's power is heard. As in the ritual of Baptism, moreover, the triumphant struggle of the human soul with the monster-infested waters is followed by the eucharistic joy of banqueting.

Once these traditional typological meanings in the poet's handling of his tale come into focus, the individual images can be seen to cohere in a highly suggestive pattern. It may even be that the memorable image of the stag pursued by hounds but terrified of the mere's waters is to be understood in the light of traditional symbolism. Daniélou tells us [16] that a frequent baptistery decoration in the early Church was

16. Jean Daniélou, *The Bible and the Liturgy* (Notre Dame, Ind., 1956), pp. 36–37.

the figure of a deer drinking at springs of water (Ps. 41), symbolizing the thirst of catechumens to receive Baptism. In some of these illustrations there was a serpent in the deer's mouth, signifying that only after the serpent had been vanquished could the deer quench its thirst. The stag in *Beowulf*, though mortally hard pressed, will not immerse itself in the serpent-infested waters. Is it in this tradition, then, that we find part of the meaning of the cleansing of the serpent-filled mere, so that "Hart" Hall may be restored to its earlier paradisal condition? Heorot is described early in the poem as *heah ond horngeap* (82, high and horn-gabled). The only other occurrence of this phrase in Old English poetry is in *Andreas* (668) where it is applied to the *tempel dryhtnes* (temple of the Lord) in Jerusalem. (It is usually assumed that *heah ond horngeap* is a Germanic gift to Old English poetry, and it may have been; there is, however, no evidence at all in the poetry to support the assumption.) As I have suggested earlier, then, it would appear that Heorot is at once a symbol of the individual soul and of God's people who must experience hell's attacks and then be restored but must also, ultimately, be subjected to destroying flames. Beowulf's total life pattern, in Parts 1 and 2 of the poem respectively, shows him willingly experiencing both traditional baptisms, that of water and that of fire. After the second of these his soul goes to the Judgment of the just.

The hero's conquest of the mere is so momentous that Hrothgar, restoring a more realistic and human perspective after the marvelous exploits of the hero, feels it necessary to preach to Beowulf a sermon against pride. Unlike the mythical *Descent into Hell, Beowulf* as a poem is concerned primarily with life in middle-earth, and Part 1 is a kind of *cyropaedia* on the training of a young prince. It is almost as if, following the destruction of God's foes and the hero's penetration into the dryht of hell, Beowulf now possesses a knowledge and experience that could destroy him. Hrothgar feels impelled to remind the young champion, whom he has adopted following the defeat of Grendel, of the limits of human power, even though it is clear to them both that it is only by God's grace that Beowulf has been enabled to survive the demonic perils of this particular flood. With all this in mind, Hrothgar, like Simeon in Luke 2, speaks of the great promise implicit in the birth of the hero who is to become the comfort and perpetual help of his people. Finally, banqueting and the giving of gifts are resumed.

The *Beowulf* poet's sense of the fleeting or mutable character of everything in middle-earth inevitably extends in Part 2 to the person of the hero. In Part 1, as a figure of vitality and superabundance, as the heroic vehicle of divine grace, Beowulf was enabled to abolish that destructive time as duration into which Heorot—this poem's main *imago mundi*—had fallen and to restore the hall to its original freshness and radiance: "the hall rose high above him, vaulted and shining with gold; inside, the guest slept . . ." (1799b–1800). The twelve years of bondage to Grendel were in a sense canceled in favor of that sacred time contemporary with Creation, and Hrothgar appropriately gave twelve symbolic treasures to his deliverer at the end of the twelve years of misery. Now in Part 2, as the central organization of images takes on the shape of *the myth of the hero's death and the return to chaos,* we find that time and *yldo* (age) have worn the hero and his kingdom. Hrothgar was described by Beowulf as "a peerless king, altogether blameless" (1885b–1886a), defeated only because of that age which toward the end of his fifty-year reign took from him the joys of power. Now Beowulf, also an exemplary king, is first threatened and then destroyed by a fifty-foot serpent, also at the end of a fifty-year reign. The tragedy of Hrothgar's life, only temporarily relieved by Beowulf's deeds, has now become the hero's own, but no heaven-sent champion appears who can act effectively on his behalf.

There is no escape from the ruins of time in this elegiac tragedy, for the basis of the tragic vision is being in time. Even as we move through the poem's romance, through its myths of creation and heroic deliverance, we are constantly made aware that death and human defeat in middle-earth

are what give tragic shape and form to the lives of the
Scyldings. It is death that defines the life of Scyld, of Beow,
of Heorogar, and, finally, of Hrothgar. Now, in the account
of the end of Beowulf's *lændagas* (loan-days, fleeting days),
again it is death that defines the shape of the heroic life.
Throughout Part 2 the poet carefully establishes a sense of
imminent and nearly total disaster, a disaster partly realized
by the end of the action. But the catastrophe described is
not apocalyptic, as in the Old English Doomsday poems. In
these latter, time as duration is brought to an end, history
is abolished, and what is pure and faithful within God's
Creation is taken back into eternity. But *Beowulf* does not
show an end of the world, a Ragnarok or Doomsday. It
shows the defeat of heroic effort in the world of time. At the
very end of the narrative the Geats are still struggling against
time; they build a great barrow on the headland called
Hronesnæs (the Headland of the Whale) that will keep alive
for other seafarers the memory of their king. Within the
barrow lie an ancient, useless treasure and the ashes of the
hero. Outside, twelve horsemen, warriors bold in battle, sons
of chieftains, circle round, uttering an ancient lament. Beowulf has died, haunted by the memory of those marvelous
times when he displayed in almost godlike manner his
greatest powers; Hrothgar earlier was forced to admit defeat
at the hands of Grendel but also looked back nostalgically,
in geardagum (in former days), to a time when he subdued
all enemies of the Danes and doled out treasures in almost
godlike manner. It is fundamental to the elegiac nature of
the poem that the acts of strength, of superabundance, and
of creativity are constantly pushed back into that legendary
earlier and better time indicated by the hoary phrase *in
geardagum*.

The poet uses various materials to convey his theme of
human defeat in time-dominated middle-earth. We have
seen how the myth of Cain can be used as an illuminating
aid to interpretation in Part 2, even though the poem no
longer explicitly mentions it by name. The dryht of hell and

the confused, chaotic society of Cain and Babylon have gained the ascendant. But the memory of something more in accord with heaven's purposes must never fade entirely from the poetry, or the tragic effect will give place to unrelieved irony. In the poet's use of the Lay of the Last Survivor (2247–2266), we have a vivid illustration of the way human splendor and achievement are made to recede into the past even as they are clung to in human memory.

This set piece, an elegy within an elegy, is a melancholy vision of vanished kinsmen and comrades uttered by the one survivor of an ancient race, who has just deposited his ancestral treasure in the earth and now laments his own fate, along with that of his people. The human tragedy presented is of a splendor two degrees removed into the distant past, a vision of pluperfect things. From the poet's perspective, the guardian of the rings is "an unknown man in days gone by" (2233); from the perspective of the lone survivor, the subject of the lament—that is, his own noble race—is also something from a glorious past that no longer exists. The immediate context of the foreground narrative, the disintegration of Beowulf's kingdom, deals with exactly the same theme in a less oblique way. The lone survivor tries briefly to enjoy "the treasure slowly accumulated through the years," but the same fate that has destroyed his kinsmen removes him as well, leaving only a memory. So too with the dying Beowulf, himself a "guardian of rings" who lives on "after the fall of heroes" (3005a), the aim is to restore an ancient treasure to its former use, but this desire is frustrated, at the cost of the hero's life.

The point of time in Geatish history at which Beowulf dies signals an imminent end for the Geats as a unified dryht society. It is true that Beowulf leaves behind him Wiglaf as the *endelaf* (last remnant) of his people, placing the young hero in somewhat the same position as that of the lone survivor in the elegy, but the social disintegration is now so far advanced that there is, so far as we are told in the poem, little hope for Geatland in the fact that Wiglaf remains. The last words of the aged Beowulf, as he gives his bright helmet, his golden circlet, his ring, and his corslet to the young spear-warrior, clearly signal the end of a race:

> Ðu eart endelaf   usses cynnes,
> Wægmundinga.   Ealle wyrd forsweop
> mine magas   to metodsceafte,
> eorlas on elne;   ic him æfter sceal. [2813–2816]

> [You are the last of our race,
> Of the Wægmundings. Fate has swept away
> All my kinsmen to their destiny,
> Men in their power; I must follow after them.]

We have seen how in this poem, as in other Old English poems, each creative human act—the emergence of Scyld from the sea, the building of Heorot, the cleansing of Heo-rot, the quelling of the mere—has its archetype in the crea-tive and redemptive acts of God or Christ. Hrothgar's throne may be only an approximate reproduction of its transcendent model existing *in æternum,* but its reality and significance derive from that model. When this reality is threatened or hidden, as in the devil worship, tragedy ensues. Similarly, Beowulf's works of cleansing and delivering may be only imitations of those of Christ, who is never named in the poem, but much of their genuine significance for a Christian audience must surely have derived from their oblique but unmistakable association with their archetype. The Grendel kin as well, however much they may be trolls with Scan-dinavian associations still clinging to them, have—unless we assume the Old English poetic mythology to be largely ir-relevant to *Beowulf*—their main symbolic resonance in the archetypal monsters of the dryht of hell. Now in Part 2 of the poem, we observe the victory, on the level of middle-earth, of those same destructive forces symbolized by the monsters and their human associates in Part 1; the outlaws and traitors of Part 2 who now make up the race of Cain are the logical successors to Unferth, Hrothulf, and the com-batants of the Finn episode. There is, however, a development. Human murder is now presented in a narrative context in which the death-bringing dragon is central and succeeds in destroying the hero.

Considerable discussion has taken place among *Beowulf* scholars as to whether the Grendel kin and the dragon are monsters of a similar kind or kindred significance. The question is important, even crucial, in any consideration of the overall tragic structure and unity of the poem, and I should like now, in terms of the concept of symbolic metaphor operating in the four essays of this book, to attempt an answer.

We have seen how Grendel's mere is a complex fusion of images from the conventional fallen world described throughout the canon, a fusion which involves the motifs of both the wasteland and the chaotic sea as these are brought into intimate association with traditional hell images. Grendel is deprived of the joys of the dryht, both heavenly and earthly, and lives in a hostile hall or death dwelling where a hoarded, unused treasure (1613) is only one indication of his membership in the demonic dryht. Like Moses in *Exodus,* leading his troop along a symbolic narrow and unknown road through the moorlands to the Red Sea in anticipation of a new creation, Beowulf has to take his troop and the Danes along the same *enge anpaðas, uncuð gelad,* to make possible the decisive encounter of God's champion with the dryht of hell and the resultant restoration of the dryht of Heorot.

The dragon's barrow is not as elaborately described as the mere, but it too is presented as a hall—*eorðsele* (2410, earth-hall); *hringsele* (2840, ring-hall); *sele* (3128, hall). It is a vault beneath the earth (*hlæw under hrusan*) near the welling sea and the struggling waves (2411–2412a). In addition, it is described as "the serpent's den" (*þæs wyrmes denn,* 2759; *dennes,* 3045) and as "an earth-grave" (*eorðscrafa,* 3046). In this barrow for many years the dragon has guarded the "ornaments of a hall" (*recedes geatwa,* 3088) which here lie utterly useless (*læne licgan,* 3129), the symbols of a vanished dryht. Like the mere, the dwelling of the treasure guardian is difficult of access: "beneath lay a path unknown to men" (2213b–2214a). Like the Grendel kin, the fire-dragon lives in "a no man's land" ("ne ðær ænig mon / on þære westenne," 2297b–2298a), from which he comes at night to harass the world of the dryht. Finally, this hall deep in the earth is called the "secret dryht-hall" (*dryhtsele dyrnne,* 2320) of the guardian of the treasure, indicating quite clearly that, despite certain obvious differences, the central imaginative idea here is that of another demonic dryht. The fact of the dragon's aloneness, like that of his hoarding, is a clear indication of the way in which he symbolizes a perversion of those dryht values championed by Beowulf.

The immediate conflict between the Geats and the fire-dragon begins with the theft by an outlaw of a cup from the serpent's hoard. Similarly, in the *Reginsmál,* the baleful influence of the Niflung hoard begins to work from the moment the mischievous Loki steals the treasure. One is reminded, as well, of how in *Elene,* when the marvelous "hoard" is unearthed, the devil appears, enraged, in Jerusalem and complains loudly about the theft of his treasure by a second Judas. His fury over the fact that the loss of treasure means the end of his possession of human souls is relevant to *Beowulf,* a poem in which human societies engaged in the free dispensing and receiving of treasure are consistently presented as spiritually healthy, as living in the way God intends. A hoarded treasure is spiritual death or damnation.

The fact that the *Beowulf* dragon does not attack until the rifling of the hoard is not an adequate reason for deducing that he does not represent general hostility to the world of the dryht in which man lives. For three hundred years "the foe of the people" (*se ðeodsceaða,* 2278, 2688) has been hoarding the rich treasure of a human society and now, when provoked, sets out to destroy every living thing in the land of the Geats (2314b–2315). Whatever his motivation (its inadequacy in terms of cause and effect is another mark of the nonnaturalistic character of the poem), the results of the dragon's attack are very similar to those of Grendel, except that his ravages are more nearly complete: Beowulf's hall and gift-throne are utterly and immediately destroyed. It is worth remembering that the poet explicitly connects the hero's final battle with all those that have gone before, in two different places (2345 ff., 2518 ff.), even as he stresses that this final struggle will be *in extremis.*

Beowulf's last monstrous foe is designated by the word *wyrm* (serpent, worm) more frequently (fifteen times) than by any other; the word *draca* (dragon) occurs several times, as do *draca* compounds: *ligdraca* (2333, 3040, fire-dragon); *frecne fyrdraca* (2689, terrible fire-dragon); *se eorðdraca* (2712, the earth-dragon); *egeslic eorðdraca* (2825, horrible earth-dragon). In Old English poetry the worm or dragon, in any of its three aspects, always represents enmity to mankind: the worms who devour man's corpse after death; the dragons and serpents who receive his soul in hell; and the dragon of sin and mortality who rules over middle-earth until Christ cancels for all time the work of the tempter. In the fallen world under the threefold curse on Adam, Eve, and the serpent, it is the wyrm that triumphs, for, like the wolf and the raven, he claims the human body. In hell it is serpents and dragons who receive human souls. In the elegiac signature to *The Fates of the Apostles,* Cynewulf anticipates the day when he must leave behind his "earthly part or corpse as a comfort for worms," and similarly, in *The Grave* it is the worms who conquer as they divide between them the decomposing body. In *Soul and Body I* again we find the idea of the worm as the devourer of the human body and of the serpent as the lowest of earthly creatures. The soul, spitefully haranguing the body, says, "Now in the earth you will feed worms." He then goes on to damn the body utterly, by saying it would have been better for the body to have become a fowl, or a fish, or a beast of burden, or a cow wandering witless in the field, or a fierce wild beast, or, finally, the basest of serpents. In *Christ and Satan* (97–98) and in *Judith* (115), to name only two examples of a recurrent motif, there is mention of the dragons and serpents who wait in hell to embrace the souls of the damned. It is the form of these last *wyrmas* that Satan assumes when he prepares to destroy the joy of the *dryhtsele* of Eden.

The serpent or dragon which destroys Beowulf's body but not his soul appears to me to have a somewhat oblique symbolic connection with the traditional idea of the four elements from which all mortal things are composed: he is an ancient *"earth*-dragon" who guards an accursed hoard in an "earth-hall" by day and by night flies through the *air* spewing out venomous *fire,* until he is killed and pushed over a cliff into the embrace of the sea *waters.* To notice this —in a poem where symbolism of fire and water and comparisons between "fleeting" middle-earth and eternal reality loom large—may not be overly fanciful, especially since the dragon obviously represents the elemental fact of death for the aged hero and for other living things in his kingdom. Like the fateful treasure over which he keeps jealous watch, he has a ringed or coiled form (*hrinboga,* 2561, and *wohbogen,* 2827), and however malignant his effect, again like the treasure, he has a certain fatal, demonic splendor: *syllicran wiht* (3038, strange or wonderful creature).

The Grendel kin and the dragon share some of the descriptive words and epithets used for monsters in the poem—*bona* (slayer), *feond* (enemy), *lað* (hostile one), *mansceaða* (evil destroyer), *aglæca* (wretch, monster, demon, or warrior), *grim* (fierce, angry), *atol* (horrid), *freca* (bold one). They all live in demonic halls; they wage war on the world of the human *dryht*; they are all enemies of societies championed by Beowulf, the "greatest of men in the days of this life." The giants and the "wondrous serpent" (891) or "dragon" (892) killed by Sigmund are clearly meant to be analogous to the Grendel kin; they are mentioned following the victory over Grendel, not following the fight with the fire-dragon. It is true that each monster is individualized to a considerable degree and presented as distinct from the others; perhaps the dragon differs from the Cain-descended monsters of Part 1, even as the evil which impinges on age differs from that encountered by youthful energy. But in a poem in which metaphorical identification brings together logically separate entities as much as in *Beowulf* this should be no reason for not seeing obvious connections, especially when the poet himself

points them out. To say that the dragon is "a mere partici-
pant in a tragedy that started many ages before" [17] certainly
minimizes the significance of a creature that dominates much
of the latter part of *Beowulf* and has close connections with
the other monsters in the poem. The fact that Satan has
been the foe of Adam's sons ever since his visit to the guest-
hall of Eden does not make him any the less guilty; nor
does the fact that the dragon in Christian iconography is
always identified with forces hostile to men and God make
an individual but typical representative of the species any
the less guilty. *Beowulf* is a tragedy about the world of the
golden or paradisal dryht going down to defeat. The dragon
has jealously kept to himself many of the treasures of that
world for three hundred years.

There is another aspect of the conflict with the dragon
which indicates the intricacy and cunning of the poem's
metaphors. We have seen that the "halls" inhabited by the
monsters are parodies or perversions of those inhabited by
the Danes and the Geats. The dryht-hall as such, then, is a
double image, existing in both ideal and "un-ideal" forms,
as well as in an ambiguous mixture of the two. We have
seen, moreover, how certain aspects of the society of Heorot,
most notably the fratricide and the devil worship, have their
metaphorical significance in the Grendel kin and the mere.
An identification of the same kind is working in Part 2, between the old king, Beowulf, and the dragon.

At the time of their encounter each is represented as an
aged protector of his hall: Beowulf is "frod cyning / eald
eþelweard" (2209b–2210a, "a venerable king, old guardian of
the homeland") and "frod folces weard" (2513, "old and wise
keeper of the people"); the dragon is *wintrum frod* (2277,
old in years); Beowulf has ruled for fifty years (2733); the
dragon is fifty feet in length (3042). Beowulf has a splendid
dwelling (2326) and gift-throne (2326–2327); the dragon has
a mighty treasure house (2279b–2280a) and dryht-hall (2320).
Both are presented as warriors who rejoice in battle: Beowulf

17. See T. M. Gang, "Approaches to *Beowulf*," *Review of English
Studies* 3 (1952): 1–12.

is called *har hilderinc* (3136, hoary battle warrior), and a few
lines earlier the poet has described the monster as *hilderinc*
(3124, a battle warrior). Early in the poem when the hero
is fighting triumphantly with Grendel's mother, the poet
uses the formula *secg weorce gefeh* (1569, the man rejoiced
at his work); a similar phrase is applied to the dragon, *wiges
gefeh* (2298, he rejoiced in the war). The hero is called *nið-
heard cyning* (2417, a king brave in battle), and his foe is a
gearo guðfreca (2414, alert fighter). The adjective *stearcheort*
(stouthearted) is used in describing both of them, Beowulf at
line 2552 and the dragon at line 2288. So also is the term
aglæca, at line 2592, where they are both included in the
phrase *þa aglæcan* (the warriors). Each, moreover, is similar
in his impact on the other: "æghwæðrum wæs / bealohyc-
gendra broga fram oðrum" (2564b–2565, "each of the hostile
pair was an object of horror to the other").

   If only one or two words, phrases, or ideas were used in
common to describe the assailants, one could conclude that
nothing very much was implied, especially since each is a
fighter in a tale of conflict and the language of the poem is
formulaic. But when several expressions are used for both,
one begins to recognize a closer metaphorical relationship
between the protagonist and his last enemy. In some mysterious and illogical way the poet's mythical mode of imagining has managed to bring the two into a relationship both
of antithetical tension and of partial identification. There
is never any doubt that the old king will die in the struggle
with the fiery monster, because the poet tells us from the
beginning of Part 2 that this will happen. It is also true
that the monster has been roused to seek vengeance by the
theft of a goblet. But in some more comprehensive way than
that the dragon is the foe of man who brings death and destruction to the land of the Geats. The hoard he guards is
under an ancient curse that extends its deadly power to
Doomsday. (Is this strange and much-discussed curse the
ancient biblical one placed on man and nature and fated to
last through all history until the Judgment?) The guardian
of the treasure who reluctantly gives up the hoard is, in his

reluctance, similar to Beowulf, unwilling to surrender the treasure of his soul to death (2422). The corpse of each is only a ruin of former power: Beowulf's is separated from his soul, crumbles in the flames of the pyre, and is buried as ashes; the dragon's body is separated from the hoard and pushed from a cliff into the surging waters of the sea. The fact that the physical treasure is consigned to the ground "as useless as it was before" is set against the more important fact that the only real treasure in Beowulf's life, his soul, faithful to the heavenly Dryhten, has gone to the Judgment of the just.

In the metaphorical design of the poem, the dragon, at certain points of the narrative, *is* the body of death, of Beowulf's death and, by extension, of the Geatish people as a unified society. If, moreover, Beowulf's gold-hall, like Heorot, is another *imago mundi,* the dragon is also the body of man's mortality. The coils of the serpent surround the warrior-king while the thanes who should be shoulder to shoulder with their lord turn away and retreat into the woods. Loyalty dies, protection vanishes, and the good society disintegrates. It is the twilight or coming winter of a society's life that we see in Part 2, as destructive fire and social chaos succeed the joys of the wine-hall, the order of the dryht. The dragon is the central unifying symbol in the whole poem for the elemental power of death; the symbols of life and divinely sanctioned human activity are the gold-hall, circulating treasures, and the hero.

Where most other Old English poetic narratives show an intensely otherworldly loyalty, *Beowulf* reveals a tension between courageous devotion to that heroic work which is necessary and good in the tragic context of middle-earth and the realization that, ultimately, human loyalty must focus elsewhere. The contempt-of-the-world theme is kept in restraint in *Beowulf,* however, in a way that it is not in the poems discussed in Essays One and Two, with the result that sustained elegy and tragedy remain possible. The guest-hall of Eden and the Promised Land gleam most splendidly near the beginning and in the central parts of the poem, but they are never entirely lost sight of, to the point where homiletic strictures on the worthlessness of earthly endeavor can take over. The basis of the poem's tragic nature is its account of being in time, the fact that the fifty years respectively of Hrothgar's and Beowulf's reigns are measured by the fifty-year habitation of a demonic dryht by murderous monsters and by a fifty-foot dragon of destruction who guards a rich treasure of the world of the dryht.

If one presses very far a rigorous Augustinian doctrine of extraterrestrial reality with this poem, one is bound to conclude that a life like Beowulf's, deeply involved in the wars and the gift-dispensing rituals of Denmark and Geatland, is less ascetically pure than that of Guthlac or Juliana, but such thinking cannot absorb the kind of experience described in the poem. To see this and accept it does not, in my view, mean that *Beowulf* is an intractably pagan poem somewhat influenced by a Christian sensibility. It means that it is a tragedy and that the experience of the tragic—Christian, pagan, or whatever—cannot be moralized or comprehended within any conceptual world-view. Hrothgar is a tragic figure whether or not he in any way is culpable in the fate of Heorot; Beowulf is consistently admirable throughout the poem, despite the old king's sermon to him on the dangers of pride and despite the possible suggestions later in the text that he is somehow caught by a worldly interest in a fated treasure.

What makes Beowulf a tragic figure is his superabundance, his capacity for superhuman acts, his strength of thirty men, his exalted sense of social obligation, and his generosity—all these being characteristics that place him above ordinary human experience, to the point where, finally, he is destroyed by a dragon. It is this heroic energy, first visible in the sea passage from Geatland to Heorot and in his account of the swimming contest with Breca, and continued in the fights with Grendel and his mother, that is the basis of the poem's romance. Heaven's plenitude has extended in extraordinary measure to this greatest of men between the seas, and his experiences show him as constantly bursting the confines of normal earthly life. His energy is directed to the protection of the most ideal form of heroic life and society in middle-earth—Heorot in its unfallen aspect. In contrast to Beowulf, his king, Hygelac, though reputed in Germanic historical monuments to have been almost a giant, falls dead in the land of the Franks while Beowulf swims away, carrying the armor of thirty men.

But Beowulf, like Heorot, becomes simply a memory. The close alignment of aged hero and dragon in Part 2 is the poem's decisive reminder that in the tragic vision even the most heroic form, perhaps most especially the heroic form, is defeated by the elemental facts of existence in time. The world that remains after Beowulf has died contains two sorts of people, cowards and outlaws, on the one hand, and those faithful to dryht loyalties (Wiglaf, the weeping woman, and the circling horsemen), on the other. By this point we have been shown the impact of heroic energy on the world of the fallen dryht and have been shown also that in such a world it is heroic energy that is destroyed while the fallen creation continues in time. The golden dryht of middle-earth and the youthful Beowulf are poetic images of the kind of joy and reality the *hæleð* want, but the irony of the tragic vision decrees that life is not shaped according to human desires. The poet, with the quiet assurance of great artistry, follows his account of the roaring flames and raging winds of Beowulf's cremation with a description of the disposal of physical things: the hero's ashes are sealed in a great barrow; the rings, necklaces, and armor of the ancient treasure are returned to the earth, hidden again and useless to men. Twelve riders circle the mound, ritually containing the grief of the Geats: they eulogize the greatness and glory of their dead king, and they mourn his passing. The closing scene expresses a pronounced tragic sense of confinement, of the putting into dark places of all that is splendid in this world. It shows the stilling of heroic energy.

Conclusion

To speak of a Christian mythology as I have done in these essays is to imply several important principles. The first and most important of these was the conviction, held by the Church fathers and by the New Testament writers before them, that the Bible is a single book or total vision of man's relation to God, a sustained and comprehensive description of the divine-human relation as it unfolds in time and space. This idea has been obscured somewhat in modern times by what is called the lower and higher criticism of the Bible, those textual, linguistic, analytic, and historical investigations of the sixty-six books of the Bible that constitute the bulk of serious biblical scholarship from about 1750 onward. According to the older view, the Bible as a unified book has both a linear and a circular aspect. Cædmon, we are told by Bede, sang first of the Creation of the world and then proceeded through the various biblical events of genuinely mythical character—the origin of the human race, the Exodus from Egypt and the entry into the Promised Land, the Incarnation, Passion, Resurrection, and Ascension of Christ, the coming of the Holy Spirit, the teaching of the apostles, Doomsday, the pains of hell and the joys of heaven —until he had comprehended the whole story of human history as this was understood in the early medieval Church. This linear narrative was viewed as an orderly arrangement with a beginning (Creation), a middle (the Incarnation), and an end (Doomsday). At the same time its pattern could be thought of as circular, though not as infinitely repeatable; the work of Christ in restoring the original unity of heaven, first broken when Lucifer rose up in pride against the throne of God, is the rounding out of that complete pattern of human life imaginatively set forth in the Christian mythology. The heavenly Jerusalem at the end of time is both Paradise restored and Paradise transcended.

In whichever of the two ways an Anglo-Saxon poet like

Cædmon and his teachers thought of the story, it is clear, from Bede's account and from a large number of Anglo-Saxon poems and sermons, that it is precisely those scriptural events of mythical size or miraculous import that most commanded attention. What scientific, analytic study of the Bible tends to explain away, or account for only with great difficulty, was the stock in trade of a poet like Cædmon or even a "historian" like Bede. It is abundantly clear that poems like those found in the Junius MS, and others, manifest an overall attitude to biblical mythology that is as far removed from sound historical methodology or from any attempt to understand the individual books of the Bible in terms of their meaning for their original authors and first readers as anything could be. The constant reading of Old Testament materials as if the New Testament preceded or was contemporary with them, the apparently arbitrary associating of widely separate biblical events in one poem, the pronounced tendency to dwell on the most fabulous parts of scripture, and the lively sense of metaphorical connections—these phenomena all indicate a body of poetry conceived in a mythical mode, and they invite a set of critical presuppositions that are not going to lead the reader to despise those poems which aspire to heavenly things even as he values inordinately those precariously attached to the physical world. This is not to suggest, of course, that the critic has to adopt as his own a supernaturally based theology, simply that he must find in modern critical theory some means of accounting for a poetry whose vision of reality is to a considerable extent attached to imaginative and conceptual structures in some ways very remote from most twentieth-century readers. Theories based on and determined by what Dr. Johnson called "the real state of sublunary nature" are not likely to make much sense of *The Dream of the Rood* or of a large number of other highly romantic or mythical Old English poems.

The "human" figures in the poetic records are not psychologically conceived, as are many in nineteenth- and twentieth-century literature; we cannot in any direct way respond to them as participants in a common social experience. There

is little dedication to the existential that bears up throughout a whole Old English poem. There are of course patterns
of tension—between body and soul, between earthly treasures
and those of the heavenly gift-throne, between physical weapons and those of spiritual warfare—but normally in this
theocentric, supernaturalist poetry it is recognized that any
earthly good must be taken into its eternal context if the *læne*
world of material things is not to drag down and enslave the
soul. Even *Beowulf* and *The Wanderer,* poems that speak
powerfully of the pull of "middle-earth," do so, as I have
argued in Essays Three and Four, only as a means to realization of *ece rædas* (lasting benefits, eternal good). We find
assertions many times of the necessity for man to take on a
saintlike nature, what might be called an "angelic imagination," so that as *godes cempa* (warrior of God) he may re-
nounce his sensual being and escape the *banhus* (bone-house,
body) in which his soul is temporarily imprisoned.

Historical scholarship's deep commitment to the existential
or the actual events of history, or, at the very least, to easily
recognizable human feelings evoked by response to nature or
to human relationships in this world, has led many critics
and students of Old English to prefer the elegiac, the tragic,
and the few ironic texts, since these apparently have a closer
correspondence with actual human life than have the more
obviously mythical or romantic pieces, like *Andreas,* for example. This, in my view, has resulted in a largely unwitting
attempt to destroy the autonomy of the Old English poetic
universe by trying to comprehend it on the level of real
emotion (we have our students read only the elegiac close of
Guthlac B, rather than the preceding theocentric account of
the saint's triumph over death) or of actual events documen-
table historically. The fact is that the majority of the poems
in the extant poetic records show a strong tendency to romance and comedy,[1] that is, to themes of triumph and re-

1. Here I use the terms *romance* and *comedy* with the meanings indicated by Northrop Frye in the third part of his *Anatomy of Criticism:
Four Essays* (Princeton, 1957), pp. 129 ff. Frye describes romance and
comedy, along with irony or satire and tragedy, as pregeneric narrative

birth by miraculous and, to us, arbitrary means, in accordance with the belief that reality is upward, chaos and hell downward.

One implication of this is that the main lines of modern critical theory can only with great difficulty be made to work at understanding the visionary nature of Old English poetry. Criticism based on what is sometimes called the "reality principle" may not even be the best instrument for understanding modern "realistic" or "ironic" texts. It is increasingly evident that it is a very weak tool for a study of our earlier literature, because its assumption that literature is made out of life, not out of literature, means that literature must be subject to existential categories. Old English poetry is made out of poetry, out of an ancestral word-hoard, and yields little or no direct insight into history. It is an imaginative art revealing a world reconstituted according to human desire, but, since Anglo-Saxon man thinks of himself as a creature of God with a rational soul, this desire normally takes the form of aspiration toward what God is believed to want for man. The heavenly visions and almost Byzantine abstraction of the early English poets may seem disembodied and unreal to a modern, man-centered criticism, but there can be little doubt that for a Cynewulf or a Cædmon there was no problem at all in mustering up a belief in the objective reality of the supernatural order. The fallen world has to be taken into account but not surrendered to. It must be left behind in favor of the creation of a properly human reality according to divine models—hence, the pervasiveness of the visionary element and the sense of a continual reshaping of an initial revelation or Word that characterizes much Old English

---

mythoi, that is, "plot patterns." Romance is the *mythos* of literature concerned primarily with an idealized world in which subtlety and complexity of characterization are not much favored and narrative interest tends to center on a search for some kind of golden age. Comedy visualizes "the world of desire, not as an escape from 'reality,' but as the genuine form of the world that human life tries to imitate." In an Old English context the genuine form of the world to which man moves is Paradise or heaven, the society of divine beings commonly described as the dryht or comitatus of the heavenly Lord and his thanes.

poetry. Chaotic, unhumanized nature, including man's, and hell—these are the enemies. The world of the earthly gold-hall and the hoarding of physical treasure, if wrongly viewed, can become the world of illusions, of false myths. Reality is glimpsed in the loneliness of the Seafarer's quest or in Constantine's vision on the banks of the Danube.

If the "reality principle," based on the assumption that the meaning of a literary work can be seen only in relation to existential forms of meaning, is a critical hypothesis of too limited usefulness for most Old English poems, it may be supposed that a different kind of correspondence to some-thing external to the literary work should be sought, that the interpretation of the poem in relation to moral and theologi-cal doctrines known to be held in the culture will be more illuminating. The great strength of this hypothesis is that it opens up as yet largely unexplored connections between early medieval theology and art, on the one hand, and Old English poetry, on the other. Its weakness, at times, is the apparent assumption of a continuous relation between the words of the poem and nonpoetic documents, usually commentaries; in other words, an assumption that Old English poetry is technical allegory. This has the advantage of trying to face up squarely to the fact of the didacticism of Old English poetry, which has too often been sloughed aside, but it also seems on occasion to induce an obliviousness to the imaginative qualities of the poetry and to take as given the idea that the only important unity in a particular poem or in Old English poetry as a whole lies in a body of doctrine or concepts out-side the poetry.

Since, however, a number of the interpretative conclusions reached in this book are similar to those offered by that group of scholars who in recent years have been gathering evidence for the "allegorical" or "exegetical" reading of Old English poems, it is necessary that I define what my approach has in common with theirs and how it differs. Prominent in this area of discussion are B. F. Huppé, D. W. Robertson, G. V. Smithers, O. S. Anderson, J. E. Cross, Marie P. Hamilton, and Margaret E. Goldsmith.[2] It is probably unfair to link together so disparate a group of scholars. All that is implied is a general similarity of scholarly approach, a recognition on my part that each of these critics appears to accept the hypothesis that one, probably the major, informing context for certain Old English poems is patristic literature and that this context suggests to them in turn the appropriateness of an allegorical reading of some or perhaps most Old English poems. Specific references to studies by these critics are found throughout this book.

The most extended statement published so far presenting the case for an allegorical reading of Old English poetry is B. F. Huppé's *Doctrine and Poetry: Augustine's Influence on Old English Poetry*. This book presents Augustine's poetic theory as it is set down in the *De doctrina Christiana*, sketches the influence of this theory in terms of its use by Isidore of Seville, Vergil of Toulouse, Bede, Alcuin, Rabanus, and Scotus Erigena, and then goes on to an interpretation of Cædmon's *Hymn* and the Old English *Genesis* poem in the light of the Augustinian tradition already outlined. The book includes also the author's brief "conjectures" about the way this kind of exegetical reading would elicit doctrinal meanings from *Exodus, Daniel, Christ and Satan, Beowulf, The Wanderer, The Seafarer,* and *The Battle of Maldon.* In my view the most important achievement of this volume is the commentary on *Genesis,* a rather neglected and, not infrequently, despised poem in modern times. As I have tried to demonstrate in the essays of this book, certain key images and themes in *Genesis* work decisively in other Old English poems, to the point that one suspects that it—or at least the poetic conventions used in it—had a seminal function in Old English Christian poetry. Huppé has also served us well by demonstrating the figurative

2. Miss Goldsmith's *The Mode and Meaning of Beowulf* (London: Athlone, 1970) has been published after this book was complete. At numerous points her reading of *Beowulf* and mine include consideration of the same elements in the poem, but our overall interpretations are in the main quite different.

meanings probably working in Cædmon's *Hymn*, these, too, having a wider relevance in the canon. One would like to see Huppé put the same critical hypothesis to work in detail on *Exodus* which, at least on its rather forbiddingly figurative surface, would seem to invite at least some measure of the kind of allegorical analysis given *Genesis*.

As to the relevance of Huppé's general thesis—that Augustinian views on literary interpretation decisively influenced, in both composition and interpretation, the whole development of Christian art and poetry in early and late medieval times—I am more skeptical. The thesis is simply too sweeping in its implications to account for even the considerable variety of styles or modes of composition in Old English poetry, let alone matters further afield. This does not mean that biblical influences are not pervasive in the Old English poetic records. They are, as I have attempted to show, but this fact does not necessarily imply allegory in an Augustinian sense. Even with poems like *Genesis* and *Exodus*, where scriptural commentaries are an obvious aid to interpretation in that they describe the current conventional understanding of the biblical materials in the period, one discerns an overreadiness in the critic to assume that the Augustinian cortex or doctrinal content must be the primary concern of the twentieth-century critic. Huppé is too ready to adopt, it seems to me, the role of the intellectual historian interested primarily in literature as documents in the history of ideas rather than in literature as an imaginative order of words using ideas and theological matters but always distinct from the discursive prose of the doctrinal or philosophical treatise. Huppé's contribution is genuine when he elucidates the themes or ideas. His commentary is also critically rewarding when it explains a conventional image— as, for example, the image in Cædmon's *Hymn* of God "adorning" the earth [3]—that is, when he identifies the likely basis for an understanding of how images in the poem work. But throughout the study one detects a curious invulnerability to or disinterest in the texture of the poems under discussion, to the way they function as an order of words or pattern of

3. Huppé, *Doctrine and Poetry*, p. 115.

images, and especially an impatience with the fact that however major the patristic influence may be the poems are still composed in the heroic diction of early English poetry.

To stress this last point is not to join the ranks of those scholars recently described as "the Wagerian school" [4] but simply to assert that it is possible, in the current zealous campaign to eliminate the excesses of an earlier Germanicist scholarship, to replace them with new ones. It would seem to me that, however massive the evidence for the influence of Latin Christian culture on Old English poetry, it is essential to keep prominent both halves of the poetic revolution Bede describes in the story about Cædmon. In other words, it would be a gross distortion of the facts of Old English poetry to so emphasize the *æfestnes* (religion, devotion) and the *arfæstnes* (goodness, piety) of the poets that we ignore or push aside the fact of the *scopgereord* (language of the scop, poetic diction) and the *Engliscgereord* (English language) in which they composed their poems. Even when there is a very close parallel for an image or group of images between a biblical or patristic text, on the one hand, and an Old English poem, on the other, it is still necessary to observe the fact of two separate linguistic contexts and, similarly, to recognize that to a high degree the Old English poetic canon has its own special character and autonomy.

Here I return to the concept of an environment of images. Because Old English poetic imagery, like that of all bodies of poetry, is deeply involved in the concrete physical realities of an actual Anglo-Saxon society—however spiritualized or allegorized the themes attached to that imagery may be—it would appear that concentration on it, in arriving at interpretations of poems, is less likely to lead to an unhistorical distortion than if one overemphasizes the doctrinal or ideological context common to the whole early medieval Christian world.

To question certain aspects of the allegorical approach is not to suggest that critics of Old English poetry should revert to romantic ideas of individual genius and creativity or of

4. John Fleming, "*The Dream of the Rood* and Anglo-Saxon Monasticism," *Traditio* 22 (1966): 48.

artists as special beings working apart from the major ideological assumptions of their society, as the way to understanding the poetry in question. It is to suggest, however, three things: that any poem, medieval or modern, is primarily a structure of images; that the reading of poetry as explicit or implicit allegory is done most successfully when it respects the balance between image and idea in the poem itself; and that a major task of the critic should be to recognize that "literature" itself, especially that from the same historical period and in the same language, is likely to be a context of major importance for any individual poem. To fail in the first or second of these, to translate, for example, the visionary poem *The Dream of the Rood* into the doctrinal concepts clearly embodied in it, is largely to ignore its beauty and power as visionary poetry, dependent on its imaginative strength, that is, on its concrete images, for its capacity to inculcate *caritas* in a particular human society. The use of the other poetry of the period as a potential informing context for each poem, although partially frustrated by apparently unsolvable problems of lineal connections, is especially pertinent in the interpretation of Old English poetry and has been the main concern in this book.

Index